The Future Shapes of An

To many people, the Church of England and worldwide Anglican Communion has the aura of an institution that is dislocated and adrift. Buffeted by tempestuous and stormy debates on sexuality, gender, authority and power – to say nothing of priorities in mission and ministry, and the leadership and management of the church – a once confident Anglicanism appears to be anxious and vulnerable. *The Future Shapes of Anglicanism* offers a constructive and critical engagement with the currents and contours that have brought the church to this point. It assesses and evaluates the forces now shaping the church, and challenges them culturally, critically and theologically.

The Future Shapes of Anglicanism engages with the church of the present that is simultaneously dissenting and loyal, as well as critical and constructive. For all who are engaged in ecclesiological investigations, and for those who study the Church of England and the wider Anglican Communion, this book offers new maps and charts for the present and future. It is an essential companion and guide to some of the movements and forces that are currently shaping the church.

Martyn Percy is Dean of Christ Church, Oxford. He is a member of the Faculty of Theology at the University of Oxford, where he also teaches in the Department of Sociology, and for the Said Business School. He also serves as a Professor of Theological Education at King's College London and is a Professorial Research Fellow at Heythrop College, University of London. He was formerly (from 2004–2014) the Principal of Ripon College, Cuddesdon, at Oxford. He writes on Christianity and contemporary culture, modern ecclesiology and practical theology. Recent books include *Thirty-Nine New Articles: An Anglican Landscape of Faith* (2013), *Anglicanism: Confidence, Commitment and Communion* (2013) and *The Oxford Handbook of Anglican Studies* (2015, edited with Mark Chapman and Sathi Clarke). He was recently described in the journal *Theology* as the British theologian who is closest to being a 'missionary anthropologist'.

Routledge Contemporary Ecclesiology

Series editors:
Martyn Percy, University of Oxford, UK
D. Thomas Hughson, Marquette University, USA
Bruce Kaye, Charles Sturt University, Australia

The field of ecclesiology has grown remarkably in the last decade, and most especially in relation to the study of the contemporary church. Recently, theological attention has turned once more to the nature of the church, its practices and proclivities, and to interpretative readings and understandings of its role, function and ethos in contemporary society.

This series draws from a range of disciplines and established scholars to further the study of contemporary ecclesiology and publish an important cluster of landmark titles in this field. The series editors represent a range of Christian traditions and disciplines, and this reflects the breadth and depth of books developing in the Series. This series presents a clear focus on the contemporary situation of churches worldwide, offering an invaluable resource for students, researchers, ministers and other interested readers around the world working or interested in the diverse areas of contemporary ecclesiology and the important changing shape of the church worldwide.

Titles in the series include:

The Wisdom of the Spirit
Gospel, Church and Culture
Edited by Martyn Percy and Pete Ward

Practical Theology and Pierre-André Liégé
Radical Dominican and Vatican II Pioneer
Nicholas Bradbury

The Holy Spirit and the Church
Ecumenical Reflections with a Pastoral Perspective
Edited by Thomas Hughson

The Future Shapes of Anglicanism
Currents, Contours, Charts
Martyn Percy

Growth and Decline in the Anglican Communion
1980 to the Present
Edited by David Goodhew

For a full list of titles in this series, please visit www.routledge.com

The Future Shapes of Anglicanism

Currents, contours, charts

Martyn Percy

Routledge
Taylor & Francis Group

LONDON AND NEW YORK

First published in paperback 2017

First published 2017
by Routledge
2 Park Square, Milton Park, Abingdon, Oxon OX14 4RN

and by Routledge
711 Third Avenue, New York, NY 10017

Routledge is an imprint of the Taylor & Francis Group, an informa business

British Library Cataloguing in Publication Data
A catalogue record for this book is available from the British Library

Library of Congress Cataloging in Publication Data
Names: Percy, Martyn, author.
Title: The future shapes of Anglicanism : currents, contours, charts /
    Martyn Percy.
Description: New York : Routledge, 2016. |
Series: Contemporary ecclesiology ; 19 | Includes bibliographical
    references and index.
Identifiers: LCCN 2016024123 ISBN 9781472477170 (hardback) |
    ISBN 9781472477187 (pbk.) | ISBN 9781315566740 (ebook)
Subjects: LCSH: Anglican Communion—History—21st century. |
    Church renewal—Anglican Communion.
Classification: LCC BX5005 .P475 2016 | DDC 283.01/12—dc23
LC record available at https://lccn.loc.gov/2016024123

ISBN: 978-1-472-47717-0 (hbk)
ISBN: 978-1-472-47718-7 (pbk)
ISBN: 978-1-315-56674-0 (ebk)

Typeset in Sabon
by Swales & Willis Ltd, Exeter, Devon, UK

For Ian
Priest, Pastor, Counsellor, Consultant, Scholar,
Wry Observer and Wit – and More Besides

Give us a man of God
Father, to pray for us,
Longed for, and insignificant,
But excellent in mercy,
And ordain him
Someone who loves the mystery of the faith
Whose conversation seems
Credibly to come from heaven
A poor man, a hungry man
Whose hospitality is endless.

Give us a preaching man,
Father, who doesn't know how to fake,
A free man, on holiday
In this parish, a still man
Good as an ikon
With a heart full of treasure;
Someone to talk to
When death comes here,
A fellow countryman of birth and death
And the dynasty of our family,
Whose eye has missed nothing.

Give us a man without sanctimony
Father, to handle what is eternal,
A private citizen among miracles
Not his, modest
Capable of silence
Someone who reminds us now and then
Of your own description
And another kingdom
By the righteousness of his judgement
Or some grace in what's done
In laying down his life even
For his friends.

Reginald Askew (source: Advisory Council for Church Ministry prayer card, Petertide, 1975. Readers are reminded that at the time, the language for vocations to ordained ministry was exclusively masculine. However, the sentiments above clearly apply to all those who are called to Holy Orders).

Contents

Acknowledgements

I am grateful to Hereford Cathedral for their kind permission to reproduce the Mappa Mundi, and to the Anglican Communion Office in London for a current map of the Anglican Communion, and to Seabury Press for the 1962 map of the Anglican Communion.

Some of the material for the Introduction is drawn from recent writing for organisations such as *Modern Church*, *Church Times* and other publications. An earlier version of Chapter 1 appeared in *Modern Believing* 55.3 2014. Chapters 2 and 3 are drawn from an article that originally appeared as an online contribution to the *Journal of Anglican Studies* (March 2015). Chapter 4 was first published Stephen Lowe & Martyn Percy, *The Character of Wisdom* (London: Ashgate, 2004, pp. 3–22). Chapter 5 was originally a short article published for the newsletter of the Centre for Study Sexuality and Spirituality in 2015. A shorter version of Chapter 6 was originally published in Jeff Astley and Leslie Francis, *Exploring Ordinary Theology: Everyday Christian Believing and the Church* (London: Ashgate, 2013). Some of the material for Chapters 7, 8 and 9 is drawn from more recent writings for the organisation Modern Church, and with a focus on the Church of England and issues in the wider Anglican Communion. Some of the material in the Conclusion is drawn from Martyn Percy, *Power and the Church* (London: Cassell, 1998). The Coda is an updated version of a story that originally appeared two decades ago in *Signs of the Times*, and was recently updated for *The Ecclesial Canopy* (London: Ashgate, 2014). I gratefully acknowledge the publishers of these essays and articles, and the opportunity to update them for this volume.

Every attempt has been made to obtain permission to reproduce copyright material. If any proper acknowledgement has not been made, copyright holders are invited to inform the editors of the oversight.

MWP, Christ Church, Oxford
Passiontide, 2016

Illustrations

Figure 1 is a map of the Anglican Communion dating from 1962, and appeared in *The Anglican Mosaic*, edited by William E. Leidt (Seabury Press, Greenwich, Conn. 1962; with a Foreword by the Metropolitan of India, and published for the Anglican Congress of 1963). It puts North America at the centre of the Communion, and relocates the Church of England well to the right. The design and colours resemble maps of that era in the American magazine *National Geographic*.

Figure 2 is a current map (2016) showing the Provinces of the Anglican Communion: The Church of Ireland serves both Northern Ireland and the Republic of Ireland; the Episcopal Church of the Sudan serves both Sudan and South Sudan; and the Anglican Church of Korea serves South Korea and, theoretically, North Korea. Indian Anglicanism is divided into a Church of North India and a Church of South India.

The Diocese in Europe (formally the Diocese of Gibraltar in Europe), in the Province of Canterbury is also present in Portugal and Spain. However, the Spanish Reformed Episcopal Church (or IERE *Iglesia Española Reformada Episcopal*, established in 1880) is also in Communion with the Archbishop of Canterbury, has its own bishops, and uses the Mozarabic liturgy, as well as having a distinct Protestant-Evangelical identity. The Lusitanian Catholic Apostolic Evangelical Church (*Igreja Lusitana Católica Apostólica Evangélica*, also founded in 1880) in Portugal is in Communion with the Archbishop of Canterbury. In Europe at least, therefore, the Anglican Communion has had overlapping episcopal jurisdiction for almost 150 years. The Episcopal Church, USA (TEC) affiliated Convocation of Episcopal Churches in Europe has affiliate churches or chaplaincies in France, Belgium, Austria, Switzerland, Italy – and more recently, Kazakhstan. The borders of the Church of England's Diocese in Europe extend east to Mongolia, where there is a Chaplaincy in Ulaanbaatar.

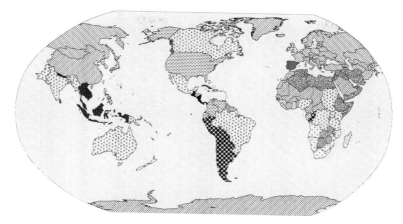

Figure 1 Map of the Anglican Communion (1962)

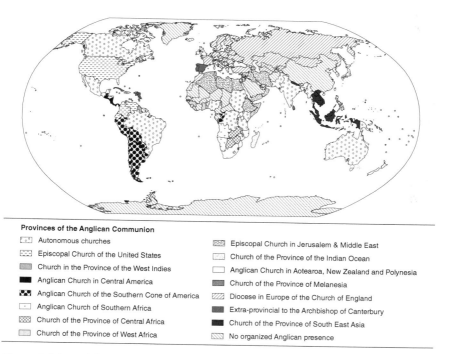

Provinces of the Anglican Communion

Autonomous churches	Episcopal Church in Jerusalem & Middle East
Episcopal Church of the United States	Church of the Province of the Indian Ocean
Church in the Province of the West Indies	Anglican Church in Aotearoa, New Zealand and Polynesia
Anglican Church in Central America	Church of the Province of Melanesia
Anglican Church of the Southern Cone of America	Diocese in Europe of the Church of England
Anglican Church of Southern Africa	Extra-provincial to the Archbishop of Canterbury
Church of the Province of Central Africa	Church of the Province of South East Asia
Church of the Province of West Africa	No organized Anglican presence

Figure 2 Map of the Anglican Communion (2016)

Figure 3 Hereford Mappa Mundi Trust and the Dean and Chapter of Hereford Cathedral

Introduction

Arguably, some of the defining issues of our age include disorientation, distraction (or dissonance) and disaster. Disorientation, in the sense that there are wholly new experiences of space and time, with new tensions between globalism and regionalism, social cohesion and consumerism, and reality and spectacle. Distraction or dissonance, in the sense that there are new instabilities of value, meaning and identity, and considerable tension between the past, present and future – and all linked, seemingly to our capacity to be distracted by small matters, whilst losing sight of the larger picture. In terms of dissonance, we seem to trust the new and not the old; and the future, but not the past. We also seem, as a church, to make bold predictions and pronouncements on the potential for progress and development; but to be rather more circumspect about processing results and indications that point in a different direction. Disaster, perhaps more obviously, ranges from speculation on climate change to the global threat of terrorism.[1]

The map of the present, then, and of the future, looks at least challenging – and some might opine that the outlook is bleak. And what of ecclesiology? The optimism invested in ecumenism in the late twentieth century has clearly given way to a more anatomised and polarised ecclesial landscape. Few would have predicted the rise of 'furious religion' and fundamentalism as major forces in religious and world affairs in the twenty-first century. So, what might an ecclesial map of the future tell us, especially about Anglicanism, with which this volume is concerned?

> A world view gives rise to a world map; but the world map in turn defines its culture's view of the world. It is an act of exceptional symbiotic alchemy.[2]

Maps are fascinating. They reveal not so much the world that might be encountered, but rather, how the cartographer chooses to view the world.

---

1 For an illuminating perspective, see Bird, Curtis, Putnam, Robertson and Tickner, *Mapping the Futures;* see also Burleigh, *Sacred Causes.*
2 Cosgrove, 'Mapping the World', pp. 65–115.

Scale, symbol, demographics, topography, geography – indeed, any number of factors – play a part. The mapmaker, in many ways, is trying to do just what the sociologist of religion attempts every time they venture into the field:

> At the risk of shocking sociologists, I should be inclined to say that it is their job to render sociological or historical content more intelligible than it was in the experience of those who lived it. All sociology is a reconstruction that aspires to confer intelligibility on human existence, which, like all human existences, are confused and obscure.[3]

Mapmakers do not just reproduce the world they see. Indeed, they cannot do that. They create that world, constructing it by sifting information, drawing lines, selecting colours and tones, devising symbols, and choosing scales and relations that invite viewers to share in that construction of reality. A map always *manages* the reality it is trying to convey.[4] No map perfectly captures the territory it surveys; there is too much to see; too much to weigh and discern; too much to be interpreted and then refracted back. All maps are partial interpretations of reality, and to some extent, inherently political. They cannot avoid being divisive in the very act of trying to be descriptive.[5]

Maps, of course, can be more than just an attempt at an interpretation of the physical landscape encountered. Some of the oldest surviving maps we have in the modern world are not so much spatial as theological or metaphysical – or perhaps fusions of religion and the prevailing cosmology of the age. There was a reason for this, of course: orientation. People needed to know where they were. In more ancient civilisations, this was not merely a matter of spatial location. It was also about knowing where you fitted in within God's ordered creation – the spheres to which each species of creature belonged. Where the sacred places were; and where places of chaos and danger might be; the known and unknown aspects of a world where redemption could be both lost and found.

Orientation was the key. Ancient civilisations vested enormous religious significance in the directions we faced, and in what we might turn away from. The sun rising in the east was often associated with renewal; and simply by setting in the west it was associated with decline and death. The north was associated with darkness and its forces; the south with light. These worldviews and theo-cosmologies, elided with the construction of early church buildings, shaped liturgies. Thus, we find the west associated with mortality (the direction Christ faces when he dies); and the un-baptised and

---

3 Aron, *Main Currents in Sociological Thought*, p. 207.
4 Brotton, *A History of the World in Twelve Maps*, pp. 8–9.
5 On this, see Marshall, *Prisoners of Geography*; see also Massey, *Space, Place and Gender*, pp. 146ff and Sibley, *Geographies of Exclusion*.

excommunicants were traditionally buried facing north – the direction of darkness. But in China, the sacred direction for many centuries was north. This was on the basis that the emperor looked to the light and warmth of the south, and as his subjects therefore looked up and towards him, they would automatically face north: the direction from which the gaze of the emperor came. Maps make meanings; and they orientate us.

The Mappa Mundi at Hereford Cathedral dates from around 1300. It is one of the largest and oldest maps to survive to the present day. But a modern reader of the map would have trouble recognising the places it purportedly maps, and thereby orientating themselves. Indeed, unless accompanied by some skilled reader of ancient maps, the casual viewer would not be able to locate themselves within the Mappa Mundi at all.

There are several reasons for this. The Mappa Mundi – for sound theological reasons in early medieval England – places Jerusalem at the centre of the world. East is at the top of the map. Britain is reduced to a sort of sausage-shaped land-mass in the bottom left-hand corner. To even begin to understand the Mappa Mundi at all, a modern reader has to turn it ninety degrees to the right, to restore north to its rightful place. But even this hardly helps. Asia, as represented, contains a griffin, scenes of terrifying tribal cannibalism, with other legendary figures and symbols stalking the lands. One finds unicorns side-by-side with familiar biblical scenes, and mythical beasts sharing space with exotic animals from far beyond the shores of Britain. Indeed, the map can be read as centred on a kind of utopia, and the edges narrated as dystopia. So this is not a map, therefore, as we conventionally understand maps: it is not a guide to geography or topography, but rather to theology. Jerusalem is at the centre: the place of Christ's crucifixion, resurrection and eventual return. As Ezekiel 5: 5 puts it, 'this is Jerusalem – I have set (her) in the midst of the nations and the countries that are round about her'.[6]

We have begun with a meditation on maps because the sociology of religion is, to some extent, the mapping of groups who in turn make maps. That is to say, all religious groups – including Christian movements and congregations – tend to try and confer intelligibility on the world they encounter through a series of processes. They will share the social construction of reality from within the culture that they inhabit even if they do so with a critical eye. But they will also attempt to confer a theological construction of reality upon that same world. This is unavoidable, and to some extent grounded in the Christian tradition. The invitation to ponder sheep and goats, the saved and the unsaved, what is to be rendered to Caesar and what is to be given to God all require separation, demarcation and dislocation. People who make maps know all about this too: where the forest ends and the field begins are clear on the map, even if it is invariably more subtle on the ground. The question that the sociologist of religion might press at this point, is why

6 Brotton, *A History of the World in Twelve Maps*, pp. 82ff.

the lines are drawn where they are, how the fields and forests come to be symbolised, and why the map-maker chose not to symbolise the ambivalent ground that forms the border between forest and field.

Mapping the present

Anglicans are essentially territorial animals. They tend to construct their catholicity more through geography than ideology. Thus, it is common for bishops in the Church of England to talk warmly of the church as 'a presence in every community' – as tangible and visible as the main village post box. Everyone knows where it is; everyone has access to one. And at the risk of extending the metaphor, it is about *presence*, and less about *performance*. Mail might only be collected from a rural post box on a minimal, infrequent basis – but it will still be timed, regular and dependable.

Anglican maps of the world – and there are such things – will often shade in the countries where there is an Anglican presence or established province. Such maps, of course (see Maps 1 and 2), vary from province to province. A North American map of the Anglican Communion places North America in the centre of the map, in a way that the Church of England's cartographical imagination would usually not. Then, there are churches 'in communion' with the Anglican Church, and issues to negotiate on how to describe older Anglican churches in countries like Spain and Portugal, that existed long before the Diocese in Europe (Church of England) or the Affiliate churches of the Episcopal Church (USA) in Europe.

Such maps – wherever they come from – can be selective, impressive and misleading in equal measures. For example, there are around 85 million 'members' of the world-wide Anglican or Episcopalian 'family', and they are scattered over an impressive 165 countries, globally. Shaded in on a map, that is an estimable sight, covering all of North America, most of South America, large parts of Africa, Europe (chaplaincy churches), Asia, parts of the Far East, Australasia and more besides. Given that there are only around 200 countries in the world, a presence in more three quarters of them is understandably impressive. Indeed, the Anglican Communion is the third largest Christian communion in the world, after the Roman Catholic Church and the Eastern Orthodox Churches.

But an Anglican map of the world may only tell a story about presence, and not about performance. There is, for example, an Anglican Church in Japan – Nippon Sei Ko Kai. *Nippon Seikōkai*, or the Japanese Holy Catholic Church (abbreviated as NSKK), is sometimes referred to in English as the Anglican Episcopal Church in Japan. It has some 60,000 members, spread across eleven dioceses. But the population of Japan is 130 million, which means that Anglicans account for 0.046 per cent of the population. Or, if you prefer, an approximate ratio of one Anglican for every 21,500 of population. To put this in some other perspective, it is estimated that there may be 30,000 active followers of Christian Science in the United Kingdom (the movement founded by Mary Baker Eddy in 1879). The population of the UK is approximately 65 million, and the percentage of Christian Science followers in the UK is therefore almost identical to the percentage of Anglicans in Japan. So to shade Japan as 'Anglican' on a map is to convey a signal about presence (indeed, the very slightest, arguably), but not necessarily pre-eminence or performance.

Yet appearances can be deceptive. The Japanese Anglican Church can boast nine colleges of higher education and universities – two in Kobe (St. Michael's, and the Shoin Women's University); St. Agnes', St. Andrew's, St. Paul's, St. Luke's and St. Margaret's universities; Ryujo Junior and Poole Gakuin College. Japan has more Anglican higher education institutions than the Church of England. So to gain a sense of ecclesial presence and performance, one usually has to look well beyond the bare, presenting statistics.

For example, the Hong Kong Sheng Kung Hui (abbreviated as HKSKH) is the Anglican Church of Hong Kong and Macau. It is the 38th Province of the Anglican Communion. It is also one of the major denominations in Hong Kong. There are three dioceses – Hong Kong Island, Eastern Kowloon and Western Kowloon. The Province also cares for Macau, which is a designated territory for mission and ministry, with clergy, churches and schools all present. The population of Hong Kong is around 7 million – so about the same size as London – and the number of active Anglicans around 35,000, constituting about 0.5 per cent of the population. Or, one Anglican per 200 of population.

However, size isn't everything here, and nor are statistics. Another map of Hong Kong would show a highly active church engaged in a range of ministries: caring for the elderly, family counselling service, spiritual support in hospitals, pastoral care in correctional institutes, the Mission to Seafarers, and ministry at the airport are some of the Church's services. The church runs numerous infant and junior schools, kindergartens, and more than thirty secondary schools. St Christopher's Home, run by the Anglican Church, is the largest non-governmental organisation in Hong Kong providing small group home services for children who cannot receive adequate family care. Founded in 1935 by Bishop R.O. Hall, it complements the St James' Settlement – a multi social service agency founded in 1949, also by R.O. Hall, which provides high quality comprehensive services to meet the diverse needs of our society, to enable the individuals to help themselves and to help others, and to build an integrated and harmonious community. Hong Kong Sheng Kung Hui may only have 35,000 active members – but its work, literally, touches millions of lives through education, ministries and welfare.

As I argue later in this book, Anglicans need to be cautious about taking the claimed numbers of followers from each province at face value. The Church of England claims 25 million of the worldwide Communion's 85 million. Nigeria claims 18 million. But there are good reasons to suppose that neither of these numbers is a reliable guide to 'core' committed membership. Indeed, as Daniel Munoz[7] has recently argued, the claim that the 'global south' Anglican churches should be treated now as the *majority* and *growing* part of the Communion should be treated with some scepticism. The claim to be the largest critical mass, and expanding, does, of course, confer certain rights in negotiations on contentious issues, and there is plenty of evidence that points to amplified accounts of numerical supremacy privileging amplified conservative agendas. The conservative alliance of GAFCON provinces and primates (Global Anglican Future Conference) has certainly used its beefed-up figures to gain greater leverage in negotiations on morality and polity. But as Munoz points out, the numbers claimed are unreliable, and probably exaggerated. Moreover, and ironically, the numbers in the (much-maligned) American and Canadian churches may be firmer, stronger and more reliable. Yet the myth persists that the northern-liberal churches are in decline, and the more southern-conservative churches are growing.

Maps reify an understanding of reality. But they are interpretative as well as descriptive: they can create facts, fallacies, fictions and fantasies. It is common in the Church of England to possess a 'social imaginary of comprehensiveness' that construes the church as providing universal coverage. Like a spiritual national health service, the church imagines itself as a free-at-point-of-delivery public utility. The reality on the ground, however, is one of increasingly stretched resources. One priest to cover several dozen square miles, and perhaps a dozen churches and parishes in a single benefice, is still a 'comprehensive service' for the people of that area – but not perhaps 'comprehensive' in the way the word was used, say three or four decades ago.

As Benedict Anderson notes in his *Imagined Communities* (1983), maps can shape nationalism, ideologies, fictions and fantasies. The map that the average foot soldier of (so-called) Islamic State carries in their mind is one of a territorial caliphate in which the tide of western influence has been stemmed and contained, and replaced by a 'pure' Islam. The reality on the ground is different. Much of the territory (currently) occupied by Islamic State is deserted of people – to which the large mass of Syrian refugees fleeing their homeland throughout 2015 bore ample testimony.[8]

Anglicans, when they 'map' their world, are curiously territorial – both globally and locally. For example, the claim to have a 'presence in every community' in England is true. There are over 16,000 Anglican churches in England – plenty for the population at large. But the Post Office can claim something similar, with its 115,000 letter boxes in the UK, and 98 per cent of the population living within half a mile of one. But letters are not always collected every day. Just as services in churches are not necessarily taking place every week. Some communities will only have one church service

---

7 Munoz, 'North to South: A Reappraisal of Anglican Communion Membership Figures'.
8 Anderson, *Imagined Communities*.

per month. A story of extensive coverage is not necessarily one that implies intensive connection.

Moreover, the kind of geographical catholicity beloved of English Anglicans (i.e., 'we have the nation covered') may occlude some debates on ideological and theological comprehensiveness. The Church of England has, in the twenty-first century, struggled to maintain its full and unambiguous commitment to the 'broad church' principles that shaped and governed its polity – drawn from the writings of Richard Hooker and the Elizabethan Settlement – which have largely flourished throughout its history. Even the Victorian era, which saw some tribal polarisation between evangelical and catholic Anglicanism, still maintained a steady commitment to providing a range of variables in a broad polity. In the twentieth century too, the Church of England was able to balance tensions between liberals and conservatives, catholic and evangelical, traditionalists and innovators. But the twenty-first century, arguably, has witnessed global Anglican polity – including within the Church of England – struggling with fragmentation, tribalism and polarisation. A church, and an ecclesial and theological polity, that was once inclusive, broad and comprehensive, has become increasingly narrow and exclusive.

Moreover, the significant shift of the church – from comprehensive institution to narrower, member-based organisation – has meant that the social imaginary of global Anglicanism, as a map, no longer gives us a full or accurate picture. New territorial and ideological alliances – Sydney Anglicans and parts of Africa, for example – suggest that geographical catholicity is now more complex than it used to be. Even on a simple parish level in the Church of England, it is quite possible to be a 'member' of an Anglican congregation or meeting that has little or no relationship to the parish church and the basic utility of ministry that is offered by the clergy who have the legal 'cure of souls' for the community. This situation has partly arisen because the Church of England has seen fit to license a series of experiments – usually referred to as Pioneer Ministries, 'Fresh Expressions', 'Missional Congregations' or other groupings – that are extensions of or links to another church that has developed what one might term 'a niche-based tribal proclivity'.

Thus, members of such groups have no need to relate to their parish church, or even, particularly, to the complex culture and context of their community. They are free to develop a relatively a-contextual congregational subculture in a given area, and then associate within a much narrower social homogeneity. But whilst this might appear to outsiders to be little more than an agreeable club – albeit with sacred and spiritual dimensions – its strength lies in its tribalism. And in terms of map-making and a new social imaginary, even a relatively small gathering, such as I am describing, is free to describe itself as 'an Anglican (or Christian) presence' in any community it chooses to meet in. But 'presence' here may only mean that there is some *location* for the gathering. A regular, *intensive gathering* of believers does not necessarily imply an *extensive repertoire* of ministries that reaches out beyond the church, into the wider community. The true church is, of course, both intensive and extensive, and rooted first and foremost in the worship of God, not growth.

On a visit to a church some years ago that had spawned a large number of 'cell churches' and 'fresh expressions', I spied a map on the wall in the foyer that illustrated the issue starkly. Maps, of course, as any sociologist or anthropologist knows, are representations of reality. They require the reader to collude with scales, symbols and other codes to develop a sense of what is on the ground. But the map is not reality; the same applies to any description of anything – it must also be interpretative. This particular map placed the church I was in right at the heart of the city it was ministering to. From this centre, ribbons flowed out far and wide to the suburbs, which were then pinned in to a significant number of peripheral locations. It was a web-like image: a centre, but reaching out far and wide with tentacles. The message of the map was clear: we touch every part of this city; we have it covered.

Yet I was well aware that a number of the identified locations for coverage were contentious. After all, I lived in this city. To be sure, there could be no question that small groups of Christians, and those who attended this church in the centre, were meeting in these neighbourhoods, week in, week out. They were praying for these localities too: 'naming and claiming' the streets in passionate and concentrated extemporary prayer meetings. But I also knew where many of these gatherings were held. And that, with one or two rare exceptions, the vast majority of the inhabitants in the neighbourhoods (including those that attended their own ordinary local or parish churches) were mostly ignorant of these other meetings. In other words, for the church identifying itself at the heart of the city centre, there was a map and a story that spoke of widespread engagement with all these different neighbourhoods. Yet on the ground, there was little evidence to support this.

So, there is a symbiotic alchemy of map-making that occurs in religious groups and is produced from the delicate fusion of the social imaginary with a prevailing theological construction of reality. The worldview that emerges will, invariably, not only determine how a church or congregation sees itself within the world, but how they see the world around them. This exercise – or rather ongoing process – rarely produces an actual map. But it does produce a kind of inner map in the mind of the believers: places to avoid; places of potential; places of plenty, and so forth. In some cases, it will produce actual maps – 'centres' of spiritual activity identified in localities that by their very presence and activity will cultivate new neighbourhoods.

In what way is such a map – the kind described above – a form of 'symbiotic alchemy'? Simply, in the way that this city-centre church continued to feed off and promote its rhetoric of *extensity*. Whereas the actuality on the ground – in missiological terms – was that the church had confused extensity with *dispersed intensity*. The two are not, of course, the same.

Dispersed intensity lacks the complex social engagement that can really only come about through dense and reticulate institutional structures that emerge out of churches that are committed to deep local extensity. The map, in other words, painted a picture that told a story.

Mapping the future?

All that said, this book is concerned with the currents, contours and charts that are shaping not only the present church, but also its future direction. It is recognised, throughout the chapters in this book, that in identifying the currents, contours and charts as broadly *descriptive*, those same features are also actively interpretative. Thus, for the Church of England to be constantly referring, as it currently does, to its imminent demise, and therefore prioritising numerical growth to combat the (alleged) decay in membership, is to acknowledge that these social, missional and theological constructions present us with maps that are interpretative of the present, precisely in order to set a preferred future course for the church. There is an inherent synergy between the currents, contours and charts that are constantly appealed to by the leadership of the church – what it is suggested can be navigated, resisted or avoided – and those charts that are then set out as alternative scenarios.

There is nothing new in this. As Amy DeRogatis suggests,[9] it was commonplace in early American pioneer mission and ministry to construct maps that narrated the theological, evangelistic and ecclesial challenges missionaries felt that they faced. Mapping, indeed, was a form of moralising – by sketching out what lay both at and beyond the frontiers of knowledge (new territory, as yet unsettled), missionaries were able to bring maps back to their congregations at home that set out the spiritual and moral needs of the lands yet to be encountered and understood. As native populations decreased, so maps moved representations of these natives to the margins of these maps, and filled the centre of the maps with representations of 'untamed' territory, abundant lands, forests and rivers, evoking images of 'natural plenty'. Just as the Mappamundi had done centuries before, the centre of the map was the object of desire. And in the case of early American settlers, this was often an empty, abundant expanse, waiting to be tamed and cultivated. In other words, the maps constituted an idealised social construction of reality.

Contemporary 'church maps', insofar as they exist, do the same. Granted, they may not be set out as a map, per se. But maps they most certainly are. A Mission Action Plan (literally, another kind of MAP) will frequently set out, in words, where the challenges and opportunities lie; where the potential for growth may be; where the present lacks abundance. Spiritual cartographies are plentiful in missional thinking and praxis. And this is partly what the study of culture and Christianity needs to press on with. In so doing, one makes new maps. These maps, indeed, will be of those who are themselves

9 DeRogatis, *Moral Geography.*

trying to navigate and chart the waters of the challenges of contemporary culture in the twenty-first century. But in describing the contours and currents of the contemporary situation, those cartographers are plotting a chart that might be described as interpretative just as much as it is descriptive.

In all of this, I write with two key concerns in mind. The first is obviously the state and coherence of the Anglican Communion, about which the essays on sexuality are inevitably concerned. And the second is for the Church of England, and its identity as a national church. One writer encapsulates this second concern in somewhat stark terms:

> The historian of the last fifty years is left only to wonder what the next fifty years will bring. Unless the societal patterns which have gathered such force in the later twentieth century are superseded by new ones which combine to benefit the cause of corporate Christianity, at some point decline must bite through the sinews of the body and into the structures, the very bones, which give it solid form and movement. Arguably, it was the achievement of the Church Commissioners between 1948 and 1998 to maintain, by a steady, ongoing reform of particulars, the contours of an order and a method which might well have decayed and even collapsed in some areas without their efforts. Perhaps a future age will observe that their legacy was simply to hold back for period of time a decline which was altogether something too formidable to be halted by the Churches alone. For how much longer can the Church of Christ preserve a pervasive presence in the patterns of individual life, and in the localities of every community, when the landscape which it inhabits shows such a relentless erosion of explicit public devotion and committed participation? Such a phenomenon, in a society which Christianity has for centuries formed, characterised and dignified, brings no clear assurances and no obvious prospects.[10]

The agenda here, therefore, is the construction of a forward-looking map, which is rooted in the enterprise of ethnographic theology. One can never claim that such a map is anything more than an interpretative impression, but drawing as I do on theology, sociology, anthropology and cultural studies, this book might be, to some extent, classed as an 'ethnographic theology' of contemporary (and future) Anglicanism. This is an exercise, however, that is grounded in an appropriate humility. For the study cannot claim to be more than an impression from ground-level; 'dispatches from the front', so to speak. As Natalie Wigg-Stevenson notes,

> as with any cartography, the particular type of map drawn over a terrain is related to and intended to produce the particular kind of activity the person who consults the map wants to perform therein. We use a

10 Chandler, *The Church of England in the Twentieth Century*, pp. 481–482.

road map to drive from Seattle to Vancouver, a topological subway map to negotiate station transfers on the London Underground, scribbles on the back of a bar napkin to lure a potential lover to our home, or an orienteering map to run wildly through the woods.[11]

Much of my work on Anglicanism, as will become apparent in this book, imagines Anglicanism in spatial terms, and as a series of complex relations between church and world. (This explains, for example, why the Titanic, as a trope, emerges in the conclusion – for the spatial potential of the metaphor). However, in mapping global Anglican polity this way, and more specifically the Church of England, I do not presume to have an elevated view of the field I survey. There is no 'bird's eye' (or for that matter, 'God's eye') view of the church. One can only write and interpret what one sees on the ground – a ground of which I, and any interpreter, am inescapably part of.

That said, more is attempted than mere sketching. As Natalie Wigg-Stevenson suggests, drawing on the work on reflexive sociology of Pierre Bourdieu and the cultural theology of Katherine Tanner, theologians dig and excavate; they look for meanings below the obvious surfaces we encounter; they look for hidden links, and the 'underlying body of rules or patterned order' which may exist. This, in part, explains why theology is not a 'pure' empirical discipline. It involves tactics, guesswork, hunches and preliminary findings – all of which are gradually refined as more material is unearthed, discerned and interpreted. Often, theology is not a matter of locating agreement, but rather of practising engagement: it is an inherently relational discourse and practice that is born of hybridity, not purity.[12]

Central to the concern of this book, therefore, is 'culture' – both the emerging 'ecclesial culture' of our age, and the contemporary cultural contexts in which the church is unavoidably immersed. The engagement with the presenting issues in the book consists of a delicate, reticulate blend of theological reflection and social theory (primarily cultural studies, sociology and anthropology). Many would see this, overall, as 'theological reflection', and to some extent I am happy to own that nomenclature, provided the reader understands that ecclesiology is the subject to which this book is devoted, and specifically Anglican ecclesial life.

The title for this book – *The Future Shapes of Anglicanism* – draws deliberately on a prescient and provocative book by the great Episcopalian contextual theologian Urban Tigner Holmes III, entitled *The Future Shape of Ministry – A Theological Projection*. Holmes' hypothesis – that ministry would need to learn to 'read' culture if it was to successfully adapt – may seem obvious. But Holmes' work, for its time, was revolutionary; Holmes saw the danger in a church that might not be able to distinguish between cultural

11 Wigg-Stevenson, *Ethnographic Theology*, p. 11
12 cf., Wigg-Stevenson, p. 24.

resonance (a good thing, in his mind), cultural *relevance* (which carried both risks and rewards) and cultural *relativism* (which risked compromising the gospel and, ultimately, the identity of the church). For Holmes, the church needed wisdom both for the present age and the age to come, if it was to successfully chart its way through the currents and contours of contemporary culture. To a large extent, this book continues that same agenda, and in following Holmes, raises questions and flags up dangers, without necessarily suggesting clear, concrete answers. This is, of course, a perfectly defensible strategy: 'proceed with care', so to speak. Faith is constantly being formed; it is not complete. And neither is knowledge. So to move forward with both caution and confidence, in a balanced, Anglican way, is to practise humility and avoid hubris.

I also have drawn on Urban Holmes' *What is Anglicanism?* – possibly one of the finest, most illuminating and most perceptive introductions to Anglican consciousness, theology, liturgy and praxis. Holmes was unafraid to confess the consciousness of the church. 'We Anglicans', he comments, 'are not given to writing great theology'. The world of Anglican life is constructed not so much through abstract doctrinal propositions (let alone strategies or tactics) as it is through music, poetry, liturgy and prose, '(creating) a world of wonder in which it is easy to fall in love with God'. There is a lineage of inspiration that runs, for example, from Julian of Norwich to Milton, and ends in T.S. Eliot. Countless other examples – Herbert, Donne, C.S. Lewis and Dorothy L. Sayers, to name but a few – illustrate Holmes' key observation, that Anglicanism is a faith of sensibility. Its absorption with aesthetics mirrors the belief that God meets us in a vast range of experiences, not just a handful of selected texts or doctrines, or a tightly defined and strongly policed sphere of dogma. In Anglicanism, the nature of God is ultimately inexpressible, and can't be reduced to simplistic notions.[13]

Put another way, Anglican polity testifies to the breadth of God. Here Holmes' writing concurs with my own 'spatial' instincts:

> We often speak of Anglican 'comprehensiveness'. If this is a way of making relativism palatable or a means of accommodating all shades of opinion with no regard to truth, then it needs to be rejected. If by comprehensiveness we mean the priority of a dialectic quest over precision and immediate closure, then we are speaking of the Anglican consciousness at its best. This sense of a community of thought as opposed to a well-defined, definitive position . . . is why Anglicanism has never been a confessional church.[14]

13 For further discussion, and for a more distinctively English elucidation, see Ecclestone, *The Parish Church?* See also Watson, *Introducing Feminist Ecclesiology*, and Gittoes, Green and Heard, *Generous Ecclesiology*.
14 Holmes, *What is Anglicanism*, p. 7.

Holmes understood that a rich, deep engagement with culture was crucial for the life of the church, if it was to live out its incarnational vocation – to be at home in the world in the here and now (and so to make our home here) so that the world might be at home with God for eternity. So for Holmes, Anglicanism is 'a mode of making sense of the experience of God', or 'a particular approach to the construction of reality', or 'to the building of a world'.[15] As a polity, it most certainly constitutes a kind of map – a social or theological construction of reality. And such a map might, for example, conflict with other maps of the present and the future.

Ecclesiology is simply the social-institutional reification of the theology, Christology and pneumatology of a denomination. The Father, Son and Holy Spirit worshipped, adored, manifest and immanent in a given congregation and ecclesial community manifests itself in aesthetics, structures, governance, polity, mission and praxis. The Father, Son and Holy Spirit we believe in and worship – consciously and unconsciously – is what we ultimately reify in our institutional life. A belief in a broad, deep, relaxed, non-intervening God will lead, most likely, to a fairly mellow, non-intense church. A subscription to an intense and passionate theology will most likely result in that being manifest in worship and polity – formal and informal. Adherence to a God who frets about the state of the world, might be angry about our state of being and is anxious to save souls will, inevitably, lead to a fretful polity that is anxiety-ridden for those who are not 'members' (i.e. saved).

In the context of this book, this simple observation matters quite a lot. Some years ago, I was present at a meeting when the then most senior Executive Manager in the Church of England told a gathering of our most senior theological educators that 'our days for doing theologies of education or for theological formation in training, or for church leadership, are finished'. What he meant to imply was this. That in the entire reconstruction of seminary or theological education, there would be no theological thinking to reflect on the content or process of the new world being ushered in, or to construct the foundation upon which this new world would rest. All the decisions to be made were pragmatic, organisational and financial. Theology had no need to involve itself with the resulting reconstruction. The decisions would be made by executive managers and strategists, and not by theologians.

This is a serious problem for the Church of England. Indeed, it is hard to know where to begin with critiquing this current approach to theological education and formation, which will almost certainly lead to a vacuous polity. The risks of investing in ever-greater 'missional activism' – whilst at the same time disinvesting in deeper theological education and formation – are significant. Moreover, this disinvestment and downgrading of theological education is occurring at a time when there is less and less religious literacy within our schools and in our wider culture. One can no longer assume

15 Ibid., p. 1.

that undergraduates, for example, will know enough about Christianity to understand the Reformation(s) (if reading history), or Milton (if studying English literature). Hymns and Bible readings seldom form part of daily worship at school. And this means that those coming to test vocations now are less enculturated in Christianity than previous generations. So the case for *increasing* investment in theological education for seminarians could hardly be stronger. What is the point of missional activism if the church does not know the faith it hopes to convert people too, and the people proclaiming the message are themselves, only partially educated in Christian doctrine? Yet the Church of England seems set to continue to disinvest in the cultivation of wisdom and theological formation, whilst increasing its investment in missional activism.

Organisational-activism and management can't fill the gap vacated by theology, Christology or pneumatology. Management can't replace God. If God – and theology, Christology and pneumatology – are not our point of origin for addressing and transforming the church, then we will simply produce a secular reification; non-sacred or anti-sacred. The glory of power is its reification. And what is reified from the power of secular ideologies will be a creed that values the material, quantifiable and reproducible: exactly what the executive managers follow. Here, therefore, the church might as well be a supermarket chain or car-plant, the only difference being that we are 'selling' God and trying to increase our customer-base through our outlets (i.e. churches). But such a viewpoint is little more than a form of idolatry. Now, the executive manager proposing to exclude theology is no idolater, to be sure. But he is proposing a production plant and line – shaped and governed by salvific management – and then placing it at the heart of our life and worship, in order to grow the number of consumers. And that is idolatry. We cannot worship systems and functions – even for ends we believe to be good: only God can be worshipped.

This short vignette gets close to the heart of the issue for the church: how to engage with culture. In the case of this vignette, the culture is managerial, and it purports to be able to run the church better, discipline it (spiritually, fiscally, strategically, etc.) and turn it into a fitter, healthier body, with 'effectiveness' and 'growth' following. The resonant cultural tropes here are multiple and manifest. But many who now see this problem in ecclesiology and theology are not rewarded for their sentinel prescience. They are, instead, experiencing something of an exile within their own church. The culture the church should be critiquing is actually the one shaping its governance and polity. To be sure, there is a risk in any volume like this of being implicated in a Canute-like parable – a desperate shake of the fist at incoming tides and rising sea-levels. All we can highlight here is the fact that, as the church produces its own ever-thickening culture of managerialism within, it incapacitates itself to act prophetically and poetically without. It suffocates in its own effluence.

The culture of church and the church of culture

Engaging with contemporary culture is invariably the most demanding task facing the church. Every generation of Christians that has ever lived has struggled with this. Michael Bailey and Guy Redden[16] point out that 'culture' is one of the most complicated words in the English language. The word seems to cover anything and everything. There are cultures of shame and abuse; alternative cultures and sub-cultures; political and religious cultures; cultures of ethnicity, gender and sexuality; of nationhood and regions; and popular culture and aesthetics. Indeed, there is nothing that is outside the panoply of culture. Of course, much of what is distinctive in the Christian faith emerges from a dialogue with culture. Indeed, there has never been a time when culture was not an issue for Christian faith. The New Testament bears ample witness to this: what to eat, what to wear, who to relate to, and how, and so forth. The contemporary form of the issue arises from new sources: the missionary experience of the western churches, the inimical secularisation thesis, and apparently declining church attendance. Correspondingly, the terms 'contextualisation' and 'enculturation' have quickly crept into western theology from the field of missiology, which for decades had been questioning the relationship between concepts of truth and revelation and the problem of relativism.

So what does the current, somewhat sketchy, map of the future suggest might be some of the key issues facing Anglicanism in the twenty-first century? Of course, authority and power in the Communion, and the vehicles and mechanisms for coherence and catholicity, will continue to be relentlessly tested. All the signs are, at present, that they are resilient. That said, we must remember that the so-called Instruments of Unity were not designed to resolve issues of gender or sexuality. These Instruments of Unity – the Archbishop of Canterbury, the Meeting of Primates, the Anglican Consultative Council and the Lambeth Conference – have all come under pressure in recent years, and show marked signs of wear and tear. We might say, therefore, that in a Communion of increasing local and regional particularisation (e.g., Sydney evangelicals being themselves, but also exporting that ethos on platforms of conservatism to preserve a version of 'orthodoxy' that is anti-liberal), there may be some serious issues to resolve about how to maintain a cohesive catholic Communion that is trans-national.

Equally, we can point to several emerging issues that are arguably most manifest in the Church of England, but are also apparent, by extension, across the Communion. These include an emerging decline in and loss of theological leadership. The church lacks articulate theological leadership in many key internal functions. More generally, theological literacy amongst the bishops is a growing problem. Coupled to this, there is a growing lack

---

16 Bailey and Redden, *Mediating Faiths*.

of intellectual public presence: with little in the way of theological depth or significance to offer, some parts of the Anglican Communion are now reduced to bishops being no more than regional managers of organisations (dioceses) struggling with money and resources, as well as being purveyors of spiritual sentiments that rarely impact outside the church.

This problem is linked directly to an observable, inward turn: managing processes, crises, anxiety levels and so forth in the body of the church. Despite a prevalent and thick veneer of 'leadership rhetoric' – one found littered all over the church – the reality is that most Anglican bishops are becoming managers, not leaders; and mired in the pastoralia, processes and proclivities that muzzle them. Ironically, the growth in numbers of diocesan staff and church administration, including senior staff with executive functions that are designed to *release* senior clergy for pastoral, theological and liturgical work, has only served to increase the amount of time bishops now seem to spend in management and committees, and not in public leadership. Bishops and churches have become organisationally absorbed with their own processes. Managerialism is therefore a key cultural construct and challenge for the present and future. Yet the emerging breed of episcopal managers tends to collude with this problem, precisely because they do not really see themselves as teachers or theologians – with some openly admitting they are not. So they inhabit a world of pastoralia (chaplain to the congregations of their diocese), internal organisational strategy, tactics, processes, marketing, branding and so forth. This is busy work, to be sure; but it really is a distraction from actually engaging the gospel with the world, and leading and representing the people of God confidently in the public sphere.

What suffers in this is leadership in public life. We no longer seem to have the theological deftness amongst our bishops that can lead us through complex public, ethical, moral, social or theological dilemmas in a way that earns national respect and admiration. As a church, we seem to spend all our time trying to balance our own proclivities and praxis within the church. Few bishops would currently command significant public attention on issues of vital national importance or public concern outside the congregations and dioceses they oversee. Increasingly, our language and practice as a church is that of 'insiders' and 'members'; as a consequence, there is little chance of any new bishop being a good outsider.[17]

Mission is also at issue here. Despite much of our own 'insider emphasis' on mission, it seldom masks what is really just a broad range of anxieties about money, resources and numerical growth. Few bishops could currently write an inspiring theology of mission; and even fewer could write about mission in context in a way that might engage the academy or public life. The Anglican Church seems to have an abundance of tacticians and

17 On this, see Woodhead and Brown, *That Was the Church That Was: How the Church of England Lost the English People*, 2016.

practitioners – who, like all managers, model varying degrees of effectiveness. There is nothing more practical than a good theory. But we have almost no theologically-literate theoreticians within the present domain of episcopacy who could craft such a theory.

The end-game of this is a gradual emergence of a vacuum – of the absence of inspiration. With so few bishops contributing to contemporary culture publicly and intelligently, the church risks turning ever-more inwards. But even here, it cannot manage itself out of its own internal crises. The women bishops or sexuality debates, for example, still need good theological minds and theological leadership, and not managerially-led or legal compromises. In consistently choosing 'safe managers' for episcopacy (indeed 'a safe pair of hands' has become a widely revered ecclesial trope), the church can quickly look bland, and lacking in depth. The public turns away.

The church has, in the twenty-first century, moved against its thinkers, prophets and educators. It fears a breadth in leadership; people who can think outside the box; and who have some theological imagination. Arguably, management has seen to that. Alas, other smaller denominations, having lost their initial generations of charismatic leadership, have already found themselves lost to the corrosive forces of bureaucratisation. If Anglicans are not careful, we will soon repeat their history. Ultimately, unless our church is truly free to be the Church again, we run the serious risk of being over-managed into a rather vapid and ineffectual form of Christian witness. English Anglicanism will be all process, but no content: a body without a soul; a kind of 'Zombie Church', in fact.

Conclusion

Earlier in this introduction, we referred to the sense of exile that some now experience *within* Anglicanism. Muriel Porter's recent work[18] records the seismic shifts over the past few decades that have changed the contours of the Anglican Church in Australia. Harsh conservative forces are threatening the historic inclusive comprehensiveness of Anglicanism, partly in reaction to the ordination of women and issues of human sexuality. Fear and anxiety about the church's future, coupled to assertive managerialism, are crippling the leadership's response. In a similar vein, albeit more positive, Greg Garrett's work laments the pessimism that sometimes drives American Episcopalians straight into the arms of uncritical and under-discerned strategies for numerical growth. Garrett argues for a recovery of nerve, and faith in a distinguished past and rich tradition of spiritual depth, which alone can lead to a vibrant present and brighter future.[19]

The Spectator magazine has recorded in the Church of England the 'reformers versus opponents' contest that underlies the growing sense of exile:

---

18 Porter, *A New Exile?*
19 Garrett, *My Church Is Not Dying.*

A new mood has taken hold of Lambeth Palace. Officials call it urgency; critics say it is panic. The Church of England, the thinking goes, is about to shrink rapidly, even vanish in some areas, unless urgent action is taken. This action, laid out in a flurry of high-level reports, amounts to the biggest institutional shake-up since the 1990s. Red tape is to be cut, processes streamlined, resources optimised. Targets have been set. The Church is ill – and business management is going to cure it . . . Provoking more anxiety, though, is the emphasis on growth in numbers. Half of the central fund distributed to help poorer dioceses is to be diverted to support thriving projects. The previous system was thought to 'subsidise decline'. The new approach, to be brought in over ten years, is meant to 'incentivise . . . Church growth and innovation and flexibility'.[20]

It is this sense of capitalism and managerialism shaping the church that formed the basis for David Hare's excoriating play focused on the Church of England, *Racing Demon*.[21] The same theme was recently revived in Steve Water's play, *Temple*.[22] For the Church of England, there has never been a shortage of literature offering the anatomy of a crisis. We should perhaps note that Anglicanism is not alone in this. One simply has to witness the range of offerings that deal with Roman Catholicism (e.g., Walert Bühlmann, Desmond Ryan, etc.); or ecclesial communities more generally (e.g., Michael Jinkins, and David Bebbington and Timothy Larsen).[23] More specifically, writers such as Paul Avis, Stephen Pickard, +Rowan Williams, Bruce Kaye, Daniel Hardy and Mark Chapman write hopefully about current crises in polity and identity.[24] From a historical outlook, apparent crises are set in a more measured perspective by writers such as Stephen Bayne and H.R. McAdoo.[25] Critical, and arguably more pessimistic, perspectives can be gleaned from Ephraim Radner, Philip Turner, Muriel Porter and Bill Sachs, amongst others.[26] More popular approaches, questioning structures (Steven Croft and Keith Elford, for example), or probing, on the other hand, creeping tribalism (Betty Saunders, Peter Selby, etc.) demonstrate that there is no shortage of 'future maps' for the Church of England and wider Anglican Communion.[27]

---

20 Greaves, 'God's Management Consultants: The Church of England Turns to Bankers for Salvation', p. 20.
21 Hare, *Racing Demon*.
22 Waters, *Temple*.
23 Bühlmann, *The Coming of the Third Church*; Ryan, *The Catholic Church*; Jinkins, *The Church Faces Death*; Bebbington and Larsen, *Modern Christianity and Cultural Aspirations*.
24 Avis, *Church Drawing Near*; Avis, *The Identity of Anglicanism*; Pickard, *Seeking the Church*; Williams, *Anglican Identities*; Kaye, *Conflict and the Practice of Christian Faith*; Hardy, *Finding the Church*; Chapman, *Anglican Theology*.
25 Bayne, *An Anglican Turning Point*; McAdoo, *Anglican Heritage*.
26 Radner and Turner, *The Fate of Communion*; Sachs, *The Transformation of Anglicanism*; Porter, *Sydney Anglicans and the Threat to World Anglicanism*.
27 Croft, *The Future of the Parish System*; Elford, *Creating the Future of the Church*; Saunders, *Oh Blest Communion! The Home Life of the Church of England*; Selby, *Be Longing: A Challenge to the Tribal Church*.

So, is there a crisis for the Church of England, and for the wider Anglican Communion? It depends on your perspective. Of course, we live in an age of cultural amnesia. It is no better in the church. But I am reminded of what Herbert Kraemer (a Dutch missiologist) often said: the fact that the church lives in difficult times is not the problem; the fact that we constantly forget the church has always lived in difficult times – that is the problem. This is partly why remembering is so vital in our time. In an age of rapid consumerism and short-term solutions, we do well to dwell on what it means to remember, and why this might be important, not so much for our past as for our present and future. Of course, remembering is at the heart of the gospel: 'do this in remembrance of me' are amongst the last words Jesus utters to his disciples. And 'Lord, remember me when you come into your kingdom' are amongst the last words uttered to Jesus on the cross. But a distracted, dissonant church may be liable to lose its poise, and confuse any kind of apparent missional momentum with progress. We may need, as a church, more pause and poise, and less proactive pioneering.

Holmes closes his exquisite meditation on Anglicanism with this powerful reminder to all who would purport to reform, reinvent, reinvigorate or re-strategise the Church of England or wider Communion:

> There is an inevitable course to our religious profession . . . that course leads to living in the world as God sees the world. We can debate the trivial points, but the vision is largely clear. To love God is to relieve the burden of all who suffer. The rest is a question of tactics.[28]

Holmes' gentle framing of the Great Commandment – love the Lord your God with all your heart, mind, soul and strength, and love your neighbour as yourself (Deut. 6: 5; Lk. 10: 27; Mk. 12: 30, etc.) – is not only the core of our vocation as followers of Jesus. It is also the only true basis for any ecclesiology.

This book sets out the terrain relating to some of the key challenges facing Anglicanism in the twenty-first century. This, by definition, cannot be an exhaustive sketch. But as we noted earlier, this is a work that sits within the field of contemporary ecclesiology; careful attention has been paid to the synergies of Christianity and culture, and the issues presented to a denomination that is attempting to negotiate the cultural currents that shape its contours and also challenge its polity and identity. This is why the story concluding this volume is present in this book. I appreciate that this is unusual for a work of ecclesiology, but it serves as a complement to the timbre of the text as a whole.

As for the main discussion in the book, the connecting thread consists of maps and charts that explore the emerging polity and terrain of global Anglicanism and, more specifically in some places, that of the Church

28 Holmes, *What is Anglicanism?*, p. 95.

of England. Part I looks at mission and management in the Church of England, and also asks some wider questions of the overall leadership of the Anglican Communion in relation to the emerging role of the Archbishop of Canterbury as an instrument of unity. Part II opens up an exploration of three contested areas – money, sex and power – and sketches some of those issues currently presenting to wider Anglican Communion, local churches and dioceses. Part III concludes with some charts and forecasts, and is a more discursive, musing analysis and conversational commentary, exploring some of the problems and possibilities that Anglican ecclesial polity and identity may need to negotiate.

This book, then, is a natural complement to my earlier *Anglicanism: Confidence, Commitment and Communion*, in which issues of catholicity and coherence are consistently probed. Inevitably, there is some slight overlap between the two, but this volume is more critical than its predecessor and emerges out of a set of conversations and reflections that have begged a number of questions. Indeed, one reader of an early draft of this manuscript suggested that if the tone of the first volume was something like *A New Hope* (from the first *Star Wars* trilogy), this might represent the rather darker sequel – the equivalent of *The Empire Strikes Back*, so to speak. (A third volume will appear in due course).

But it also flows out of a deepening conviction. Namely, that Anglican polity is at its best when it is intentionally broad. By 'broad', I do not use the word in a tribal or exclusive way. 'Broad' means the intentional cultivation of a breadth of perspectives – each one held passionately, intelligently and humbly – and entails being respectful of, while perhaps disagreeing with, alternative perspectives. One could perhaps refer to this as 'Angliclusivism' – a rather infelicitous portmanteau word, admittedly. By this, however, I mean to leave almost nothing out; to include, and to hold in as much as possible. Not to exclude. It is a catholic vision of the church – it has the quality of being comprehensive and inclusive. 'Pan-', in other words, embracing all; but with limits, and borders to hold in all and contain the mass. Or, the kind of comprehensiveness to which we referred earlier, articulated by Terry Holmes.

Like Terry Holmes, I believe that the best polity Anglicans have combines both hesitancy and conviction. To be broad and open is, strangely, to be deeply confident and profoundly rooted in Christian faith. And this may be a far better vehicle and guiding ethos for Christianity in the twenty-first century than the kind of shrill, tribal, amplified voices that insist on exclusivity and certainty – only to succeed in repelling and recruiting in equal measure. In contrast, the heartbeat of good, broad theology and ecclesial life, is in some respects slow, chilled and steady; but can also work at pace, and can be given to exuberant spiritual excess, passion and overflow. I hold that every denomination is, to borrow a phrase from John Caputo, an attempt to express the 'mood of God'. Ecclesial life is, essentially, simply the social reification of any group's theological priorities and spiritual proclivities.

The mood of a denomination of congregation essentially captures and communicates what it thinks is the heart, mind and nature of God.

Anglicans are broad because, simply, they think God is much broader than the measure of our minds (as Faber's Victorian hymn suggests).[29] They are also economic and poetic – there being such a thing as 'Anglican aesthetics'. Sometimes Anglicans don't need to spell things out, because art, beauty, music, liturgy and space say more than words ever can.[30] Anglicans, when they use terminology, often revert to broad and deep words like 'Communion', 'catholic' and 'comprehensive' because, deep in the ecclesial DNA of Anglicanism, is a breadth and inclusiveness that is fundamentally resistant to tribalism and sharp, high borders that only serve exclusivists. Anglicans, like the Kingdom of God that Jesus preached and embodied, are radically inclusive. As the epigram 'Outwitted', by American Edwin Markham (1852–1940) put it:

He drew a circle that shut me out –

Heretic, rebel, a thing to flout.

But Love and I had the wit to win:

We drew a circle that took him in!

In some sense, then, this book is partly an elegy, and partly re-vision. It laments what is currently lost (or mislaid) within Anglican polity and ethos in our time. It takes the current threats of tribalism and managerialism seriously; it asks questions of the movement from broad institution to narrow organisation. But it also has a map of what and where the future for Anglicans may lie: theological, spiritual, wise, inspiring, public, open, invitational, passionate, liberal, conservative, radical, orthodox, political, local, national, heavenly, earthly, prophetic, measured, cool, humorous, serious, rational and mystical. Or, put another way, broad.

29 Faber, F.W., *1854* 'There is a Wideness in God's Mercy'.
30 I note, however, that confidence in Anglican aesthetics is receding, and in its place are propositions and statements that are somehow deemed to be more comprehensive. One diocese in the Church of England recently promoted their visionary 'Statement of Purpose' – summarised in a 58 word strap-line. In contrast, the Great Commandment (Matthew 22: 37–40) needs only 47 words to explain the heart of the gospel.

Part I
Currents, contours and charts

1 Growth and management in the Church of England – some charts[1]

The Church of England, in every age, has faced fundamental challenges. Many would cite the challenge of secularisation or consumerism in our time as one of the tougher trials the church has had to negotiate. I am less sure, however. But I do think there are two distinct challenges facing the church today. Or rather, it is one challenge but with two faces, much like a coin. The single-most pressing challenge that the church faces today is that of distraction; and its two sides are mission and management. We appear to be preoccupied with both, and to such an extent that the Church of England now finds that its energies are consumed with perpetual drives towards efficiency and productivity.

Yet the church exists to glorify God and follow Jesus Christ. After which it may grow; or it may not. Its performance may improve too; or it may not. But it is imperative that faithfulness is always put before any search for success. Indeed, for the vast majority of the population of England, church-talk of mission and numbers tends to drive away far more people than it ever draws near. Evelyn Underhill, writing to Archbishop Lang on the eve of the 1930 Lambeth Conference, reminded him that the world was not especially hungry for what the church was immediately preoccupied with. Underhill put it sharply in her letter: 'may it please your Grace . . . I desire to humbly suggest that the interesting thing about religion is God; and the people are hungry for God'.[2]

Preoccupied with productivity?

As any student of early church history will know, the beguiling attraction of the very first heresies and heterodoxies lay in their simplicity. They presented the most attractive solutions to any immediate and apparently unsolvable problems. For the first generations of Christians, these usually lay in the

1 The first part of this article is drawn from a short piece that appeared in the *Church Times*, February 28, 2014 ('It's Not Just About the Numbers').
2 See M. Percy, Easter Sermon, 'More Than Tongues Can Tell', April 13, 2013, delivered at Christchurch Cathedral, New Zealand, reprinted in *Anglican Taonga*, May 2013.

sphere of doctrine and praxis. For us as a church today, the presenting problem appears to be declining numbers in our congregations. Ergo, an urgent emphasis on numerical church growth must be the answer. Right, surely?

Wrong, actually. The first priority of the church is to follow Jesus Christ. This may be a costly calling, involving self-denial, depletion and death. Following Jesus may not lead us to any numerical growth. The first priority of the church is to love the Lord with all our heart, mind, soul and strength, and our neighbours as ourselves (Lk. 10: 25). There is no greater commandment. So the numerical growth of the church cannot be a greater priority than the foundational mandate set before us by Jesus. As Stanley Hauerwas and William H Willimon warn,

> [t]he church lives not by savvy, worldly wisdom, and techniques for church growth but rather lives moment by moment, in every time and place, utterly dependent upon the gifts of the Spirit . . . Christians are people who dare to live in the power of the Holy Spirit, that is, live lives out of control, coming to God dependent, empty-handed, lives driven by and accountable to someone more interesting than ourselves.[3]

It was Karl Barth who observed that the true growth of the church is not to be thought of in mainly extensive terms, but rather in those that are intensive. He argued that the vertical (or intensive) growth of the church – in both height and depth in relation to God – does not necessarily lead to any extensive numerical growth. He added that 'we cannot, therefore, strive for vertical renewal merely to produce a wider audience'. Barth concluded that if the Church and its mission are used only as a means of extensive growth, the inner life of the church loses its meaning and power: 'the church can be fulfilled only for its own sake, and then – unplanned and unarranged – it will bear its own fruits'.[4] That would seem to settle the matter. Moreover, many parish clergy, and those working in all kinds of sector ministries, already know this to be true. The church does not exist to grow exponentially. Mission is deeper than that. The church exists to be the body of Christ.

The pastoral theologian Eugene Peterson once commented that the one thing he had learned in mission and ministry is how complex measurable growth can be. Here, Peterson draws on the theologian, essayist, poet and farmer, Wendell Berry. Peterson says that under Berry's tutelage he has learnt that 'parish work is every bit as physical as farm work: it is about *these* people, at *this* time under *these* conditions'.[5]

The pastoral turn towards an agrarian motif is arresting. Jesus told a number of parables about growth, and they are all striking for their

3 Hauerwas and Willimon, *The Holy Spirit*, 2005, p. ix.
4 Barth, *Church Dogmatics*, Volume IV, Part 2, chapter 15, p. 648.
5 See Peterson, *Under the Unpredictable Plant*; Bonzo and Stevens, *Wendell Berry and the Cultivation of Life*.

simplicity and surprise. Especially the allegory of the sower (Mt. 13: 3–9, etc.). This parable probably should be the template for all Diocesan Mission Action Plans. For what Jesus is saying to the church is this: have regard for your neighbour's context and conditions. So, you might work in a parish with the richest soil, where every seed planted springs to life. The seasons are kind; the vegetation lush; the harvest plentiful. But some places are stony ground, and faithful mission and ministry in that field might be picking out the rocks for several generations. Others labour under conditions where the seeds are often destroyed before they can ever germinate. Or perhaps the weather is extreme in other places, and here we may find that although initial growth is quick, it seldom lasts.

The question the parable throws back to the church is this: what kind of growth can you expect from the ground and conditions you work with? And this is where our current unilateral emphasis on numerical church growth can be so demoralising and disabling. Is it really the case that every leader of numerical church growth is a more spiritually faithful and technically-gifted pastor than their less successful neighbour? The parable says 'no' to this. It implies that some churches labour in harsh conditions; some in fairer. So be wise to the different contexts in which our individual and collective ministries take place.

I mention this for one very obvious reason. If we continue to place the heterodoxy of numerical growth at the heart of the church, we risk eroding our character, and our morale. Some will argue, no doubt, that if you aim at nothing, you'll hit it every time. Better to have a target and a plan than to just keep plodding on. Maybe. But the Charge of the Light Brigade (1854) had vision, courage, objectives, and some strategy; these were not in short supply. But the rest, as they say, is history.

Factors producing numerical church growth and decline are always complex. But the church might need to do some basic work on our maths. In the secular world, one plus one equals two. But counting and adding whole numbers in the church is fuzzy logic. Is a newly baptised infant 'one unit' in terms of believers? Does the person who comes every week, but has more doubt than faith count as 'one' or a 'half'? Is the regular, but not frequent churchgoer 'one', or less? Does the person who comes to everything in church, but has a heart of stone, count as one? Or less?

We know that God counts generously. The poor, the lame, the sick, the sinners; all are promised a place at God's table in his kingdom. That's why Jesus was seldom interested in *quantity*; the Kingdom is about enriching *quality*, even in small numbers. Yet we live a culture that is obsessed by measuring things numerically, and judging success from this. Fortunately, God is loving enough to tell us lots of counter-cultural stories about numbers: going after one, and leaving the ninety-nine, for example. Or, dwelling on a single sparrow; or numbering the hairs left on your head.

God's maths are different to ours. And God does not easily concur with our cultural obsessions with 'growth-equals-success'. No-one denies the urgency of mission, and for the church to address numerical growth. But the church does not exist to grow. It exists to glorify God and follow Jesus Christ. After which it may grow; or it may not. So faithfulness must always be put before the search for success.

So the key to understanding numerical church growth might be to engage in some deeper and more discerning readings of our contexts – the very soil we seek to nourish and bless, so the seeds can flourish. This will usually be more a complex piece of work than simply announcing another new vision or plan for mission. The metaphor is intended here: there is work to be done on the ground.

To be sure, we need leaders who can ride the cultural waves of our time. But we also need other leaders who can read the tides, and the deeper cultural currents of our age. Our recent emphasis on numerical church growth – borne largely from fear, not faith – has led to the unbalanced ascendancy of mission-minded middle-managers.

It is hard to imagine a Michael Ramsey, William Temple or Edward King receiving preferment in the current climate. If all leaders must now make obeisance before the altar of numerical church growth, we will erode our character and mute our mission. The veneration of growth squeezes out the space for broader gifts in leadership that can nourish the church and engage the world. As with all things Anglican, it is a question of balance. No-one can or should say that an emphasis on numerical church growth is wrong. It isn't. The issue is one of proportion. There are no bad foods, only bad diets. And the continued over-emphasis on numerical growth skews the weight and measure in the body of our leadership.

This is a more subtle disproportion than it might at first appear. It was said of the late Cardinal Basil Hume that 'he had the gift of being able to talk to the English about God without making them wish they were some-where else'. The value of this gift should not be underestimated. And for our national mission, this is precisely why we need a leadership that incorporates space for the holy and devout; the gentle pastor; the poet and the prophet; the teacher and theologian; and possibly a radical or two for good measure.

The church may not always draw near to such leaders. But the nation often does – especially those who don't usually go to church. For the first time since the Reformation, we now have no bishops who have held a uni-versity post in theology. The nation may not notice this explicitly, but at a subliminal level, it will certainly sense the lack. So for the sake of national mission, and our credibility, we may want to intentionally develop a broader range of leaders than the very singular objective of numerical church growth currently allows for.

But let us return to numbers. Some of the most recent figures for numerical church growth in the Church of England offer up some surprising anomalies. In the 2010/11 Church Statistics,[6] many dioceses that had well-developed

---

6 *Statistics for the Church of England in 2010/11*, published 2012.

mission strategies showed continuing numerical decline. Only a few did not. Perhaps the greatest surprise was to discover one diocese that had enjoyed significant numerical growth – a whopping 17 per cent in average weekly and usual Sunday attendance. Ironically, this was led by a bishop who had seemingly little in the way of experience in mission and ministry. Like Basil Hume, the bishop had not been a parish priest, and could not tick any of the boxes that indicated he had led any congregation to numerical growth.

The diocese was Canterbury. And the bishop was someone who also had the gift of being able to talk about God in public. Having a knack for imaginative, reflective and refractive public theology and spirituality does indeed intrigue and draw in people who might not otherwise pay attention to the rumour of God.

So by welcoming some teachers, poets and prophets amongst our leadership, and those who point us imaginatively and compellingly to Christ, we might yet discover an even richer, more effective purpose in our mission. And in so doing, also find some other routes to numerical growth along the way.

Over-managed, theologically under-led?

What then, of management? Here, I do not propose to rehearse the extensive and helpful contributions of Richard Roberts to the debates on management and leadership in institutions such as universities, and by implication and extension, our churches. His recent work in this field is sublime and matchless. Instead, I want to begin with a story.[7]

A few years ago, a guest of mine waited in the Common Room of Cuddesdon with a cup of tea until it was time to meet. She sat and read, but quickly found herself tuning in to a conversation some distance away between three ordinands, gathered around the fire. The subject was 'how to get on in the church' – granted, a tiresome-though-typical conversation between students at any theological college. One said it was important to make sure you went to a high-profile parish as a curate. Another, that the key was connections – making the most of who you knew, not what. The third said that what was needed were intellectual qualifications – ideally, a doctorate in theology.

What my guest found strange was the way the first two ordinands rounded on the third. Being theologically well-qualified was fine if you wanted to specialise, they said. But as for getting on in the church, it was surely more of a hindrance than a help. Good management and good connections were the way forward. Good theology would most likely hold you back, and might even marginalise you as 'a specialist'.

---

7 See Roberts, 'Contemplation and the "Performative Absolute": Submission and Identity in Managerial Modernity', pp. 318–337; Roberts, *Religion, Theology and the Human Sciences*; Lewis-Anthony, 'Promising Much, Delivering Little'.

My guest left at this point and headed over for our appointment. She reported the conversation with some bemusement. She asked whether or not I thought it was true. I said I hoped not; though I feared so. This is partly because our current appointments process serves a nest of core priorities: numerical church growth, management and organisation. Being a 'teacher of the faith' or offering cogent public theology has now moved from 'essential criteria' into the 'desirable' column. Theologians amongst our leadership may be appealing, but are not actually necessary. We can manage without, apparently.

As a church, we are now management-led, albeit with an added emphasis on mission. We tend not to choose leaders with rough edges, or who might not fit the mould. The managerially-led process delivers what the managers say the church wants: growth, organisation and management. So, predictability is preferred to prophecy. More alarmingly, consistency and compliance are mistaken for catholicity. As a church we have now confused management and leadership to such an extent that our system of preferment is geared up to the evisceration of truly creative theological leadership.

But there is a further problem here. The managers driving such processes believe and act as though they are leading the church. As Adrian Wooldridge and John Micklethwait claim, 'managers have always fancied themselves in the officer class'.[8] Most key policy areas in the church today are governed not by theological leadership and vision, but by management.

In some ways it is true that leadership is a process similar to management. Leadership entails working with people; so does management. Leadership is concerned with effective goal accomplishment; so is management. But whereas the study of leadership can be traced back to Aristotle and Plato, management science only emerged around the turn of the twentieth century with the advent of advanced industrialised society. Management was created as a means of reducing chaos in organisations, to make them run more efficiently and effectively.

The primary functions of management – identified by Henri Fayol – were planning, organising, staffing and controlling.[9] These functions are still representative of management. Fayol worked for one of the largest producers of iron and steel in France. He became its managing director in 1888, when the mine company employed over 10,000 people.

Fayol realised that the goal of management was to serve processes that produced predictable results. We make round pegs to fit round holes, and square for square. Management eliminates rough edges. Any creative friction tolerated will have to be subordinate to the processes and their goals. So, management will not have a vision for an organic institution, where the wrong shapes might eventually meld together, or even ultimately make something better. As with management, so with the church, perhaps?[10]

8 Wooldridge and Micklethwait, *The Company*, p. 11.
9 Fayol, *General and Industrial Management*.
10 On this, see Malloch, *Practical Wisdom in Management*.

Comparing management with leadership, John Kotter's work argues that the two are contrary, but also connected.[11] The task of management is to provide order and consistency. The task of leadership, in contrast, is to produce change and movement. Management focuses on seeking order and stability, whereas leadership is about seeking adaption and constructive change. That's why management and leadership will always need each other, of course.

Abraham Zaleznik's work went one step further, however, and argued that managers and leaders are actually different types of people.[12] He maintained that managers are reactive, and prefer to work with people in order to solve problems – but tend to do so with 'low emotional involvement'. Essentially, they act to limit choices. In contrast, leaders are usually emotionally engaged. They try to increase the available options in order to resolve problems. Leaders seek to shape ideas; managers just respond to them.[13]

Whether or not one accepts this leadership–management distinction, it is my contention that the church today is primarily a *management-led* organisation. Which is why the relatively new procedure for selecting diocesan bishops is so interesting to reflect upon. It has become a management-led process, driven by executives who run the Crown Nominations Committee (CNC).

The procedure is as follows. Interviews are held in Lambeth Palace, London or Bishopthorpe, York. So there is no opportunity for the candidate to see the place to which they might be called. Families and spouses – their needs (or indeed gifts) – are not part of the consideration process. There is little sense of this being a broader vocational discernment that involves a wide range of potential stakeholders. After a candidate has made a brief presentation, there is an interview lasting barely one hour. All candidates are asked the same questions. There is a nest of issues that all interviews focus on: the priority of numerical church growth, the need for management and clear organisation. But there is no time for vocational dialogue or the development of shared wisdom. There is no space for serious discussion about public theology and national issues requiring theological reasoning, or questions on international issues.

There is no time to test the financial acumen of a candidate, despite diocesan budgets measured in millions. Questions on how candidates might approach divisive issues are mostly avoided. There are 16 people present at the interview, but around two-thirds of the interviewers will sit in total silence – there is not time for them to ask questions, or engage in conversation. All candidates are processed identically, thereby ensuring fairness and organisational compliance. When voting takes place, the preferred candidate needs a

11 Kotter, *A Force for Change.*
12 Zaleznik, 'Managers and Leaders: Are They Different?'
13 See also Torry, *Managing Religion.*

two-thirds majority. Compromises are perhaps inevitable at this point. Yet everything remains subordinate to 'the process'.

Management-led processes tend to reproduce in their own image: more management. So the process cannot receive candidates, for example, who may be artful in the practice of 'loyal dissent' – a charism often thought essential for the church, not least for its own good health and conscience. Instead, the premium is placed on managerial compliance.[14]

The advent of women bishops to some extent occludes this; but it will do so only briefly. The chance of a genuinely radical woman being appointed to a See remains remote. An emphasis on managerial amenability will, alas, see off any serious consideration of women who have prophetic or theological gifts.

A one hour interview for a position of major ecclesiastical responsibility will seem curious to most outsiders. Especially since many clergy, when applying for an incumbency, might spend the best part of the day being interviewed by a very broad array of people. So, for a bishop who will have hundreds of 'employees', and most likely sit in the House of Lords, a one hour interview seems a rather slight process of discernment.

At this point, some additional observations on the CNC interview process may provide further confirmation of the 'management-led' dynamics with which this section is concerned. All the candidates (up to four) arriving for a CNC interview are 'pre-processed' – required to fill in their DBS form (Disclosure and Barring Service check), and produce other relevant documentation before being seen by the panel. After all the candidates have been interviewed and sent home, the panel discussion and voting takes place. The first and second names eventually forwarded to Downing Street each require a two-thirds majority. At present, an STV (Single Transferable Vote) system is in operation, by secret ballot. (See *General Synod Standing Order 122, 2009*, p. 11, and recently amended in July 2013.) Under STV, an elector has a single vote that is initially allocated to their preferred candidate. But as the count proceeds, and candidates are either selected or eliminated, that vote is transferred to other candidates according to the elector's stated second and third preferences.

However, such a process can produce some strange results. For example, it is possible for the panel to select a first choice candidate (who has secured a two thirds majority), but not reach agreement on a second name: in which case the whole process must be re-started from scratch. More generally, STV systems tend to eliminate the potentially more creative candidates, and coalesce around a compromise. So an STV system, on the face of it, might seem like a good 'fit' for the Church of England. It can engage seriously with the kinds of tribalism that might be represented in the various wings and factions of the church, but the eventual outcome tends to lead to a

14 On this, and for a different perspective, see Scruton, *The Uses of Pessimism and the Danger of False Hope*, London: Atlantic Books, 2010.

compromise candidate. (This does of course help explain why poets, prophets and teachers are seldom selected.) But the system has other flaws that can be exploited. There is some anecdotal evidence that in the past, local panel members may have run a 'party whip' for their preferred candidate – effectively blocking the selection of any other nominee. So some tribalism can triumph in the process, after all.

Yet in all of this, the operation of such a complex system places managers, and managerial method, at the very heart and centre of what should actually be a process of *spiritual discernment*.[15] Ultimately, the whole process, and any discussion of it, tends to keep theology and theologians in a subordinate relationship to management – on a short lead, so to speak. But this situation is hardly unique in the church today. Similar tales could be told of theological courses, colleges and programmes being controlled and shaped by central management; or by bishops, of pastoral and missional priorities being determined by executive managers. Some may ask, at this point, why doesn't the leadership of the church *do* something about this? The answer is, simply, that our current leadership is now being led by management. And now that managers are in power, it is highly unlikely that they will put themselves out of office.

In replacing older vocational processes for discerning diocesan bishops with a newer set of managerial procedures, there is a sense of subduing the work of the Spirit – of managing the transcendence of God. To be sure, management never intended this. But in the relentless pursuit of control, compliance and consistency, the result is nearly always the same: predictability. The casualties are obvious: theological prescience and perceptiveness, both effectively eviscerated from the episcopacy. As Timothy Radcliffe OP warns, writing in the foreword of Nicholas Bradbury's study of Pierre Andre-Liege,

> Christianity will disappear in Britain unless we rediscover our Churches as communities which expand and challenge our sense of who we are. They should be oases of resistance to the 'management speak' which deforms contemporary culture.[16]

An excursion in to the *Green Report*:[17] a critique

So, appropriately enough, we turn to the incorporation of managerialism in the Church of England, and its increasing reliance on numbers ('ecclesionomics') and growing faith in the power of organisational and administrative directives ('ecclesiocracy'). To be sure, the Church of England

15 Apparently, +Justin Welby's interview for the post of Archbishop of Canterbury lasted around 75 minutes – a far cry from a conclave to elect a Pope, or any head of a global church.
16 Radcliffe, in Bradbury, *Practical Theology and Pierre Andre-Liege*, Farnham, Surrey: Ashgate, 2014, p. x.
17 *Talent Management for Future Leaders and Leadership Development for Bishops and Deans.*

is a complex and demanding institution, and good management, at all levels, will always be important. Some of the ideas listed in the training section of the *Green Report* would seem to be sound. Managerial insights clearly have a place in the Church, and I readily affirm that. There are a number of serious problems with this report, however, and not only within the text but also in the manner in which it was conceived.

First, and in terms of process, there is a problem about the composition of the group that produced the report. Not one ordained woman was on the review group – and at a time when the Church was about to welcome women bishops. This is breath-taking. Nor was there a recognised theologian, or an academic specialising in continuing professional or vocational education. And, despite the fact that the report raises secular 'MBA-style' programmes to a level of apotheosis, no recognised scholar with expertise in management or leadership from the academic world formed part of the core working party. •

In the actual text of the *Green Report*, there are a couple of serious issues to wrestle with. First, it has no point of origination in theological or spiritual wisdom. Instead, on offer is a dish of basic contemporary approaches to executive management, with a little theological garnish. A total absence of ecclesiology flows from this literature. A more notable absence is any self-awareness in the report: unaware of critiques of management, executive authority, and leadership that abound in academic literature, it is steeped in its own uncritical use of executive management-speak.

Second, a small 'talent pool' of potential future leaders, we are told, will be selected and shaped by a handful of executive managers, and their selection and training facilitated by them. The criteria for joining the talent pool are controlled by these executive managers, who, in turn, have determined the vocation of the Church, its strategic priorities, its goals and, to some extent, its identity. The report highlights 'high', 'outstanding' and 'strong performance' as key indicators of leadership potential. An individual's potential will be measured against 'growth factors'.

Entry to this new talent pool will be strictly limited to around 150 people (so fewer than four potential leaders for each diocese) who have demonstrably built 'healthy organisations, [are] leading for growth, contributing to the common good, [and] re-shaping ministry'. (No prophets or pastors, then; and a final fond farewell to those tiresome theologians.) Members of the talent pool will be allowed to be part of this elite group for up to five years. The report predicts that about 30 people will go into posts each year. 'If there is a decline in measurable performance or potential, an individual will be asked to leave.'

The report expects to see all senior leaders equipped with a standard toolkit of MBA-type organisational skills. But it does not say how this might connect with the primary calling of bishops as 'shepherds of Christ's flock and guardians of the faith of the apostles'. Or what the implications for public ministry might be if bishops now move from being chief pastors to chief executives? Despite the report's stated aspiration to increase diversity in senior leadership (much needed), there seems to be no space for the bishop as scholar, evangelist, contemplative, theologian, prophet or pastor. Or scope for senior church leaders who might be visionaries, risk-takers and pioneers.

Ultimately, the report is coy about the problem it is actually trying to solve: ecclesiastical preferment. No definition of leadership is ever advanced in the text. The report at no point solicits the views of the led. Or of former church leaders. The executive managers already know what they are looking for in preferment – folk like themselves. There is no critique offered on the expectations placed upon church leaders. The text focuses on training people for management tasks that the review group takes as givens. No different models of leadership are discussed, such as servanthood, collaborative ministry, or pastoral care. Although executive managers are patently not the leaders of the Church, they nonetheless aspire to be in charge. If this report is put into practice, they will be. A few administrative offices either side of the Thames, based in Church House, Westminster, or at the Wash House at Lambeth Palace – secretariats that once served the Church – will become sovereign.

Serious problems with the *Green Report* will become all-too apparent. Elliott Jaques, in his *A General Theory of Bureaucracy*,[18] argued that the church was an 'association', and clergy 'members', not its employees. He argued that once clergy come to be regarded as employees in a manager-subordinate relationship, congregations become customers, and the sacred bond between laity and clergy becomes broken, and turned into one of consumer–provider. Jaques specifically praised those churches that promoted life tenure for clergy, because it guarded against centralised managerial interference, and protected the deep communal and personal ethos of the clergy–laity bond. Overt central control and monitoring by churches, argued Jaques, slowly destroyed local spiritual life, because the clergy would be subject to demands on two fronts. Namely, those targets and priorities set remotely by central management, and the local consumerist demands of congregations. The combination would erode public–pastoral ministry to the whole parish, with the clergy becoming demoralised and alienated.

So, this work on leadership in the Church really needs to begin in a different place with different people, starting with deep spiritual, intellectual and theological interlocutors. They would produce something less presumptuous, with a clearer methodology and a cogent argument rather than a set of assertions. Consultation on the report was promised. But I have already received a summons, urging early booking on the new MBA-style programme for senior church leaders. Comments were welcome, it seems, but the agenda still forged ahead.

We appear to live in an age in which all bishops must now fit the 'executive mission-minded-middle-manager' paradigm. Our executive managers who run

18 Jaques, *A General Theory of Bureaucracy*, pp. 344–347.

the Church tell us this is what is needed. Before ordination, +Justin Welby was himself both a product and proponent of this executive-management culture. But as an Archbishop, he should arguably exercise far more caution when giving sweeping powers to unrepresentative task forces such as this. Convening a group like this may initially look like appealing, dynamic leadership; but the tactic can quickly lead to demoralisation and alienation. For example, the task force reviewing ministerial education brazenly excluded any serving theological educators from the core group.

The *Green Report* represents a straightforward bid for power from a small group of elite executive managers, who seek to reign over the selection, training, and oversight of church leadership. This needs challenging and resisting, and the proponents reminding that their ministry is serving and supporting the Church, not leading and controlling it. It is ironic that the *Green Report* begins by quoting the Archbishop of Canterbury's first address to General Synod in July 2013: '[We are] custodians of the gospel that transforms individuals and societies . . . called by God to respond radically and imaginatively to new contexts.' The inexorable rise in power of ecclesiastical executive-managers is just one of those challenging new contexts the Church faces. It does indeed need some radical, imaginative responses.

Conclusion

What might the bishops of 50 or 100 years ago make of the present situation? How might they read the currents and contours of ecclesial life in the Church of England? They might conclude we are essentially over-managed and theologically under-led. They would certainly be alarmed at the weakening of theological acuity amongst our leadership, and the impact this now has on wider public theology. They would be concerned about our attempts to cope with crises and debates (on sexuality and gender, for example), that present us with socio-moral issues which refuse to be managed – but do in fact require rich theological engagement and thoughtful directing.

All this, in turn, leads to some additional problems for the church. It becomes hard to avoid a form of ecclesial narcolepsy if we have unintentionally muted theologians who have the necessary vision and urgency to cause the church to awaken. The revolutionary patience that Ched Myers speaks of, or the loyal dissent advocated by Gerald Arbuckle,[19] can lose their place and value within a managerially-shaped ecclesial body. The possibility of radical theology – from the Latin, *radix*, meaning 'root' – that gets to the heart of a matter, is quickly subsumed in cultures and agendas of conformity, management and productivity. Indeed, and to return to the parable of the sower, we can find that the forces of management and growth, weed-like, 'choke' the rarer border plants that contribute richly and differently to our fields of life, vitality and abundance.

19 See Myers, *Binding the Strong Man;* Arbuckle, *Refounding the Church.*

Leadership, it is often said, is doing the right thing; and management is about doing things right. The church needs both, of course. But it is perhaps not unfair to say that the church of the post-war years has moved from being over-led and under-managed to being over-managed and under-led. Kenneth Thompson addressed this in his classic thesis, arguing that our post-war internal organisational reforms have been driven by two major external forces.[20]

The first, affecting the church in the late nineteenth and early twentieth centuries, was the differentiation of institutions as they became more specialised in their functions. The church, for example, ceased to run adoption services in the way that it once did – or hospitals, universities and colleges, for that matter. The second to affect the church was an increased emphasis on rationality, accountability and productivity – such that we are increasingly pre-occupied with immediate, empirical and pragmatic ends. In other words, we try to justify our value through measuring success, and then driving that success by the criteria we chose to measure it by.

But what are often neglected by focusing on the measurable are more nebulous and extensive forms of engagement in public ministry. Indeed, a singular focus on growth-related targets may suggest a *lack* of vision.[21] Prophetic engagement with issues of justice and peace, for example, may suffer: this can be time-consuming, and may not yield any immediate 'measurable results'. Pastoral work, too, is hard to quantify and measure. In all of this, the organisational-managerial star tends to rise, whilst that of the institutional-leadership wanes. Indeed, as one senior retiree from a branch of a major institution recently opined, 'I used to be well-led in a first-class institution; I am now inadequately managed in a second-class organisation'.

The potential losses in moving from an institution to becoming an organisation are considerable. Ministry – especially ordained – is a calling and vocation without clear and prescribed boundaries. It is not 'work', or a 'profession', as such, but rather a sacred calling in which character and virtues matter as much as, and perhaps more than, aims, objectives and outcomes. Clergy need to be *called* – hold a vocation to an ordained ministry. Clergy need to be *competent* – have some skills and expertise relevant to the vocation. And clergy need to be people of *character* – moral exemplars. Those so called, with competence and character need to offer, in turn, three more things: word, sacrament and pastoral care. And they are not at work or in professions. They are, rather, in an occupation, and so need to be thrice occupied: with God (worship and contemplation); with what God occupies (his body, the church); and with what occupies God (the care and concern of the world, in its brokenness and pain, and in all its needs – what we might call 'mission'). This is the work of ministry – nothing less than the same work of Christ, reconciling the world to God.

20 Thompson, *Bureaucracy and Church Reform*.
21 cf., Spencer, 'Goals for Growth Expose a Vision's Limitations', *Church Times*, 14 August 2015, p. 10.

Describing the church in this way is not a retreat into romantic-sacral language. It is, rather, a simple reclamation of the pure, deep pulses that drive many vocations, and most forms of local church. What the imposing and intrusive managerialism currently at work in the Church of England risks is undermining and demoralising clergy and congregations alike. Managerialism is not neutral; and despite its laudable attempts to scrutinise, organise and police, it often fails to empathise, mobilise and inspire.[22] The dominant hegemony of executive managerialism in the church – as other institutions can testify in education and healthcare – has presumed to rule, when it was only ever there to serve. Its needs to recover its vocation as servant, not master.

Some years ago, John Milbank argued that the social sciences had little to contribute to our understanding of theology and religion.[23] He suggested that sociology or anthropology attempted to 'police the sublime'. Whilst I have always felt that social sciences and theology are rich in their complementarity, I am deeply concerned that the management sciences are now shaping our ecclesiology – and so yes, 'policing the sublime'. Certainly, managerialism is reining in the radical, patrolling our pastoralia and taming the theological. Wisdom is pushed to the edges; 'management strategy', masquerading as vision, has become central.

Some will doubtless opine that the church cannot wean itself off its absorption with management and mission – albeit one with such a narrow accent placed on efficiency and productivity. But as Wendell Berry has pointed out, the conviction that we cannot change, because we are dependent on what is wrong, is always the addict's excuse. Deep down, we know it will not do. We need to be free of our distraction-dependency, and of being satisfied with anything that sates the quantification of expectation, and our innate yearning for conformity and control. We need more emphasis on wisdom and depth; less dependency on orientating our life (and happiness?) by pursuing bigger and better numbers.

Only when the church is free of imposed ideologies and agendas, can it begin to reclaim an identity as an institution that radically speaks of and embodies God – rather than being consumed by shallower mission and management targets. To be sure, there is no doubt that the value of theological governance amongst our senior clergy has been steadily eclipsed by the current unchecked promotion of our own managerial culture, and by our absorption with numerical growth. I hope that the tide will turn. But in truth, I fear it is still rushing in, and fast. The time has surely come to stop, reflect and radically review.

---

22 Indeed, managers can often confuse empathy with compassion. Empathy is valuable, to be sure. But it is a learnt human skill in which one can be trained – in personnel work or counselling, for example – and which can, to some extent, be commodified and purchased. Compassion is, however, a virtue that cannot be manufactured or bought. The church is clearly more than a place for encountering empathy; it is called to be a body of compassion and mercy.

23 See Milbank, *Theology and Social Theory*.

2 New currents in executive and archiepiscopal leadership

The emerging British Empire – not formed until the second half of the nineteenth century – is partly what enabled the Church of England to move from being a national church to becoming a global Communion. The expansion of Anglicanism was both an ordered and untidy affair; simultaneously systematic and unsystematic. But the purpose of this essay is not to elaborate on how one national church has become a global Communion. We need simply note that, now, the Anglican Church has over 80 million followers – a 'household of faith' that comprises 38 provinces and 65,000 congregations and is spread across 164 countries. After the Roman Catholic Church, it is the most widespread denomination in the world (and the third biggest, if one counts the Eastern Orthodox as a single group or family). The Archbishop of Canterbury is the spiritual leader of Anglicans worldwide. The office of the Archbishop of Canterbury has, therefore, undergone a significant transformation over the last 150 years. Since the more formalised formation of the Anglican Communion – arguably to be dated from the first Lambeth Conference in 1867 – the office of the Archbishop has essentially moved progressively from being one of straightforward *primatial* ecclesial authority within England to that of *primus inter pares*, globally.

Each Archbishop, since the nineteenth century, has sought to inhabit this role, naturally mindful of the ecclesial issues, global politics and cultural challenges that were facing both the national church and wider Communion. In recent times, +Rowan Williams sought to foster listening and mutual learning between warring factions on the divisive issue of human sexuality. An irenic style was a hallmark of his primacy. But this had some downsides. As Rupert Shortt notes, +Rowan's distaste for management and strategy, coupled to his tendency to agonise inwardly at the expense of decisiveness, led to a lack of firm leadership in several key areas.[1] In contrast, his predecessor, George Carey, sought to bring a distinctive kind of ordering and organisation to a complex institution, and for the purposes of enabling a keener focus on evangelism throughout the national church and wider Communion. It is perhaps still too early to say exactly what +Justin Welby's

---

1 Shortt, *Rowan's Rule.*

legacy will be (although some possibilities are lightly sketched later). But, like each Archbishop before him, his own style of leadership is, inevitably, shaped by the prevailing grammars and cultures of leadership to be found in wider society.

Since becoming Archbishop of Canterbury in 2013, +Justin Welby has brought a distinctive style of leadership to the office. So far, Archbishop Welby seems to be more of a strategist – one who sets targets, and works out routes to reach them.[2] Some opine that this has something of a 'Blair-ite' flavour. This is generally meant favourably, albeit cautiously: for example, perhaps placing 'pragmatism before principle', managing diversity, and an emphasis on the primacy of personal mission. One should always counsel caution in comparing Archbishops to British Prime Ministers. Nevertheless, the comparison may have some partial validity in at least three areas.

First, a warm, charismatic and personal style of leadership that cuts through established party lines and tribal divisions. +Justin has already shown himself to be adept at this, and significant rapprochement has been achieved on divisive issues where the earlier, irenic styles of his predecessor seemed not to have made much progress. Second, the energy and fresh dynamism of the Archbishop sets a tone across the wider Communion. This can be enabling and inspiring, and generates positive 'spiritual capital', creating a climate of possibility and expectation. Third, the capacity to be directive and decisive enables the church to shift in its self-understanding. Instead of being captivated by a sense of impasse and un-decidability, it now appears that deadlocks can be broken, and the church can move forward more confidently. So, comparisons to Tony Blair's style of leadership have some partial validity.

But there are also comparisons to be made that are perhaps more ambivalent. Early on in +Justin's primacy, he set himself the ambitious and eye-catching target of visiting every Archbishop within the Communion, and each in their own country. Thirty-eight Primates to see in two years is a tall order, to be sure. These visits were, however, to be very much a 'personal' mission. The officers and infrastructure and representation of the machinery of the Anglican Communion have tended not to travel with him.

Many of these visits simply consist of the Archbishop and his wife, Caroline, travelling to stay in the home of an Archbishop overseas. The personal and

---

2 Atherstone, *Archbishop Justin Welby*. Some of the potential implications of this are discussed in more depth in the third part of this book, in relation to the *Reform and Renewal* agenda – especially its adoption of secular reasoning, business-think, pragmatism and passionate intensity as key drivers in the proposed reforms. Personal proclivities often manifest themselves in wider public ministry. In an earlier phase of Welby's ministry, some commentators noted the absence of a deep uniting theological vision or coherent spiritual ethos underpinning much of his (undoubtedly laudable) activism. The lack of theological frames of reference for this ministry led to a growing sense of alienation within the various support bases. This, coupled with a tendency not to consult with colleagues or supporters, led to a consequential depletion in the sense of shared ownership for this ministry.

warm tone of this initiative should not be underestimated. But it carries risks. Briefings on potential pitfalls in local contexts might be hard to come by if you travel without advisors. (Indeed, there is some evidence to suggest that gaffes and avoidable errors have been made). This problem cannot be corrected if the pattern of visits continues as it is currently configured. Advisors are there to help direct and target meetings with key people, and help avoid meetings and encounters that might be ill-advised. They also spread the workload, and help manage the exposure and energy of a busy Archbishop. Without them, the attendant risks will be greater.

Arguably, however, the biggest risk of the 'personal visit' is the implicit message it sends across the Communion – one wholly unintended, I suspect. For it places the accent firmly on 'who' – the personal charisma, capacity and character of *this* Archbishop – rather than the 'what' he represents. Part of the secret ingredient of Blair's likeability and electability lay in his ability to persuade voters to direct their gaze towards him, and trust him *personally*, rather than the Labour Party he represented, or to dwell upon the messy contingencies of party-political in-fighting, or the potential influence of the Trade Unions. Hence, 'Vote Blair', and not 'Vote Labour'. Tony Blair, in other words, began to *personally* embody those likeable and electable qualities that were *drawn* from socialist principles; but he was not necessarily asking voters to invest in those same party-political principles that lay behind him as leader.

Now, this dynamic is hardly unique to Blair. Similar things could be said about recent American Presidents. The issue here is not, perhaps, personal charisma, but rather the *amount* of it in relation to the body being led – it is a question of balance. It is simply the case that in certain socio-political cultures we tend to place more trust in charismatic figures that embody particular qualities of leadership, rather than in institutions – which can, by comparison, seem to be sluggish, divided and wasteful. But this dynamic, if it indeed exists, is more of a problem in ecclesiology – and specifically in this case, for Anglicans. For we need our Archbishops – present and future – to really *engage* with the institution that is the Communion, in all its complexity. A 'personal communion' between the Archbishop of Canterbury and the thirty-eight other Primates is undoubtedly important, and a fine platform on which to build. But it is only one element in enabling the Communion to cohere.

The danger of starting and stopping at a drive towards a 'personal communion' between the Archbishop and Primates is that the Communion itself further disintegrates into a set of warm reciprocal relationships – which is not, of course, a *theology* of the Communion. The next step down this road would be *not* to call and convene a Lambeth Conference again. (After all, is it not just a tiresome and cumbersome institutional apparatus that simply gets in the way of getting things done?). This is where a theology of the Communion might help. The twentieth and early twenty-first centuries have seen the Anglican Communion at subsequent Lambeth Conferences argue on divorce, contraception, sexuality, gender and other issues. But in truth, all denominations squabble – it is a sign of life and vibrancy.

As Luis Bermejo SJ points out in *The Spirit of Life*, all our creeds were formed through fractious meetings that were rooted in controversy. Christians – and perhaps especially Anglicans – sometimes forget that the Holy Spirit works through meetings (often taking a long time, and over many years); it is how we arrive at truth. Bermejo SJ argues that there are four stages of ecclesial life: communication, conflict, consensus and communion.[3] Issues in the Anglican Communion tend to get refracted through this four-fold process. This is how the Holy Spirit moves the church; it is not the case that only the last of these stages – communion – is the 'spiritual' stage. The work of the Holy Spirit is also manifest in conflict – helping the church to be pruned and refined. Thus, Anglicans agree on what the Bible says – but not always on what it means. The polity is often more relational than propositional – Anglicans can sometimes be characterised as more interested in how we disagree, and a little less in what we actually disagree on.

Paradigms and polity

Bermuda and the Caribbean might almost serve as paradigms of polity at this point. Many people assume that Bermuda is part of the Caribbean. The images of the islands to which the public are mostly exposed seem to suggest the warm, balmy climes of the Antilles that nestle between North and South America, and off the Mexican and Central American coasts. But in fact, Bermuda is closer to North Carolina and Nova Scotia than it is to Miami in Florida. It is a group of remote islands in the North Atlantic. Bermuda is also the oldest remaining British Overseas Territory. Its first capital, St. George's, was established in 1612 and is the oldest continuously inhabited English town in the New World.

And as one might expect from such a quirk of history, the Church of England is still, in some sense, 'established' there. St. Peter's, the parish church, is the oldest Anglican Church in the New World. Bermuda's Anglican 'establishment' – though unique – is perhaps comparable, in part, to that of the Channel Islands. But it is different from the Channel Islands insofar as the Diocese of Bermuda is, today, one of six extra-provincial Anglican churches relating directly to the Church of England, and overseen by the Archbishop of Canterbury. The Anglican Church of Bermuda comprises a single diocese consisting of nine parishes, and although a part of the Anglican Communion, is not part of any ecclesiastical Province.

The Caribbean is quite different. Politically, it consists, as a region (identifiable, though with contested boundaries), of an area that stretches

3 Bermejo SJ, *The Spirit of Life*.

from Grand Bahama Island in the north to Curaçao in the south, and French Guyana in the east to Belize in the west. Even ignoring the many Central and South American nations that border the Caribbean Sea (whose cultural and linguistic heritage sets their history out of the scope of the region) there are a total of 16 independent or sovereign states and nine island groupings that remain dependencies (in one form or another) of the United Kingdom, France, the USA and the Netherlands. There are at least eight currencies in circulation. If one includes the South and Central American Caribbean countries, the total number of nation states and dependencies is 35. In Anglican terms, some of these countries are part of groupings of dioceses in the Episcopal Church of the USA (TEC): Haiti or the Dominican Republic, for example. Others are part of the Province of the West Indies, which includes Barbados, Belize, Guyana, Jamaica, the Bahamas and Trinidad and Tobago. The current Archbishop of the Province resides in Barbados, which is an independent sovereign state. It is a complex zone – politically, culturally and ecclesially.

Archbishop Justin visited the Province of the West Indies in August 2013. Or, more accurately, he visited the Presiding Archbishop in Barbados. The other bishops were invited – quite late on – to join this meeting. But few of the Caribbean bishops made it. For some, it is not even their Province, as they are part of TEC. For others, the distances – several hours of flight to Barbados – made the journey at such short notice far too difficult. True, the gesture of the visit is worthy. But one could not, in all sincerity, claim to have 'done' or 'ticked the box' on visiting the Province. One territory visited within 30-plus nation states and dependent territories, only leaves time for a few personal conversations. One cannot engage with the complexity of the Province in any depth. Seeing one Presiding Archbishop in their own country, for example Barbados, could be akin to travelling to Brussels, seeing the European Union President, and claiming to have 'done Europe'.

But given the complexity of this Province, it is difficult to see how a single personal visit can cover the ground adequately. Indeed, it might risk more harm than good. Even the name of the Province is potentially awkward for colonial and post-colonial identities. From 1958 to 1962, there was a short-lived country called the Federation of the West Indies composed of ten English-speaking Caribbean territories, all of which were then British dependencies. The West Indies cricket team continues to represent many of those nations. The very name of the Anglican Province reflects this experiment in post-colonial organisation. But it did not last long politically or economically.

So what are the potential hazards in these 'personal' visits? First, they might be too 'light touch', and risk confirming some rather impressionistic views of the provinces of the Communion. A recent trip to Hong Kong was valuable – the newest and smallest Anglican province, consisting of three dioceses (East and West Kowloon and Hong Kong Island)

and a missionary diocese (Macau).[4] But however good the visit was, it took less than 48 hours, and could not possibly begin to engage with the complexity of the Province and its multifarious ministries. Second, and following on from this, the visits exchange a deep engagement with institutional density and complexity for a briefer meeting imbued with personal warmth. Whilst this has a value, it is too fleeting. Third, and again sequentially, it is not clear how this 'strategy' – if that is what it is – really helps the Communion cohere. One simply cannot substitute exchanges of personal warmth for those that deal with the gritty business of engaging with institutional diversity, complexity, differences and disagreements that characterise the Communion. For that, there cannot be an easy alternative to meetings – often tense, slow and well-represented ones (so yes, expensive and difficult to organise) – which enable the Communion to both know and own its identity. This is why, of course, for all their many faults, Lambeth Conferences have a value. Because they confer upon the Communion an obligation to meet with their differences, and work through – in fellowship – the things that both bind us together and cause division. Such features of ecclesial life cannot be skirted around. As Archbishop, +Justin is himself one instrument of unity in the Communion. But the other conciliar entities that offer unity and communion are necessarily different as they are complementary.

Ecclesiology: institution, organisation and leadership

So what is at issue here? The nature of the problem probably lies in understanding the nature of the body that is the church, or the Communion, and appreciating that it needs a kind of leadership that may be less obvious to the secular, commercial, corporate sectors one usually finds in business.[5] Governance is an issue here, since (as Rollo May opined),[6] structure is an expression of value. How the church is shaped and re-shaped reveals what its leaders (currently) value. A homogenous, pasteurised polity, in which all leaders are compliant and 'on message', will reveal a tight structure that resists diversity and an investment in celebrating a wide range of theological viewpoints. Of course, it is important to grasp here that the church is not simply an organisation struggling to cope with the complexity of cultural

---

4 'Archbishop visits Hong Kong', http://www.archbishopofcanterbury.org/articles.php/5168/archbishop-visits-hong-kong, 28 October 2013.

5 On this, see three discussions of patterns of ecclesial governance: LeRoy, *Patterns of Polity: Varieties of Church Governance*, Cleveland, OH: Pilgrims Press, 2001; Ryan, *The Catholic Parish: Institutional Discipline, Tribal Identity and Religious Development in the English Parish*, London: Sheed and Ward, 1996; and Mudge, *Rethinking the Beloved Community: Ecclesiology, Hermeneutics, Social Theory*, Lanham, MY: University Press of America, 2001.

6 Discussed extensively in *The Meaning of Anxiety*, New York: W W Norton, 1950 (revised edn 1996) and *Love and Will*, New York: W W Norton, 1969 (revised edn 1989).

change. It is, rather, an institution. The distinction is a vital one to comprehend if one is to address the kind of archiepiscopal leadership that might be required. Here, the contrasts between organisations and institutions, usefully characterised in the early work of Philip Selznick, might be helpful in understanding the nature of the church.[7]

Selznick argues that organisations primarily exist for utilitarian purposes, and when they are fulfilled, the organisation may become expendable. Institutions, in contrast, are 'natural communities' with historic roots that are embedded in the very fabric of society. They incorporate various groups that may contest with each other over the very nature of the institution and its values. Following Selznick, a church is much more like an institution, thereby requiring a particular kind of moral leadership from its ordained leaders (including character, compassion and wisdom), rather than (mere) management.

For Selznick, the very term 'organisation' suggests a certain rudimentary bareness; a kind of lean, no-nonsense system of consciously co-ordinated activities. It refers to an expendable and rational instrument engineered to do a job. An institution, on the other hand, is more of a natural product of the prevailing social needs and pressures – effectively a responsive, adaptive organism. This distinction, claims Selznick, is a matter of analysis, rather than of direct description. It does not mean that any given enterprise must be either one or the other. While an extreme case may closely approach either an 'ideal' organisation or an 'ideal' institution, most living associations resist such easy classifications. They are complex mixtures of both designed and responsive behaviours. But assuming the Communion and its churches are more akin to an institution than an organisation, this of course requires an extensive investment of time. There can be no quick-fixes in the church. Those conversations that are moral and theological need to engage with the reality of complex institutional life.

Thus, and according to Selznick, organisations tend to use 'tools' or means as they reach for definite goals; and their leaders deliver on this, in target and performance-related ways. The institutional leader, in contrast, is primarily an expert in the promotion and protection of values. And in one sense, this distinction between organisations and institutions can act as a helpful aid in reflecting upon and discerning the contrasting attitudes in the wider Communion. Put bluntly, is the Anglican Communion an inefficient, tangled and complex body that needs to be re-shaped organisationally? Or, is it an institution in which its tangled and complex structures are, in fact, part of its very identity and value? Indeed, it may be something like a family, perhaps, or even a 'household of faith' if one wanted to be more biblical about this – so not easy to organise, and not always obvious where membership begins and ends, and who belongs? It is neither fully one nor the other,

---

7 See Selznick, *Leadership in Administration; Avis, Authority, Leadership and Conflict in the Church*.

of course. But on balance, a church – even one single local one, let alone a complex Communion of 65,000 congregations in 164 countries – is far more akin to an institution than it is to an organisation.

But how is something of such complexity to be led? One of the more creative and prescient writers in this arena is Simon Western.[8] Western argues that 'leaders are authentically transformational . . . they increase awareness of what is right, good, important and beautiful'.[9] Western believes these common characteristics of leadership have expressed themselves in three primary forms of discourse during the twentieth century. He proposes a fourth, but the three main ones identified are Controller, Therapist and Messiah.[10] Controller discourse is aligned to social management, and the progeny of early twentieth century scientific rationalism. The focus lies in efficiency, with transactional behaviour that rests on finding a balance between rewards and deprivation. Therapist discourse is a later development in the twentieth century, highlighting personal growth and wellbeing, and individual concern. Finally, Western suggests that the latter decades of the twentieth century saw the emergence of Messiah discourse. With the elevation of leader over and against managers, Messiah discourse validates charismatic and visionary leadership in the face of uncertain environments for institutions. Messiah discourse feeds off the tensions between salvation and destruction, and hope and despair. Typically, the discourse promises order from chaos, and pitches charismatic authority against institutional ennui, promising a 'third way' forward, which will be transformational. Typically, it sits light to detail, and stresses heroic feats and redemptive, visionary outcomes (e.g., 'we can't go on as we are – we must move forward if we are to be faithful to the vision and succeed', etc.).

This latter form of discourse is clearly a prominent 'accent' (no more) in Archbishop Justin's rich, blended style of leadership.[11] There is a considerable tendency for the media to play up to the Messiah–Hero motif, in an almost *Boy's Own* fashion. The *Daily Mail* reported on Archbishop Justin, whilst a Canon of Coventry Cathedral and in his work for the International Centre of Reconciliation (ICR) as follows:

> Soldiers with machine guns circled in helicopters as rebels blindfolded +Justin Welby, the future Archbishop of Canterbury, bundled him into a speedboat and took the mild-mannered Old Etonian into the heart of Nigeria's darkness. Although in extreme danger, the bespectacled father of five remained 'completely relaxed', according to a colleague who was with him on the peace mission for a church body.

8 Western, *Leadership*.
9 Ibid., p. 22.
10 Ibid., pp. 80–126.
11 See Atherstone, *Archbishop Justin Welby*.

On another occasion, fresh from negotiating with Al Qaeda operatives, Welby was arrested by the Nigerian army. As he heard shouting and pounding footsteps of soldiers storming up the stairs, he spoke calmly down the phone to a colleague. 'I'm going to count to ten and when I finish, they'll be here. Don't worry, I'll leave my phone on, so I can be traced,' he crisply informed Canon Dr Stephen Davis, who was on the other end of the line in Britain. He then completed the countdown, placed the muted phone in his pocket and passively accepted the rough shoves of his captors as they bundled him out of the building.

Only hours later the former oil executive was located and released at the embarrassed behest of the Nigerian authorities, desperate not to lose one of their most prized peace negotiators. That incident, in 2005, was just one of an array of extraordinary secret acts of courage which mark out +Justin Welby as a remarkable resolver of conflicts. Dr Welby has had to shake hands with warlords, negotiate with kidnappers and endure multiple arrests in some of the most dangerous warzones in the world, where the slightest mistake could have seen him lose his life.[12]

Similar 'heroic' tales have also been reported by the media since Bishop Welby became Archbishop. The alleged refusal to take a brief from Lambeth Palace staff ('I'll run my own diary, thank you'), and apparently handing back the carefully prepared schedule that had been devised for his first three years in office. Or the veiled threat to General Synod of what might happen if the vote on the Measure to ordain women to the episcopate was thwarted again. The media have invested in something of a trope: a heroic leader who gets things done; who cuts through red tape; that does not spend time in stuffy meetings, but gets out and about; a man of action, not merely words. (A kind of ecclesiastical 'Action Man', in fact.) As with all media creations, it is hard to discern the difference between image and the reality; the media highlights preferred tones and accents – boundary lines are often blurred. But there are dangers, here, in accepting the plaudits that the media might pour upon a hero. It can become difficult to maintain a necessary balance under these conditions – to be yourself, and the person God calls you to be, indeed.

Western acknowledges that Controller, Therapist and Messiah discourses are not mutually exclusive. Bishops and Archbishops will inevitably be under some pressure to conform or relate to all three – offering control, therapy and heroic forms of liberation in equal measure. However, Western believes that leadership within institutions needs to pass through these three discourses and enter into something altogether more holistic and engaged. He acknowledges that the search for leadership models and ideas is now driven by several factors: the need to find solutions to changing social, political and

12 'Revealed: Archbishop Blindfolded by Rebels with Kalashnikovs on Jungle Mercy Mission', *The Daily Mail*, 11 November 2012.

economic conditions; the need to sustain the 'leadership industry'; enormous social pressure to modernise ('new sells, old doesn't'); and some compulsion to establish perpetual relevance, leading to what Marx dubbed a 'commodity fetish' – the institution, once commodified and marketed, starts to take on an identity that bears little relation to its original purpose.

Western proposes, in place of the three models outlined above, a discourse of 'eco-leadership'.[13] Inevitably, perhaps, this 'model' emphasises a variety of traits that are already apparent and emerging in twenty-first century leadership studies, but which perhaps especially draw on our contemporary cultural absorption with organic, natural and sustainable concepts. Thus – and somewhat against the Messiah discourse – Western identifies the 'post-heroic discourse' which emphasises 'the genuinely human . . . [drawing] on all their humanity, intelligence and emotions . . . remember[ing] what they know from their experiences'. Leadership spirit is also identified as a trait, and in particular the capacity of the leader to 'learn from the middle'. This was, of course, the normal *modus operandi* of Archbishop Rowan Williams. Whilst this led to some inertia, as well as failures, the strength of the model is that it can build collegiality in the medium and long term. Messiah leadership discourse, in contrast, tends to foster cultures of followership; and it marginalises the critical voices that are essential for developing balance and breadth.

So here we could say that Western's plea for the leadership of institutions is more for a portfolio of skills and charisms that may be familiar to those who are deep reflective practitioners: self-awareness, spontaneity, holistic skills, reframing skills, vocation, people who are vision and value led, who have reflexivity, (feeling with) compassion and engagement. Correspondingly, a deep systemic understanding of the institution that is being led is required. Or, and for our purposes here, leadership might be the cultivation of heightened ecclesial intelligence, and its visionary application. It cannot just be predominantly the super-hero or messiah at work; there must be balance. The form of leadership (for institutions) that Western therefore advocates is one that is ecologically sensitive. Western quotes John Donne here: 'no man is an island entire of himself; every man is part of the main'. Western understands that:

> solutions in one area may create problems in another . . . short-term gains may have immediate benefits, but may have longer-term consequences . . . [thus] there are interdependent parts which make up a whole . . . it is about connectivity, inter-dependence and sustainability.[14]

Western's stress on inter-dependence, connection and sustainability might serve as something of a warning for institutions that might be inclined to

---

13 Western, *Leadership*, pp. 173–197.
14 Ibid., pp. 183–197.

invest too much in 'messiah discourses' of leadership. Some wariness seems appropriate here. Because for all the good that any messiah can do for a body in crisis, the solutions proffered often don't engage with and redeem the whole of the institution. The experience of charismatic leadership often *feels* transformational whilst in motion. But the eventual reality is often somewhat different, and can lead to deeper forms of disengagement, and ultimately disenchantment.

Conclusion

At face value, the proposed managerial reforms of the Church of England, recently presented to General Synod, would appear to be just the ticket. Several Task Groups, all grappling with apparently intractable problems that have dogged the church for decades, are addressing key issues. The groups have wrestled with talent management, discipleship, simplification, financial equity, resourcing ministerial education and national church structures. As the Archbishop of Canterbury said, defending the *Green Report*, 'we can't simply go on as we are if we are to flourish and grow as the Church of England . . . our call is not to manage decline' (Press Statement, 16 December 2014). Those same sentiments were echoed by John Spence in the *Church Times* – 'we've got to find new ways of doing Christ's work'.

Of course, if the church is failing, ('we can't simply go on as we are'), who might benefit from this proposition? Usually, it is those who promote such negative narratives. The proponents of the change-or-decline storyline argue that the body of Christ is sick, and left untreated, will die. That's the prognosis; subsequent diagnosis offers suggested treatment.

The two proposed forms of treatment – which have existed for 75 years, courtesy of the American church growth movement and sacralised pragmatism – are mission and management. Books and programmes advocating this treatment for the body of Christ place measurable growth and tangible success on a pedestal. This brand of missiology, however, risks narcissism and breeds unhealthy competition. My church is bigger than yours; our mission strategy better than theirs.

Clearly, no-one can be against mission and management. But we need some balance. Those who promote the body of Christ as being in sickly, terminal decline – afflicted by a range of illnesses and conditions said to be broadly rooted in secularisation and secularism – are also proffering their own preferred restorative tonics.

The elements of the twofold cure – medicinal doses of mission and management – are both imbued with apparently quantifiable data. They typically eschew the poetic, pastoral and prophetic in favour of numbers and apparent results. These cures seek to take control of, discipline and shape the body, delivering the 'fitness' now deemed to be necessary for survival. This is a kind of 'Charles Atlas' approach to ecclesiology and missiology. How do I know I am 'fit' and strong? Feel my muscles; admire my form; look at my growth.

But those panacea-promoting groups seeking cultural resonance and relevance for the church – often unwittingly – can also encourage relativism. In so doing, they unconsciously develop a secular identity for the church that erodes its sacred ethos. Like 'missional steroids' promising maximum growth, this does the church few favours in the medium and long-term, even though the short-term results appear attractive. But when you are desperate – or repeatedly told you ought to be – you'll swallow any medicine.

The new reports – the *Reform and Renewal* agenda[15] – also appear to share a common DNA, insofar as they claim to be rooted in research, listening and wide consultation, and responding (of course) to a crisis. Those that are not full of management-speak are saturated in membership-speak. Most of the reports assume, sometimes in a manner that is both shrill and amplified, that unless something is done urgently, a church that is allegedly already very sickly will surely die. This gloomy diagnosis and the proposed treatments – all of which are asserted rather than argued for – form the foundation for the suggested exigent changes. But as with other recent work, these new reports are deficient in at least three key areas.

First, there is a problem with coherence, highlighted in the general claim made by John Spence (Chairman of the Archbishops' Council Finance Committee, and member of General Synod) that the proposed reforms are 'not to be seen as a centralising initiative'. Some sentiments from Mr Spence seem to match this – that the drivers of the change must not become a kind of 'head office' for the wider church. But there is inconsistency too, when he talks of developing a single 'perfectly formed engine room at the centre'.

Secondly, there is the claim that the reports are rooted in research. Whilst this is true to some extent, too many recent reports have been guilty of the thesis directing the facts. For example, findings drawn from a report from the Archbishops' Council in 2014,[16] counted parish numbers according to the standard 'one (usual) Sunday (of attendance) in October' approach (uSa). In contrast, Fresh Expressions were allowed to count *anyone* who came at any stage over a six month period. Had parishes been able to do the same, the results would have been completely different – for they would have counted the hundreds at funerals, the midweek services, the afternoon baptisms, those attending weddings. The figure for attendance at a parish church in six months would have run into several hundreds, if not thousands. But this comparison would not have suited those promoting Fresh Expressions, who want to establish these new forms of ecclesial manifestation as 'different-but-equal' to parish churches.

Third, there is a claim that consultation forms the heart of the work – a less than credible assertion. Theological colleges and courses, for example, were pointedly excluded from the consultation on Resourcing Ministerial Education. For a report that was essentially on theological education, the

15 https://www.churchofengland.org/renewal-reform.aspx, accessed 8 August 2016.
16 *From Anecdote to Evidence.*

lack of rootedness in theology is inexcusable. It is as though the group simply set about an organisational task, and had no appetite for creating a theological foundation that might have been genuinely formative. The resources were available, but ignored.

Overall, there are nagging doubts about the reports, taken as a group. Is it really the case that all that was needed to help shape the future of the church was a cocktail blend of organisation, rationalisation, simplification, centralisation and deregulation? Can anyone really explain why theological education needed deregulating, but other aspects of the church centralising?

The implications for authority and ecclesiology would take time to spell out, but perhaps the biggest risk to emerge now is the rise of the so-called 'mission-led' or mission-shaped' church. Because it is at this point that theology – whether 'blueprint' or 'concrete' – and the super-natural authority of the church, which she is called to embody and proclaim, might simply be replaced with what is often termed 'consecrated pragmatism'. I suspect that this is a virus that is already well-advanced and at home in the Church of England's body. It produces symptoms such as panic, frenetic anxiety, ennui and low morale.

Yet the deepest problem with the Task Groups and their reports is simply this: trust. The groups who have written these reports don't seem to trust the wisdom of the past, and how it has formed the church and teaches us. They don't seem to trust theology – certainly not enough to root any of the reports in a generative and creative theological imagination. They don't trust our theological institutions enough to consult with them about theological education. They don't trust the clergy, church or wider public sufficiently to listen and consult more broadly, or conduct proper recognised academic research – an essential foundation in any reform programme.

This lack of trust has been present from the outset, and continually highlighted by the hurried, assertive and non-consultative processes leading to the final reports. Furthermore, it has been driven by a small, powerful, elite cabal, who have no immediate accountability to the wider church. They have largely worked in the shadows, listening only very selectively to what they wanted to hear. These reports are already 'done deals', even before they get to Synod. This cavalier attitude to reform risks treating the church with contempt.

So, the manner in which the Task Groups have set about their processes and written their reports can only ever produce one result: mistrust. It is not easy – or wise – to trust leaders and managers who set about the work of reforming in such a way. Alerting the church to the potential dangers we face is, of course, responsible and prudent. Passion and zeal for a better future is all fine and good. But there is a world of difference between proposed reforms and initiatives located in contested narratives of despair and optimism, but which are naively aspirational, and those that might be rooted in a rich, shared theology of hope.

Trust and obedience are cornerstones of Christian discipleship. But they are related and reciprocal; neither can be blind to the other. Trust is an essential sponsor of obedience. The concept of trust is rooted in mutual confidence, fidelity, support, faithfulness, truth and integrity. Many will rightly feel quite uneasy about 'entrusting' the future of our church, ministry and mission to a small cabal who do not seem to return that same trust. In proclaiming a crisis all the time, and offering the only solutions – TINA (there is no other way), the leadership becomes both arsonist and firefighter. Those who question the reality, source or nature of the crisis are simply told they are in denial, and they need to be immediately removed, and if necessary, opposed and castigated.

But this is not a healthful way to lead. The model of heroic leadership (firefighter and rescuer) is something that robs the collective of participation in comprehending the nature of their issues and challenges. Michael West's recent work on collective leadership – which is evidence-based – shows that there are better outcomes, wider buy-in and longer-term followership for managers and chief executives who practice collective leadership. Heroic leadership, in contrast, can quickly lead to demoralisation, mistrust, sullen consent, and the rapid unravelling of the organisation or institution.[17]

The concept of leadership has achieved a somewhat totemic status in the Church of England. And while the concept is seemingly necessary, innocent, non-partisan and neutral, the reality is very different. The term and concept carries greater weight in less liturgical expressions of Anglican polity – especially amongst Evangelicals, whether conservative, open or charismatic. But in ecclesial environments where the terms 'deacon', 'priest' and 'bishop' are set aside in favour of 'leader', valuable characteristics and charisms can be lost. The older, richer and denser ecclesial terms of reference contain within them notions of service, obeisance, widespread public ownership of the role, and richer spiritual readings – including a serious point of origin and reference to the person of Christ.

Evangelicals, in seeking to dissolve the clergy-laity gap, frequently succeed – only to open up an even wider gap between the leader and the led.[18] 'Leadership', is a thinner, more private and personal concept, and also subject to expendability. Christ's 'leadership' – whatever that might be construed to be – is also a hard paradigm to discern, let alone follow. His ministry is arguably not one of leadership, but rather of example and exemplar. Christians are called to follow a servant, not a winner. Christ did not dominate; he served. He led not by triumphing, but by sacrificing. He led not by being first on the podium, but by falling and dying. It is in dying that we rise.

17 http://www.kingsfund.org.uk/publications/developing-collective-leadership-health-care?gcl id=CPyTg8GY0ccCFUu6GwodKDUHwA, accessed 8 August 2016.
18 cf., Philip Johanson, 'Top-Down Tinkering Will Not Serve the Kingdom', *Church Times*, 4 September 2015, p. 10.

So the Church of England should be wary – very wary – of trading in its rich nomenclature for pastoral, priestly and teaching oversight; and in exchange for 'leadership', which is arguably far too vacuous. 'Leadership' is, in any case, not a biblical term, and is often a highly-gendered concept which favours alpha-males in organisational mode. 'Leadership' risks a narcissism which richer forms of institutional oversight arguably avoid, mostly.

So do we need more leaders? Well, certainly not the ones crowned by the dominant caste of executive managers. The business world is instructive here; for it is full of shipwrecked institutions. Some of these were the once-great galleons of the financial oceans – mutual companies and building societies that were rooted in values and ideals that both guaranteed their longevity, and the trust the public placed in them. They were wrecked – entirely unintentionally – by a new breed of bosses: new captains of an industry promising stronger leadership, exponential growth and ever-greater speed. Many institutions, duly rapt and enthralled by the potential rewards, placed their souls and futures in the hands of a new generation of uber-leaders. But those same leaders mostly failed to understand the intrinsic values of the bodies they led; and many ruined hulks and wrecks now testify to this.

So can we really trust this package of new reforms – rooted as they are in quite sparse consultation and such weak research – and the competence and capacities of those who produced them? Not enough, alas. The church is a complex collective heart, mind and body, and on a very long pilgrimage. As the African proverb has it, if you want to travel fast, go alone. But if you want to travel far, go together.

3 The emerging contours of archiepiscopal leadership

A great bandwagon has been rolling by for some years now. Its name is 'leadership' – leadership in industry, in commerce, in the military and in the Church's mission. In magazines acres of print are devoted to the subject. Bookstalls are stocked with an array of leadership titles. In ministerial training there is a heightened emphasis on leadership. Some of this material is sound and helpful. But all too often the idea of leadership that is deployed is an uncritical, naïve one, drawn from the world of business and secular organisations . . . The rhetoric of leadership has almost taken over Christian literature about ministry and mission. Notions of leadership derived from organisational or management studies or social psychology threaten to displace ecclesiological reflection on the Christian ministry. These disciplines have their uses and are not to be despised, but they can hardly replace theology.[1]

To be sure, one of the key issues for bishops and other senior office holders in the Anglican Church is the way in which symbolic authority has become attenuated and strained in recent times. This may be rooted in the difficulties of resolving disputes on gender and sexuality, and the solutions which, however well-meant, have tended to legitimise fissure and fracture. This weakens the symbolic sense of the church and its leadership, and it undermines the possibility of immediate and close access to authentic confidence, since the representational role of the church is to some extent guilty of deconstructing itself. That said, there is sufficient within Anglican identity and practice to permit both implicit and explicit forms of the church coalescing around leadership, even if there is a recognition that the church is bound to a series of creative tensions: problems that can be resolved, and some dilemmas that are endemic within Anglican polity, and cannot be resolved, but are rather meant to be encountered as tense framing mechanisms that give the church both its boundaries and freedom, its order and its non-order. So meetings or gatherings – even those that are lengthy and long-established – often carry

---

1 Avis, *Becoming a Bishop*, p. 59; see also Avis, *Authority, Leadership and Conflict in the Church*. Simon Western points out that there are more books in the English language on the subject of leadership than all the books available on any subject published in Portuguese.

important theological cadences within them, even when they appear to be 'unproductive' for long periods of time. Christianity is rooted in *corporate* meeting – it is what makes us *corporeal*.

Arguably, the Church of England is currently over-managed, with spiritual judgement and theological wisdom increasingly subordinated to multiple layers of executive management-led domination. Yet the danger of charismatic authority hastily and clumsily cutting through these same layers of management is that the narcolepsy of the whole institution is still not awakened to the danger it was in, and new dangers it now faces. Indeed, the institution finds that neither the layers of managerialism, nor the singular sharpness of charismatic authority that now purports to cut through them to get to the heart or the core of the purpose of the body, is what the institution actually needed. What the body of Christ does need is this: *to be comprehended*. It needs its complex anatomy to be understood, before either more management is added, or charismatic authority cuts it away. It needs deep, rich leadership and not just dramatic, heroic feats of rescue. The risk of the 'rescue rhetoric' – as with all forms of messianic leadership – is that short-term gains eventually yield longer-term damage. Like steroids, the mass and bulk of the body is quickly restored, and perhaps improved. But like steroids, long-term dosage brings other dangers. All styles of leadership carry risks. The questions are what are the potential hazards in this current style of archiepiscopal leadership? And how can these be addressed, and where possible, corrected?

For most senior leaders in the church, including Archbishops, this is no easy task. The church, like any institution, can often feel like it is mired in a kind of sludge of its own making. There is much floundering between patience and decision-making, and between learning from (or sifting through) the slurry of ecclesial life and achieving some kind of clarity. The sludge is, of course, a 'given'. Just as Christ gives himself to the Church and God gives Christ to humanity – the Word made flesh – so leaders struggle with the received nature of the body they are working with. Of course, the church is not a clarified and settled organisation; its genius lies in its contestability, and even ambivalence. Indeed, the 'sludge' may be part of what God intended. From the moment that the Risen Jesus first establishes the company of witnesses through the outpouring of the Spirit ('then he breathed on them and said: 'Receive the Holy Spirit . . .', Jn. 20: 22) the church moves outward, and each local expression of the church continues to witness to that same Risen Christ. The consequence of this is that church is founded on something that is *received* – not something invented or haphazardly discovered, then organised.

This places a special demand on all Christian leaders, but most especially those called to a ministry of oversight. For this communion and church cannot be merely led and shaped as though it were any kind of 'normal' body that responds to ordinary temporal rule, secular reasoning, or hard and clear manifestations of controlling power. It is, rather, the recognition that what we receive – a complex institution – we also pass on.[2] That there is a rich interdependence in leading, for the leaders can only be those who have been led. This is fundamental to the life of the church, the transmission of the gospel and the vocation of oversight. As +Rowan Williams commented, in a paper given to a conference in New York on archiepiscopacy during 2008,

> [t]his, of course has implications for our understanding of the bishop's ministry. If it is true that, as Tertullian said, 'one Christian is no Christian', then by the same token we should be able to say, 'one bishop is no bishop', and so 'one local church alone is no church'. A bishop is not an individual who 'represents' the local church as if he is empowered to speak for its local identity like a politician for his constituency. The bishop is above all the person who sustains and nourishes within the local church an awareness of its dependency on the apostolic mission, on the gift from beyond its boundaries – and he does this, of course, primarily and irreducibly as the celebrant of the 'Catholic oblation'. Hence, again from the earliest days, the clustering of local churches and their bishops around metropolitan sees which represented the channels through which the gospel came to be shared; and hence the insistence (an insistence that might almost be called fierce in many instances) that bishops received ordination from their neighbours in the *metropolita* under the leadership of the local primate – and hence too the seriousness of communicating Episcopal election by letter to the region, and the severity of the sanction of removing a bishop's name from the formal intercession list.[3]

So, one Archbishop on his own is 'no Archbishop'. We Christians are persons in communion; and as Anglicans, we are Churches-in-Communion. So a sole hero on a personal mission is, per se, *not* a helpful Archiepiscopal model – in the long-term. Primacy then – a further and specific calling in oversight – is about being one of the signs of the continuing reality of a living and active tradition, which is shared as a gift, and continues to be received, reified and re-lived in the church. This is why it is problematic if a local church innovates or interprets to such an extent that it cannot share what it has received with its neighbours. And here the role of episcopacy and primacy – in terms of leadership – is sometimes to challenge or limit the amount of local innovation in order to preserve and promote catholicity. This is not to make light of one of the tasks of the church, namely to live out the gospel faithfully in a specific context. But it is a reminder that the local assembly and its chief pastor (i.e., Archbishop) are bound to pass on what they have received, and not merely to adapt and innovate in order to address

2 For further discussion see Brown, *The Myth of the Strong Leader.*
3 'Rome, Constantinople, and Canterbury: Mother Churches?'

a set of contemporary pragmatic issues, no matter how (seemingly) worthy the missiological urgency may appear.

It is for this reason, perhaps, that even apparently innovative, heroic initiatives – such as Archbishop Justin appointing the Revd Dr Tory Baucum, Rector of Truro Church in Fairfax, Virginia, as one of the Six Preachers of Canterbury Cathedral – is rather double-edged. Tory Baucum is a member of the Anglican Church in North America – ACNA – which does not derive its episcopal oversight from the Presiding Bishop of the Episcopal Church (TEC), Katharine Jefferts Schori. True, the Anglican Church in North America (ACNA) is 'in the Anglican tradition' – but it is not part of the Communion. The church claims to have 29 dioceses and almost 1,000 congregations, serving more than around 100,000 members across North America. The Anglican Church in North America is affiliated with the Fellowship of Confessing Anglicans (FOCA), but is not a member of the Anglican Communion, and is, in effect, a rival to the Episcopal Church in the US and the Anglican Church of Canada. Friendly relations, however, do exist with other parts of the Anglican Communion. The ACNA is in 'full communion' with three member churches in the Anglican Communion: the Church of Nigeria, the Church of Uganda, and the Episcopal Church of South Sudan and Sudan. It has also received recognition and support from the Global South Anglican churches, an organised grouping of 24 Anglican Communion provinces. Archbishop Justin clearly hoped that through this he would promote ecclesial 'reconciliation and unity'. But the heroic gesture – if indeed that is what it is – risks the identity and composition of those who sense that a gesture such as this might eventually be counter-productive.

This gesture undoubtedly enables warmer relations with bodies within the Anglican Communion, such as GAFCON – the Global Anglican Futures Conference, which some would argue is a 'virtual' Province in all but name. And the Archbishop's bridge-building here is well-motivated, clearly. Yet this reflection takes us to the heart of the paradox in senior church leadership: both framing and creating capacity. Creating capacity – vital and necessary if the body is to live, move and have its being – emerges from a vision for how that development might take place. It needs space, and a generative vision that longs, with the Spirit, for the children of God to come into their own. At the same time, there is a framing dimension (a constant dynamic in Christian leadership), which necessarily delimits the amount of innovation and change that can take place, since the body must, in the future, still be faithful to what it has received – to what it was, is and will be.

The current vogueish elevation by the Archbishop of the *Five Marks of Mission* in Anglican polity perhaps points to the problem. There are several points to note here. First, there is nothing to object to in the *Five Marks*, per se. The *Five Marks* have won widespread acceptance amongst Anglicans as a practical and memorable 'checklist' for mission activity. They constitute an important statement on mission, and express the Anglican Communion's common commitment to, and understanding of, God's mission. The *Five*

Marks of Mission are: to proclaim the Good News of the Kingdom; to teach, baptise and nurture new believers; to respond to human need by loving service; to transform unjust structures of society, challenging violence of every kind and pursue peace and reconciliation; and to strive to safeguard the integrity of creation, and sustain and renew the life of the earth.

Second, however, the *Five Marks* are now being used slightly coercively – under the seemingly unquestionable guise of the urgency and priority of mission – to define 'orthodox' Anglicans and Anglicanism. So, to those who might have deep and legitimate theological questions about the very phrase 'marks of mission' (e.g., surely they might be the nail marks in the hands, side and feet; or perhaps the sign of the cross marked at baptism – or death etc.?), the 'marks of mission' become a coercive tool for denigrating more liberal visions of the church, and replacing these with (hyped-up) evangelical activism.

Third, the uncritical promotion of the *Five Marks of Mission* suggests that the current leadership in the Church of England is finding the very breadth of Anglicanism too complex to police. By leadership here, I mean not only bishops, but also the small cabal of executive managers who actually run most of the church these days, and for whom a 'checklist' (and yes, form-filling and the like) represents a much easier way of controlling the church. Deep, rich processes of theological and spiritual discernment are deemed to be far too difficult, time-consuming and woolly. The *Five Marks* have therefore become a tool for managers in delineating and controlling 'membership' and 'leadership'; and they allow cultures of ecclesial and theological exclusion to flourish, where there was once a thriving culture of inclusion.

Fourth, rather like University Christian Union Statements of Faith, checklists of orthodoxy appear to be necessary and essential for channeling and focusing energy and endeavour. But they quickly become reductive and sectarian. As Kathleen Boone noted in her study of fundamentalism, it is never the Bible that rules in such groups, but always the interpreter. It is the same with the *Five Marks of Mission*. Can an LGBT Metropolitan Church qualify as a valid 'Fresh Expression' of church, and come to be seen as a fulfilment of the *Five Marks of Mission*? It seems unlikely any such congregation will be permitted to qualify.

So, all are now to be signed up for the *Five Marks*, even though they have not gone through Synod, or through a rigorous theological discernment process. To be sure, the Archbishops mean no harm in promoting the *Five Marks of Mission* as a benchmark for discerning Anglican orthodoxy and orthopraxy. But much harm is already being done. The *Five Marks of Mission* are inherently 'Open Evangelical' in character, and whilst there is nothing wrong with that, the putative application of these Marks across the penumbra of the Church of England means that most of our bishops are now Open Evangelicals – or sufficiently fluent in that rhetoric to pass muster. If Boone is right – that in fundamentalist churches, it is not the Bible that rules, but the interpreter – then the implications for the uncritical imposition and implementation of the *Five Marks* in the Church of England are potentially grave. Because the test of Orthodoxy – and entry into that privileged 'inner ring' of adherents and leadership – will rest on agreeing with the *interpretation and value* that any Archbishop places on those *Five Marks*. The depleting theological sagacity of the Bishops will be replaced by unquestioning episcopal fealty.

Like a Maoist culture of old, we are now being asked to assent to the Great Leap Forward (i.e. 'growth, growth . . .'). In Mao's China (1949–76), it was not good enough to profess to be a good Communist and loyal Chinese citizen. Chinese Communism was turned into a cult of personal followership: to survive and prosper, you had to demonstrate that you were *a loyal disciple* of Mao. Because Communism was simply too broad to police, and China far too diverse to control, Mao set additional tests of orthodoxy to be sure of whom he could really trust. In the end, the only ones were those who truly followed him: the obeisant.

We are arguably beginning to arrive at the same juncture in Anglicanism. The *Five Marks* are being used to silently disenfranchise and marginalise our liberals, questioners and thinkers. So in some respects, the uncritical top-down imposition of the *Five Marks of Mission* might be said to be the beginning of an end game. It represents a descent – from a broad, diverse church for all, to a much smaller body of followers who are in personal agreement with the current leadership. In terms of everyday episcopal leadership, the results can be somewhat alarming. A bishop currently serving in the Church of England now asks all his clergy to subscribe to (his) 'Three Ps': Prophetic, Pioneering and Passionate. The intention is, as ever, laudable. But the narrowing of the missional and ecclesial agenda to one of praxis-based concurrence with the bishop is a full-scale retreat from an Anglican polity of breadth, and a descent into narrow tribalism. At the risk of suggesting other 'Ps', where might be the space and permission for prayer, pausing, pastoral or public presence, as well as priestly and prescient engagement? But as with the promotion of the *Five Marks of Mission*, these latter candidates are too broad for episcopal control.

The nature of this ecclesial body

The traditional Anglican Trilateral is usually to be understood as scripture(s), tradition and reason. The Anglican quadrilateral in the nineteenth century, serves a different purpose. The trilateral is a form of theological method (capacity-orientated?), and the quadrilateral a set of ecclesial markers (framing?), with the combined matrix in contemporary ecclesial life having both a clear and nascent identity in Anglican polity. The fourth point of negotiation in the quadrilateral – 'the historic episcopate, locally adapted' – is often translated into 'experience' or 'local culture'. It is this that makes the Anglican Communion so difficult and demanding to preside over. However, that is not *the* 'problem' to be fixed; it is an inherent dynamic of the dilemma of communion. To try to fix it would be also to break it.

Clearly, the Anglican Trilateral – a theological method for addressing and resolving tensions and hermeneutical disagreements within the Communion – cannot be replaced by a set of personal qualities that any individual Archbishop may embody. To be sure, it is undoubtedly a blessing to have an Archbishop that can offer something of a 'personal trilateral', which to some extent the current Archbishop of Canterbury has. That 'personal trilateral' is, first, a warm, charismatic and personal style of leadership that cuts through established party lines and tribal divisions; second, energy and fresh dynamism; and third, a capacity to be directive and decisive. Granted, adeptness in negotiation and forms of reconciliation are also to be welcomed. But the spiritual capital of the Anglican Communion is substantial, layered, historic, dynamic *and* given – so not an object or subject to be moulded by one person's gifts or character. The great danger for an Archbishop who is (probably, through no fault of their own) – cast in the lead role by both the media and many in the church as the 'heroic' and perhaps 'messianic' leader who will deliver the Communion from its crises – is that the need for *relatedness* gets replaced by *relationships*. The two are different.

Relatedness requires the whole institution, in all its complexity, to work with and through the office and role of Archbishop. It is slow and reticulate work. This is both the gift and burden of a multifaceted compound institution. Lambeth Conferences, the ACC, or a meeting of Primates, provide a platform for complex and conflictual conversations to be conducted. Any heavy accent on (personal) relationships, however, does something different in this context. It moves quicker, to be sure, but at a cost. It tends to demarcate between followers and resistors. Both of these categories are problematic in ecclesial polity. Detractors speak with just as much prophetic prescience as those who are seemingly collaborative. Prioritising relationship over relatedness will also inadvertently form cabals and inner circles of followers, who will typically 'buy into the vision' – whilst leaving other groups left out in the cold, who hold to other, no less valid truths. They will form alliances – even a significant critical mass – of powerful supporters.

There is already some evidence of +Justin's 'inner circle' having some morphological resonance with Tony Blair's so-called 'kitchen cabinet'. There are additional problems to note here. It was common for this kind of leadership (i.e. under Blair) to create a very small tight-knit group of ardent loyalists, and then develop a larger devoted cadre. This was often done through off-the-record briefings and seemingly indiscreet remarks that sought wider fealty. But this is generally a sign of weaker leadership searching for security and allies, and a sign of a weak institution that entertains this behaviour pattern. As a short-term tactic it often gains considerable traction. In the longer-term, it disenchants and alienates, whilst the cadres and elite become both increasingly powerful and paranoid. As for its place in the church, it clearly constitutes poor ecclesial practice, and less than wholesome discipleship.

This kind of leadership lacks self-awareness, and flows from unconscious forms of anxiety, which in turn are rooted not in humility, but rather in over-confidence over-compensating for unacknowledged insecurities. It will lead to many feeling dis-counted and un-consulted. This is why the 'eco-leadership' championed by Western is preferred to any of the 'heroic' models. Eco-leadership respects the character of the body it works with, and any transformation in transitional times through such leadership will only ever be a by-product of the character and multiple intelligences (i.e. emotional, theological, institutional, etc.) of the leader. Heroic modes of leadership, in contrast, tend to problematise or demonise the present state of an institution, requiring followers to reject what they have known and trusted in exchange for something new. The recent promotion of 'Fresh Expressions', 'Pioneer' and 'Re-imagining Ministry' form perfect vehicles of rhetoric and topoi for practitioners of heroic leadership.

In short, the quick results achieved through the exercise of personal charisma and organisational verve can, unintentionally, cause significant long-term damage to the institution as a whole. But by the time this is realised, the leader has invariably moved on.[4] Linda Woodhead, commenting on styles of leadership amongst the recent Archbishops of Canterbury, follows Troeltsch's distinction between 'church' and 'sect'. The former 'has fuzzy boundaries and embraces the whole of society'; the latter 'has hard boundaries and tries to keep its distance from society'. She claims that until quite recently, the Church of England has been the former – a church 'by law established' for the whole nation. But since the 1980s, 'the Church has veered towards sectarianism'.

> In the 1960s and '70s the Church of England was travelling with society in a broadly liberal direction, with prominent Anglicans supporting the liberalisation of laws relating to abortion, homosexuality, and divorce. But after Runcie, Anglican leaders made a U-turn . . . Under the leadership of +Rowan Williams and +John Sentamu, the Church of England campaigned successfully to be exempted from provisions of the new equality legislation, took a hard line against homosexual practice and gay marriage, and made continuing concessions to the opponents of women's progress in the Church . . .
>
> Although Archbishop Welby supports women bishops, he remains opposed to same-sex marriage and assisted dying, and takes very seriously the relationship with African churches and their leaders. The sectarian fringes of the Church remain influential, and the bishops remain isolated from the views of ordinary Anglicans. The Church as a whole creaks under the weight of historic buildings, unimaginative managerialism, and sub-democratic structures.[5]

4 On this, see Minkin, *The Blair Supremacy*. Minkin shows how Blair's leadership substituted consultation for personal charisma and executive authority.
5 Woodhead, 'The Vote for Women Bishops'.

So in terms of the overall leadership of the Church of England, understanding the socio-political, economic and cultural changes over the last century that have affected the control and management of institutions might be important. Frank Parkin, Pitrim Sorokin and Talcott Parsons distinguish between the proletariat and the bourgeoisie, the transformation of the capitalist class into the managerial class, and the identification of vested interests in ownership.[6] Thus, the patrician, landed-gentry who once occupied important Sees and Deaneries in the Church of England gave way to a new capitalist class in the Edwardian era, which in turn was quickly transformed into the managerial class of the post-war era. Ministry in the Church of England, and the emerging training and education that now shapes individuals as clergy, has increasingly focused on executive management and growth, and steadily marginalised theological wisdom.

One by-product of a tightly-controlled and dominant executive managerial class, and the focused targets which the Church of England is currently shaped by and pursuing (i.e. management and growth),[7] is the *inevitability* of an emerging charismatic leader, who as well as presiding over organisational structures, also serves as a *compensator* for the clergy and laity now dominated by management structures. Both English archbishops currently correspond to this pattern. Both have been able to establish a charismatic leadership style that is supported and enabled by layers of executive managerial culture. Welby's background may be important here. The elitism of Eton and a privileged, though personally difficult childhood, coupled to his career in executive management, are important factors in shaping his ecclesial leadership.

Indeed, the two Archbishops collude; they leave each other alone, largely, but can call on one another for mutual support as required. This largely leaves both managerial hegemony and charismatic leadership free to dominate in different ways: one rules through controlling and regulating structures; the other is left to improvise, and deploy visionary rhetoric that heightens expectation and maintains momentum. Both appeal to the rhetoric of 'enabling', but also have the capacity to dominate and control those who believe they are being liberated.

The net effect of this behavioural pattern is beginning to emerge. The current English Archbishops are now functioning much more like corporate chief executives within their respective provinces, and nationally. The role of a diocesan bishop is thereby reduced in scope to that of an area manager, left with targets, aims, objectives and outcomes set by executive managers, and endorsed by 'visionary' Archbishops. The bishops, as area managers, are further controlled through tightly regulated training processes. In all this, the parish clergy are reduced to the status of local branch managers,

---

6 Parkin, *The Marxist Theory of Class*, pp. 45–46; Sorokin, 'What is a Social Class?'; Parsons, 'A Revised Analytical Approach to the Theory of Social Stratification'.

7 See Percy, 'Growth and Management in the Church of England: Some Comments'.

thinly stretched in resourcing, but made to chase the (unreachable) targets set by the area managers. Incentives and rewards (i.e. preferment, additional resourcing, etc.) are offered to those who deliver.[8]

Yet this alliance of executive managerialism and 'heroic leadership' – beguiling as it is – only further distances wisdom, critical reflection and theological acuity from the very centre of rich theological and spiritual discourse, and the ensuing governance that flows from within the church, which is precisely what is needed to enable ecclesial institutions. The Labour party was subject to similar dynamics under the leadership of Tony Blair: controlling structures that distanced dissent, coupled to charismatic leadership that gave vision, in the Weberian sense. It goes without saying that the bulk of control rests with an executive authority vested in elite executive managers. The number of charismatic leaders permitted to act as a balance and compensator to managerial control will, in turn, be policed and restricted by that ruling elite. Furthermore, those permitted to join the elite will need to be 'on message', and therefore unable to indulge in theological or prophetic wisdom that might challenge the status quo. At present, the signs point to Archbishop Welby becoming a wholesale proponent of executive managerial culture, just as surely as he was a product of that culture as an oil industry executive, prior to ordination. Elliott Jaques, in *A General Theory of Bureaucracy*, argued that the church was an 'association', and clergy 'members', not its employees and that once clergy come to be regarded as employees in a manager–subordinate relationship, congregations become customers, and the sacred bond between laity and clergy becomes broken, and turned into one of consumer–provider. Jaques specifically praised those churches that promoted life tenure for clergy, because that guarded against centralised managerial interference, and protected the deep communal and personal ethos of the clergy-laity bond. Overt central control and monitoring by churches, argued Jaques, slowly destroyed local spiritual life, because the clergy would be subject to demands on two fronts. Namely, those targets and priorities set remotely by central management, and the local consumerist demands of congregations. The combination would erode public–pastoral ministry to the whole parish, with the clergy becoming demoralised and alienated.[9]

'Leadership', as we noted earlier, and for all the investment currently placed on the term in the contemporary church, is not a word that appears in the New Testament. Neither does 'executive' or 'manager'. So the emergent style of governance that the Archbishop seems to be so keen to promote – at least in the Church of England – may benefit from some deeper biblical, ecclesial and theological reflection. One is tempted to ask what the uncritical promotion of leadership and management can add to the *Ordinal* that shapes much of clerical praxis and identity?

8 Ibid. pp. 257ff.
9 Jaques, *A General Theory of Bureaucracy*, pp. 344–347.

Of course, it could be that the focus on leadership and management is inimical to normative patterns and channels of ecclesial governance. Currently, and under the Archbishop's leadership, there are several Task Groups, all grappling with apparently intractable problems that have dogged the church for decades. The groups have wrestled with talent management, discipleship, simplification, financial equity, resourcing ministerial education and national church structures. Yet the Task Forces sponsored by the Archbishop have largely worked outside synodical structures, as well as at some distance from the Archbishops' Council and the House of Bishops.[10] Senior managers at Lambeth Palace adjudged not to be 'on message' have been firmly moved aside. Little, it seems, can stand in the way of the heroic leader and a preferred cadre of executive managers. Yet whilst this may cause significant problems in the governance and shaping of the Church of England, there is little sign, so far, that +Justin's method will carry over into any non-English Provinces.

There are sufficient critiques of 'heroic' kinds of leadership in business, organisations and institutions to raise concerns in the church over the emerging pattern of +Justin's archiepiscopacy.[11] There are considered theological critiques of episcopacy that can be drawn upon too.[12] There are also numerous more popular and polemical works that are rooted in critical practical theology.[13] The issue for archiepiscopal leadership is how to engage with such interlocutors. If ignored, it does of course become possible to 'macro-lead', with heroic leadership patterns tending toward distancing the necessary critical voices within governance that help to season the character of wisdom.

In +Justin's early months as Primate, much was made in the media of the apparent similarities between himself and the new Pontiff, Pope Francis – especially in their warm and immediate rapport with their followers, and their apparent amiable accessibility. But their leadership styles have quickly bifurcated. Pope Francis, in contemplating changes to the practice of the Roman Catholic Church, seems to canvass widely, and listen carefully. The Archbishop, in contrast, seems to move quickly, with few signs of broad consultation. The former model is rooted in genuine humility: the Holy Spirit speaks through all the church, so all must listen attentively. This theological worldview helps preserve true catholicity; but it can mean achieving ecclesial consensus or direction is an elusive, slow

---

10 Despite considerable ferment, the *Green Report* was not allowed to be debated at the February 2015 meeting of the General Synod. The censoring of the criticism of the *Green Report* is reported in *Church Times*, 13 February 2015, p. 3.
11 See Badaracco, 'We Don't Need Another Hero'; Mintzberg, 'Rebuilding Companies as Communities'.
12 Webster, 'The Self-Organizing Power of the Gospel of Christ: Episcopacy and Community Formation'; and Roberts, 'Lord, Bondsman and Churchman: Identity, Integrity and Power in Anglicanism'.
13 See, for example, Pattison, *The Faith of the Managers*; Oliver, *Ministry Without Madness*.

and stuttering process. The latter model is unduly over-confident, and tends towards being overly directional and non-consultative. And even though this latter mode of leadership appears to make significant ground quickly, catholicity is quickly eroded by the alienation, marginalisation and disenchantment of other values.

For the Church of England, there is a serious theological issue bubbling away in all of this. Augustine argued that the human mind could be divided into two; not left and right, but upper and lower. The higher part of the mind was for the contemplation of God, and the lower for calculation and reasoning.[14] A fourth century monk – Evagrius of Pontus – went further, and argued that there is something called *nous* – a kind of spiritual and intuitive intelligence, which only arises as the mind is in communion with God.[15] It is this, I think, that the current executive managerial processes of the Church of England lack – and perhaps even wish to eviscerate from ecclesial governance. And it is this theological *nous* that charismatic and heroic forms of leadership may be slightly tempted to shun too, as theological wisdom could easily incl[...] [...] ower of executive management as w[...] [...] heroic leadership.

As Daniel Hardy note[d] [...] today is . . . that the personal wil[...] [...] of sectional interests in the Church [...] [...] ogic of Coleridge's own aphorism, the result can only be a downward spiral to self-love'.[16] Correspondingly, the inherent 'dynamic tension' of the church is not something it needs rescuing from; rather, this is precisely what needs valuing and cherishing. The dynamic tension that is inherent within the church acts as a counter-balance to claims of perfection and truth. That same inherent dynamic tension also keeps open that essential space for the Holy Spirit to teach the church new things. The risk of a singular, heroic–charismatic leader emerging who believes that they embody the claims of church – even in the name of orthodoxy – is that truth and love become both personalised and individualised, with the ultimate risk being the development of a kind of sectarian narcissism. The only way to counter this is to embrace demanding theological density and diversity as a *gift* to the church. That same density and diversity constitutes a *sign* of God's all-encompassing breadth and wisdom (which no one person or group can either own, or be said to embody), and is a foretaste of the teeming life and vitality of the Kingdom of God.

So, it becomes hard to avoid a form of ecclesial narcolepsy if the church unintentionally mutes the acuity of its theologians – those who might have the necessary foresight and urgency to call the church back to some more

14 See Augustine, *On the Trinity*, 12.1–3; see *The Trinity* trans. S. McKenna C.Ss.R.
15 Evagrius, 'Chapters on Prayer'.
16 Hardy, 'Anglicanism in the Twenty-First Century; Scriptural, Local, Global'.

self-critical reflection. As Loren Mead predicted in *The Once and Future Church*, chasing targets and investing in (so-called) 'evidence-based indices of success' – prioritised by executive managers in the church – is in fact a sign of weakness and failure in the church, and does not, as many suppose, represent a salvific or visionary-missionary horizon.[17] Such foci inspire a few, but will disenchant many, corroding both morale and identity.

The trouble with trusting in measurable growth as an indicator of fitness is that quantity tells us little about quality. Christian life is as much about character, virtue and wisdom as it is about numbers. Yet many think measurable effectiveness is the yardstick. But faithfulness is arguably more important than success. We may need to recover some of our spiritual and theological wisdom here. We are currently some way down the wrong road.

So, what kind of 'body' is the church? We need to know if we are to be led and managed well. Studies of church leadership often fail to appreciate that the church is a complex institution, and not a simple organisation. As Philip Selznick observed,[18] organisations exist for functional purposes; when they are fulfilled, the organisation may become expendable. Institutions, in contrast, are 'natural communities' with rich, historic roots embedded in the whole of society. They incorporate various groups that may even contest with each other, the institution, and its values. In Selznick's categorisation, a church is much more like an institution. It is a 'bodie politick', to quote Hooker.

Biblical conceptualisations of church are also illuminating. As an institution, it is often compared to a family or household (oikos); sometimes to a human body; or even a bride in marriage. It is seldom described as a rational, organisational venture – even in relation to tax-collecting, tent-making or carpentry. True, households and families need organising. And even marriages need managing, sometimes. But the early church, by appealing to ideas of 'family', 'household', 'marriage' and 'body', emphasised the intricate, organic and intimate bonds forming this complex institution. That is why our bishops are mothers or fathers in God, not managers. They are chief pastors, not our chief executives.

Like a family, the church exists for love, formation and growth; a 'bodie mysticall', as Hooker would say. The authors of the *Green Report* failed to grasp this. If the church was an organisation – like a business – then, yes, of course, teach our leaders about management through the very best business schools. But if the church is a family or household, a different wisdom for leadership is needed.

Conclusion

We are at a fork in the road. Essentially, we are debating what kinds of senior leaders we apparently now need, and the future shape of our church.

17 Mead, *The Once and Future Church*.
18 Selznick, *Leadership in Administration*.

The choice is stark. It is between believing in an institution that has richness and depth in worship, wisdom and eternal values; pastoral cherishing, nourishing others and social flourishing. Or colluding with narratives that say the church is a struggling organisation in terminal decline, in need of dramatic rescue. It is far too easy to say 'we simply can't go on as we are'. Such talk promotes panic and pragmatism – causing us to clutch at almost any straw, just to stay in business. We should be asking much harder questions of our leaders, not using such rhetoric to justify all manner of exigent and expedient change.

So, a key issue for +Justin Welby will be the extent to which theologians – especially those with critical voices and dissenting wisdom – are allowed to help shape the current church from the centre, in this new era of Archiepiscopacy. It is still not clear that the Archbishop might recognise these dynamics, understand them, and act; but the early signs are not promising. To be sure, there are multiple ironies here.

But let us return to Bermuda, which we discussed in the previous chapter. It stands alone, and is not part of a collective Anglican Province. The danger of a warm 'personal communion' with the Archbishop becoming the *person* rather than an *instrument of unity* for configuring the Anglican Communion, is that Bermuda will cease to be the anomaly it is, and instead become normative. Provinces are local expressions of the inherent diversity and consequential tensions embedded within wider Anglican polity and praxis. A close, personal relationship with the Archbishop of Canterbury may be helpful, but it does not resolve the *essential dilemma of relatedness* that lies at the heart of Anglicans' dense, mature ecclesial polity. The individualisation and personalisation of leadership – especially in roles within complex institutions – carries significant risks. Consequently, if a pattern of charismatic–heroic leadership and 'messiah discourse' is nurtured, we'll soon discover that, rather like the proverbial Bermuda Triangle, some things will mysteriously start to disappear. We won't quite know where they went to in this new, emerging 'personal trilateral', which seems to rest on a quite singular heroic-messianic discourse and the ever-increasing hegemony of executive managerial power vested in a small elite cadre who have pledged uncritical fealty. But miss them, we will.

Part II

Money, sex and power

Divisions and diversities

4 Future possibilities for funding the ministry of the Church of England

One of the most vexing questions faced in the Church of England today is this: how can it be afforded? The question permeates almost every level of debate on structure, viability and mission. From theological colleges to continuing ministerial education, and from diocese to national headquarters, there is no escaping the financial vagaries and uncertainties that question every appointment, initiative and commitment. At the beginning of the twenty-first century, an editorial in *The Economist* (US edition) explained the problem plainly:

> The Church of England is suffering from poverty. It has been in a financial fix before, most famously in the 1980s when the Church Commissioners lost money in high-risk commercial property deals. The commissioners, who manage the church's large portfolio of stock exchange and property assets, do better now . . . [but] the current problem is that the church has underestimated how much it will have to pay in pensions . . . the income from the Church Commissioners that would normally go to the parishes to support the everyday work of the church now largely has to make good the shortfall . . . [income handed] over to the parishes has dropped . . . retired clergy live longer . . . As a result, the dioceses, which rely for their income largely on gifts from churchgoers, are being asked to provide an extra eleven million pounds a year to keep the church running. Already it is estimated that three-quarters of the dioceses are in the red. The dioceses are urgently exploring ways of preventing the church from going broke.[1]

Yet this analysis only scratches the surface of the problem. As I argued some years ago,[2] the Church of England has yet to adapt to the emergent paradigm in which it finds itself; one in which a comprehensive national ministry is now funded by *congregations* rather than its parishes. True, as a 'spiritual public service' to the nation, the Church of England continues to enjoy a high degree of public support at many levels. Occasional offices

1 'Counting the Doomsday Option: Church of England – Another Public Service is In Crisis'.
2 Percy, *Salt of the Earth*, pp. 336–341.

(e.g., baptisms, weddings, funerals), national religious rites and service (e.g., at times of national grief or celebration), or involvement in politics, education and social situations and in regional representation (e.g., regeneration initiatives, etc.) all underline the fact that the Church of England continues to serve its people. But its people do not fund the church, and have only done so haphazardly throughout its history.

In bygone eras, the tithing of the whole community supported the local parish church – both the building and the clerical stipend. Up until the sixteenth century, non-payment of tithes could mean excommunication; non-attendance could merit a fine. But fines were always difficult to collect and seldom imposed; excommunications were almost unheard of. The practice of tithing was always haphazard, and it waned quickly in direct proportion to the growth of industrialisation throughout the eighteenth and nineteenth centuries.[3] Parliamentary reforms in 1836 tried to regularise tithing by replacing the notoriously chaotic 10 per cent levy imposed on all produce (e.g., hay, milk, fish, cheese, and any other harvest), with a rental charge imposed on land. But even this could not last, and in 1864 the law abolished the 'Church Rate' (which had been re-imposed in 1661). The practice of paying a tithe on land was finally abolished by the Tithe Act of 1936.

What the Church Rate had tried to do was to put established religion on a more comfortable footing, as it obliged parishioners to financially support their parish church (irrespective of their beliefs). But the cultural and industrial revolutions of the seventeenth and eighteenth centuries questioned this arrangement intensely. Parliament passed the Toleration Act in 1689, enshrining religious freedom in law: and the freedom to worship where you wished inevitably implied permission to support your own religion in your own way – and to not subsidise the established church. By the last quarter of the nineteenth century, the foundations for the present anomaly were already laid, namely the bifurcation of the economy of the parish with that of the welfare of the parish church. However, parish churches were to be open and available to their respective resident populations, and were to minister to them accordingly. But the cost of that ministry was borne, not by the parish, but by the congregations themselves, and in collaboration with the Ecclesiastical Commissioners.[4] In the twentieth century, further reforms to the financing of the Church of England placed more power in central and diocesan hands. In 1976, the Endowments and Glebe Measure vested all land and its management in the hands of the diocese.

For Church of England congregations and their ministers, there are three interrelated problems that need addressing which will have a bearing upon the

---

3 See Pounds, *A History of the English Parish Church*, pp. 213ff; Russell, *The Clerical Profession*, p. 128; Percy, 'Finding Our Place, Losing Our Space: Reflections on Parish Identity'.

4 The Church Commissioners were created in 1948, an amalgamation of the Ecclesiastical Commissioners and Queen Anne's Bounty (Russell, *The Clerical Profession* 1980, p. 268).

future provision of parochial ministry. The methodology used for reflection is primarily drawn from the field of practical theology. Here, it is my contention that in order to reform or afford the ministry of the Church of England in the future, local congregations and their narrativity will need to be listened to and understood as the place where emergent structures and theologies of ministry are rediscovered. The corresponding suggestions arise out of a 'problem-posing' theological strategy that locates the debate in the grounded reality of parish and diocesan life, rather than in 'ideal' theologising on the nature of gift, reciprocity or mutuality. There are three concerns to mention briefly.

The first concern to outline is the rising cost of ministry and the manner in which the money is raised by the church. Most dioceses have a 'quota' or 'parish share' system for each parish, and calculate the worth of the parish using a variety of complex formulae. The income raised from the parishes supports the work of the diocese (i.e. its central infrastructure, which may be concerned with parsonages, legal matters, development, mission, education, etc.) and makes contributions to clergy pensions and stipends. In addition to this, money raised by the congregation must pay for the expenses of ministry and the upkeep of the church and its buildings. Clearly, some congregations, for a variety of reasons (e.g., size, wealth, geography, etc.) raise more money than others. Yet the problem that is now emerging is that many congregations see the significant amounts of money they contribute to parochial ministry, and to their own churches, being swallowed up in central diocesan infrastructures.

Second, this leads to questions about the necessity of so much diocesan infrastructure, and the viability of other churches. A century ago, there were no 'diocesan centres' employing large numbers of staff. A parish church, it must be said, normally understands its need of a bishop, but it is normally less clear about the need for a large number of diocesan employees. The multiplication of centres and staff over the last 50 years has led to the enhancement and intensification of 'diocesan identity', and the deepening and extension of what a regional resource can offer to the local. To be sure, this has been a valuable (but expensive) development. But fundamentally, parishes remain the basic unit of ecclesial order and identity in the Church of England. Parishes need a bishop (occasionally), but a diocese seldom. The concerns of parochial congregations remain endearingly local and contextualised, focused around the state of the church (building) itself and the availability and effectiveness of ministerial provision.[5] Anything provided after that is a welcome extravagance; but increasingly, the financial accountability of dioceses is becoming an issue for parishes.[6]

Third, the evolution of clerical stipends is probably incomplete, and at its present stage, problematic. There is, for example, an obvious incoherence in

5 Percy, *Salt of the Earth*, p. 87
6 Laughlin, 'A Model of Financial Accountability and the Church of England', in Percy and Evans, *Managing the Church*, pp. 49–77.

paying a parish priest of 25 years' service and considerable experience and expertise little more than someone who has just emerged from theological college. The former may have significant numbers of dependents (children of college age that need funding, frail parents that need financial support, etc.); the latter may have no dependents at all, but their 'living allowance' is virtually the same. The stipend takes no account of the income of a spouse either. It is, paradoxically, a kind of proto-socialist form of payment. All receive more or less the same income, irrespective of the range of responsibilities, output, capacity and ability of the person. Housing is standardised. Of course, the origins of the 'standardised' stipend are well understood, even if it is a relatively recent development; a valiant attempt to address the substantial inequalities that existed under the previous systems of glebe land,[7] absent incumbents and private patronage. But the present difficulty is that where there was once some social equivalence in clergy pay, clerical incomes have now fallen dramatically in comparison to other professions.

For example, in 1957 the average clerical income was one fifth of the pay of barristers, doctors, solicitors and dentists – a radical shift from the comparative parity of the mid-nineteenth century. Today, as Russell notes, 'a clerical family with no other income other than a stipend and with two children qualifies for . . . income supplement . . . in some parishes both the vicar and assistant priest are dependent on social security for some part of their total income'.[8] Furthermore, it should be noted that those clergy who are 'preferred' (i.e. promoted) in the church, perhaps becoming a canon residentiary, archdeacon, dean or bishop, do receive higher stipends. However, this leaves many priests with considerable experience and expertise, exercising valuable ministries, on a 'basic' stipend, and potentially resentful.

These three financial problems are, I hold, all interrelated, and rooted to the future of ministerial provision in the Church of England. But how are they to be addressed? What strategies might there be to enable the priest-like task to continue and flourish? In what follows, I want to first of all outline how practical theology, in conjunction with James Hopewell's stress on local narrativity,[9] can help the church address the multiplicity of issues. Then secondly, I want to reflect upon the Church of England's self-understanding of ministry and identify specific strategies that might enable the future organisation of the church.

Congregations and the financing of ministry

In what way is money or finance a serious theological issue for a congregation? Clearly, congregations tell stories about money and funding all the time. They also listen to the stories of others: poor clergy on low incomes, the Church

---

7 Russell, *The Clerical Profession*, p. 238.
8 Ibid., p. 269.
9 Hopewell, *Congregation: Stories and Structures*, London: SCM Press, 1987.

Commissioners losing substantial sums, 'the minister down the road who does nothing, but is paid the same as our tireless priest', the church up the road 'with plenty of financial reserves', 'the amazing fundraising scheme or stewardship development of a neighbouring parish', 'the sacrifice of a single benefactor', the 'looming crisis in pensions', and more besides. Whatever balance sheets and financial reports might be issued by the diocese or the Church Commissioners – in other words, whatever the facts or spin – it is *stories* about money that also constitute the lives of congregations and condition their expectations.[10]

Hopewell sees money as a powerful symbol in the life of the congregation: 'money is frequently an *emotion*-laden metaphor that both expresses and provokes the identity of a particular congregation'.[11] The symbolisation is diverse. Some hide its symbolisation altogether: the subject is seldom mentioned, money or cheques are presented in sealed envelopes, discreetly, and all campaigning is done quietly (but efficiently). At another congregation, money may function as 'a potent expression of superabundance and fertility': it is a sign of spiritual fecundity. At another church, money is seen as an agent of the material and an adversary to the spiritual, and its power to dominate agendas is fiercely resisted. Still at another parish, financial difficulties become the foundation for expressing disappointment with the world (which ignores the congregation), the lack of resources from the wider church, and the apparent 'success' of neighbouring churches, which is resented. In this last form of symbolisation, the lack of money is normally correlated with the loss of power and membership.

These insights are important for three reasons. First, the presence or absence of income and capital, however that is construed in a congregation, is part of the overall *symbolisation* within their theological framework. A congregation sees that its wealth or poverty says something about their relationship with God and the world (e.g., blessing, suffering solidarity, social marginalisation, empowering-pivotal centrality within a locality, etc.). Second, money is an issue for the *orthopraxis* of the congregation or denomination; its use is *value*-laden. It may be obvious that it is not easy to pay the heating bills year on year, but that will not stop the same congregation raising money for a new window, or the restoration of a beloved pulpit. Third, income and capital remains, stubbornly part of the *local* narrativity of a congregation first and foremost (inevitably), and is therefore not easily assigned a role in a larger regional or national 'plot'.[12] In other words, before congregations worry about the fiscal viability of a diocese, they are first and foremost

---

10 Readers are also referred to Quattrone, 'Governing Social orders, Unfolding Rationality, and Jesuit Accounting Practices: A Procedural Approach to Institutional Logics'. Quattrone shows how Jesuit organisation and ecclesial praxis can be understood through any analysis of its fiscal history.

11 Hopewell, 1987, p. 8.

12 On this, see Ammerman (et al.), *Organizing Religious Work*, in which the authors compare ten mainstream denominations in the USA, and note that local congregations invariably resist and resent the larger regional or national organising structures.

concerned with their leaking roof, the expenses of their minister, and adequately endowing local outreach, of which a care of buildings is inevitably a part. Correspondingly, there is understandable resentment or reticence about large amounts of income 'disappearing' into central or regional sources, since the local, historically, invariably precedes the meta-structures of the hierarchy, which often lack definition or comparable narrativity.

Paying proper attention to congregations and their fiscal narratives is an important theological and ecclesial task. It serves to remind church leaders and dioceses that the primary resourcing of the Church of England is from the local *to* the local. Moreover, the local and the congregational are theologically significant locations where the story of witness and its recollection continues to shape and characterise the ministry of the church. Too often dioceses or central church structures assume that the meta-organisation is essential and that the local is small and therefore expendable. In truth, the reverse is true. The Church of England survived more than adequately for many centuries without the substantial national, regional and diocesan resources it presently enjoys. For many parishioners, their primary experience of the Church of England is a local one, occasionally tempered with a visit from the bishop, or an incident in the media in which the Church of England, as 'established' religion, provides occasion for what Wesley Carr calls 'national gossip'.

Behind these assertions lurks a deeper question: what kind of creature is the clergyperson? It is normal for most trained clergy today to assume that they are 'professional', and that in being ordained, they join, in effect, a profession. But this understanding of the clergy is comparatively recent, and a brief understanding of the history is essential if we are to move forward with the parallel financial questions. In Anthony Russell's ground-breaking *The Clerical Profession*,[13] we are introduced to the idea that the clergy only became 'professionalised' in the late nineteenth century, as they gradually lost their stake-holdings as landowners, gentlemen, magistrates, almoners, arbitrators, essayists, political figures and generators of improvement in health, education and overall social well-being. The rapid industrialisation of society squeezed clergy out of many 'soft' mainstream public roles or diffuse role obligations, and created the pressure for a new intensification of identity, or what we call 'professionalisation':

> As a result of these processes, the clergy of the mid-nineteenth century were disposed to accord greater significance to that central and irreducible religious function of the priestly role, the leadership of public worship. In this element of his role at least the clergyman had a monopoly of legitimate function. In an age which came to accord high status those who possessed socially useful technical knowledge, the clergy, by their emphasis on liturgical studies, attempted to become technologists of the sanctuary.[14]

13 Russell, *The Clerical Profession*.
14 Ibid., p. 40.

The Oxford Movement helped this process along, with its emphasis on frequent celebration of Holy Communion. Less than 50 years earlier, most English people had only been used to receiving the sacrament once a year. The Evangelical revival also encouraged the intensification of professional identity, with an emphasis on discipline, systematic visiting, and schools for preaching and catechising. Within a very short space of time, English clergy began to dress differently from other 'gentlemanly professions' in everyday wear by sporting dog-collars, something they had not done previously.[15] Furthermore, clergy were now being 'trained' at special theological colleges rather than taught divinity at university (another new development), which also enhanced the emerging professional identity.[16]

This rapid development in professionalisation would normally be something that is welcomed in the vocational or occupational spheres of work. But in ministry, its status as a 'profession' has never been something that could be easily agreed upon. Neither, for that matter, has it ever been something the Church of England could easily afford. As Russell notes, the number of paid clergy dropped steadily throughout the twentieth century: there were 25,000 in 1901, and less than half that number 100 years later.[17] The number of residential theological colleges in the same period has dropped from forty to ten. Yet in the midst of this, clergy have shown a marked reluctance to be reformed in line with other professions, even as their social and cultural 'capital' has steadily declined. The Paul Report of 1964 (*The Deployment and Payment of Clergy*) recommended the abolition of freehold, but aligned it with better proposals for pay and working conditions. The Report and its recommendations were defeated by the Church Assembly, the precursor to the General Synod. The Morley Report (1967: *Partners in Ministry*) made similar suggestions on the security and status of clergy, but it too was defeated by the clergy, who feared for the loss of their freehold. The attitude of the clergy towards too much professionalisation is summed up neatly in a letter to *The Times*, written by a clergyman in 1957:

> the parochial clergy of the Church of England are becoming transformed into the salaried members of a diocesan staff, living in houses provided and maintained for them on incomes fixed and guaranteed by diocesan stipend funds.[18]

The disdain towards equality and uniformity expressed in this letter may seem paradoxical to some. After all, do the clergy not want to be treated like professionals, in which their rights, privileges and salaries are guaranteed?

15 Parsons, *Religion in Victorian Britain*, p. 25.
16 For an American perspective on the nineteenth century, see Scott, *From Office to Profession*.
17 Russell, *The Clerical Profession*, p. 263.
18 Ibid., p. 271.

The answer is both 'yes' and 'no'. 'Yes', in the sense that they want to be regarded as specialist purveyors of knowledge, rites and techniques – 'technologists of the sanctuary'. But 'no' in the sense that they do not want to be rationalised or organised into a properly hierarchical or accountable body, in which their right to freedom and dissent is jeopardised.

Perhaps inevitably, various categories of minister have sprung up in the gap created by the smaller numbers of paid priests in the Church of England, and also to reflect the ambivalent attitude that prevails in relation to ministerial provision. As Russell candidly notes, 'proposals have been placed before the Church in almost every decade in the last 120 years'. Schemes have ranged from a voluntary diaconate (first proposed in the mid-nineteenth century, but regularly resurrected as an idea) to Auxiliary Pastoral Ministry (APMs), which was later to become known as Non-Stipendiary Ministry (NSMs). Many dioceses now have Ordained Local Ministers (OLMs). In addition to these categories, the number of 'sector ministers' – chaplains in hospitals, the armed services, prisons and education – has risen significantly. The blurring of the boundaries between full-time and part-time ministry, and the emergence of 'house-for-duty' clergy, has also meant that there are difficulties in specifying what constitutes 'professional' ministry in the Church of England; it no longer means 'paid', if it ever did.

Having a very basic understanding of the convoluted evolution of 'professional' ministry is important if we are to return to the question of financing the ministry of the Church of England in the near future. We have already noted that, nationally, resources are stretched. We have also noted that at the level of the local congregational, much of the narrativity about funding is conditioned by anxiety and pressure. Clearly, the impasse has to be broken. One answer may be to have more and more OLMs and NSMs, but this might undermine the value of those who are in paid full-time ministry. There is also some ambivalence about providing more and more 'cheaper' clergy, which, hitherto, few in the Church of England have been willing to face. At what point does the 'supplement' become a major part of the staple diet? Other solutions will undoubtedly include reducing the number of churches in cities, towns and villages, in effect reversing the avaricious tendencies of the Victorians, who built too many churches. In consulting Odom's history of Anglican churches in Sheffield, it is interesting to note that some of those churches built in the mid and late nineteenth century did not even survive to be counted amongst the congregations of the city when the diocese was inaugurated in 1914.[19] But the closure and merger of parishes creates resentment, and of course whilst saving some money, may also lead to the further loss of income: a parish church that no longer exists ceases to contribute funds to its diocese. Another solution may be to slim down diocesan staffing to skeletal levels, sharing out the work across regions (trans-diocesan) or amongst ministers. But each of these options is fraught with difficulties,

19 Odom, *Fifty Years of Sheffield Church Life – 1866–1916*, p. 31.

and will not make a decisive difference to the endemic financial crisis the ministry of the Church of England faces.

Power in partnership?

So how might the problem be addressed? The advantage of engaging in serious theological reflection is that it might just take the grounded experience of the life of congregations seriously, and treat their local spiritual knowledge as a source of primary theological material rather than secondary. Furthermore, good theological reflection also adopts a 'problem-posing' stance in addressing issues, which it borrows from Liberation Theology. The other dimension the methodology permits is a thematic approach rather than a dogmatic or systematic one, and in what follows I want to suggest that the key to resolving the problem lies in the rehabilitation and redevelopment of the notion of *partnership*, a major foundation of the *Morley Report*.[20] However, when the *Morley Report* deployed the term, it meant a reconfiguration of relations between clergy and the hierarchy. I am using the term rather differently, to imply the establishment of mutual *trust* between congregations and the hierarchy in the mutual support of clergy and parochial ministry. The appeal to trust implies a sense of reliability, commitment, strength, confidence, expectation and responsibility. It is my view that the modern structuring of dioceses (and their method for collecting quota payments) no longer demonstrates adequate trust in congregations and their ability to minister locally in ways that they deem to be suitable.[21] I am conscious that the proposals set down here are only lightly sketched at present, but I also hold that the ideas laid out could lead to a productive and fruitful strategy for developing the future parochial ministry in the Church of England.

First, there should be a new sense of the partnership that forms the paradigm for ministry: between parish, congregation, diocese and priest. This partnership, recognising that the main funding comes from the congregation, could be more substantially enhanced if there was a redistribution of capital resources, increasing the stake-holding of congregations in the development of local ministry. At present, local Church of England congregations do not own their churches or vicarages. Clergy must usually live in tied-housing, all of which is policed by a diocesan hierarchy, which the congregation funds. However, I believe that the lack of ownership (increasingly coupled to their financial *obligations*) is an extremely difficult dilemma for the Church of England to address. Increasing payments to central and diocesan centres, but no incremental increase in, say, running the affairs of the church, is a dis-empowering experience, and ultimately a rudimentary recipe for revolution: 'no taxation without representation'. To address this, I want to suggest

20 Morley (ed.), *Partners in Ministry.*
21 For a useful meditation on trust, see O'Neill, *A Question of Trust.*

that the Church of England needs to find more flexible ways of building financial partnerships with local congregations and parishes, in order to enable the mission of the church locally and nationally.

One way forward would be for the Church of England to sell much of its tied-housing stock to local congregations. Parishes or congregations, in a few instances, would be able to buy such properties outright, and would thereafter hold the property for future incumbents in trust, the management of the housing becoming the responsibility of the congregation, but in line with agreed minimum standards laid down by the diocese. For congregations that could not afford to own tied-housing, the option of a mortgage would be available, or a split-equity option whereby the diocese and congregation jointly owned the house, or shares therein. Bills for maintaining the tied-housing would be the responsibility of the owner or owners. For congregations in UPA or inner city parishes, where ownership was either undesirable or uneconomic, the diocese concerned could continue to own and invest in tied-accommodation for clergy. Of course, clergy would not be permitted to purchase tied-housing, as this would complicate local church polity when it came to new appointments.

A simple scheme such as this would create and release substantial new funds to invest in mission. It would also begin to allow clergy the freedom to choose between tied-housing and a stipend, or a salary and a housing allowance. Where a clergyperson wished to invest in housing themselves, the housing allowance could be paid by the parish from the proceeds of renting the tied-housing. This is increasingly becoming an issue for the clergy. The rising number of parish offices attached to churches, coupled to working spouses, means that many clergy choose to keep their tied-housing primarily as a family home, and not as a place of work. Furthermore, rising house prices may mean that some clergy are now forced to take out substantial first-time mortgages upon retirement, or, enter into joint equity deals with the Church of England Pension Board. Greater flexibility on housing and incumbency in the future might help clergy to avoid some of the economic problems that many presently face). In some cases, congregations could insist that the tied-housing and the church were an integral unity, and that the local expectation for ministry would continue to be that any clergyperson becoming the incumbent of the benefice would need to live in the tied-house provided, and that this would be a condition of accepting the post.

Second, this flexibility could also begin to pave the way for parishes, congregations and dioceses to enter into a new partnership on patterns of pay for clergy. If parishes were given more autonomy over the resources that they are already stewards of, new patterns of ministry might emerge from the material *and* the spiritual. In reality, this has already begun: we have already mentioned the rise in the phenomenon of the 'house-for-duty' priest. In many rural areas, there is no reason to doubt that the provision of pastoral care is more than adequate under such arrangements. Furthermore, we have already alluded to the fact that clergy should be properly regarded as 'semi-professional'. With greater flexibility, churches can determine whether or not they need someone full-time or part-time as their parish priest, and the level of expertise that is required. Furthermore, suppose that, within certain limits, parishes were also able to set levels of remuneration? This would encourage a more realistic appraisal of many ministries, and allow congregations to value experience, responsibility, energy, challenge and more besides. Of course, there are some who would complain that this is precisely what the stipend system sought to get away from: the creation of inequality. But in reality, the enforcement of equality can be potentially morale-sapping and incoherent. Again, a partnership on pay and conditions between congregations, parishes, clergy and the diocese might open up rich possibilities for the re-evaluation of ministry. In UPA, inner city and certain rural areas where increased pay differentials might be problematic, the diocese should be able to guarantee minimum standards, and perhaps add the novel twist of providing incentives to consider such ministries. The new capital sum that would be created from the sale of tied-housing – in effect the result of significant redistributions of wealth and responsibility, in which power-relations between parishes and diocese now acquire much greater equilibrium – could easily be used to augment mission and ministry in areas that were identified as being especially needy or vital to the overall work of the church. In the USA, for example, many dioceses can augment the salaries of UPA and inner city priests, precisely because the suburban parishes own their own tied-housing.

Third, an appropriate adoption of pay differentials for clergy would allow a partnership between parishes, clergy, congregations and the diocese to emerge, and then to continually value the experience and expertise of their clergy, independent of any type of preferment. A recent review of stipends suggests linking the pay of clergy to teachers and head teachers, but bearing in mind that the tied housing is worth several thousand pounds per year.[22] The recognition that there are *four* partners in parochial ministry might begin to tap new sources of revenue for certain types of work: urban regeneration, community development or certain types of youth work. (In many dioceses, this has already happened, with certain types of funding from government in effect 'buying' the time of a clergyperson.) For the clergy, although minimum standards would need to be maintained, the effect of adopting pay differentials would be to create a richer diversity of possibility within the Church of England. Can one, for example, envisage a future in which a clergyperson turns down the offer of a Suffragan Bishopric, because the pay would be no more (or perhaps less?) than they presently receive as a Team Rector of seven years standing, and following 25 years of ministry? The decision may come down to weighing up other pros and cons. Would the responsibility of serving one town or large urban council estate be more appealing than the endless rounds of confirmations, church fetes and clergy interviews

22 See Turnbull, *Generosity and Sacrifice*.

that might be the lot of the average Suffragan Bishop (a caricature, granted)? At present, with stipends linked *only* to preferment, the Church of England simply does not create the right *material* conditions in which imaginative (or even vocational?) decisions can be made about an individuals' future. (The issue of payment and gender discrimination belongs to another essay, but we do note that women cannot be consecrated (or paid) as bishops: their salaries or stipends are 'capped'.)

Finally, it may be that dioceses need to *listen* to their local congregations more deeply than ever, and begin to build a missiological strategy that is more collaborative and less hierarchical. With congregations now mainly responsible for funding the priest-like task, and this being done on an entirely voluntary basis, dioceses will have to show that they are increasingly accountable to their main benefactors. I suspect that this will lead to leaner diocesan structures in the future, and, perhaps, slimmer national-central structures. Indeed, I would go further and suggest that a reasonable goal to strive towards would be the radical *shrinkage* of the parish quota system and diocesan infrastructure. Heavy pruning of diocesan and central staffing levels would allow congregations to take more responsibility for the money they generate, and invest this locally in mission and ministry. For example, in many Episcopal dioceses in the USA, congregations contribute between 5 and 12.5 per cent to their dioceses. The congregation remains responsible for fixing and paying the salary of the clergy, which it does through the diocese. The congregation also maintains and normally owns any tied property. The bishops' diocesan staff will probably number no more than 15 persons. By the same token, many parishes can afford several staff working in ministry locally, because they are not paying sizeable sums to the diocesan quota.

But such a move would not represent the 'collapse of the system'; far from it. If this evolution can be conceived of in terms of *trust* and *partnership*, it may well be that even more resourcing emerges from local situations to enable the work of the church. Instead of the typical congregational experience of financial disempowerment – being bled dry year on year by an increasingly demanding hierarchy – the Church of England might discover that it has hidden riches at local levels that have hitherto remained untapped.[23]

To tap such resources will require partnership and the establishment of trust; the central giving way to the diocesan; the diocesan giving way to the congregational; the congregational re-engaging with the local; and to close the circle, the local redistributing to the national and regional. There could even be some partnership with business – corporations, commerce, companies and industry understand something of the value in spiritual capital

---

23 See https://www.churchofengland.org/media/2265027/2013financestatistics.pdf for the 2013 Church of England Finance Statistics, London: Archbishops' Council, 2015. The statistics record that almost one billion pounds was raised in 2013 by Church of England parish giving. Parishes raised these important funds from a combination of regular and one-off donations as well as investments and legacies. However, the larger amount is being given by a declining number of parishioners.

nourishing social capital.[24] It will require a far more flexible approach to mission and ministry to enable the priest-like task of tomorrow: nothing less than a radical practical theology of the church and its financing to imagine what the future might be. It will require a recognition that ministry is now a real partnership between laity and hierarchy, and is not simply a matter of what the diocesan leadership might decide. Indeed, my research reveals that some large Evangelical congregations – which provide sizeable contributions to diocesan funding are now arguing that their financial support should allow them a much greater say in the shaping of ministry in those parishes that their giving supports. In other words, the Evangelical parishes are seeking the status of partner or stakeholder; they want a say in how the diocese spends the money it receives from them. In many cases, such initiatives do not represent any kind of colonialisation, but rather demonstrate a desire to move from maintenance to mission in some of the neediest areas of any given diocese.

NB.

We began this chapter by briefly noting three interrelated financial problems that have implications for the future provision of pastoral and priestly ministry: the lack of money at national, diocesan and parochial levels. Under the present arrangements, the laity of the Church of England (congregations) are still being treated as though they were providing marginal supplements to enable ministry. But in reality, they are now substantially under-writing the cost of ministry. Yet in return for this, they have received no incremental increase in their power or capacity to shape and form local ministry. Congregations and laity have been slowly educated by the Church Commissioners into becoming 'fundamental units of funding' for the ministry of the church. But the laity have seen no growth in their power, or greater trust placed in them.[25] They have, in effect, been burdened with ever greater forms of responsibility, which incrementally increase year-on-year, whilst they continue to languish in a financial system that patronises them and presumes upon them. They have been given responsibility; but not power or authority.

As we have seen from our discussion, some congregations accept their lot stoically, and others cheerfully, depending on their worldview. But this, I venture, cannot continue indefinitely: there are finite limits on the burden of central or diocesan 'taxation' that can be tolerated by most congregations. Furthermore, there are already signs that a few congregations in the Church of England that object to certain of its theological stances (e.g., on sexuality or gender) already either withhold part of their quota payment, or may even go as far as to pay their clergy directly, no longer contributing to the diocesan purse or to the Church Commissioners.

Our solution to this problem is found to be a sharing out of the economic power that has hitherto supported the ministry of the Church of England, and

---

24 See Foundation, Tufano and Walker, 'Collaborating with Congregations: Opportunities for Financial Services in the Inner City'.
25 Percy, *Salt of the Earth*, p. 337.

the creation of trust between partners. It is to allow congregations to come into their own as important constituents within the overall equation for funding ministry, and to give them a stake and responsibility within that framework. Partnerships are, when all is said and done, a vital sign of commonality, and involve a mutual commitment that fosters vision, shares authority, and is clear about interests. The idea of conceiving of a new partnership between clergy, diocese, congregations and parishes is to re-determine the value and need of ministry in any given context, and to create the conditions whereby the church could respond more adequately to changing social situations.

To achieve this, the sale (or mortgaging) of tied-housing would generate significant funding that could be used in existing or new areas of ministry. For example, I estimate that the sale of three quarters of the tied-housing stock in an average northern diocese could create a significant endowment fund. The interest from this fund could then support new mission initiatives, supplement stipends and generally enable ministry in the locality. Preliminary research in northern dioceses suggests that something approaching two-thirds of parishes could afford to 'buy-back' their benefice housing, creating an enormous pool of funds for generative mission in deprived areas, as well as providing sufficient resources to increase clergy pay where appropriate. It must be stressed, however, that the primary purposes of this proposed initiative are to give parishes more autonomy (through judicious financial subsidiarity), with checks and balances placed on centralised power, but with new mission funds for dioceses created through the greater financial autonomy granted to parishes.

Furthermore, such a programme would also usher in a new era of flexibility for clergy (and congregations), on agreed working hours, pay and conditions; creating, in effect, a significant new pastoral subsidiarity based on *trust*. Trust is that underrated theological virtue which is seldom appealed to in the ongoing debate on the financing of ministry. Trust and partnership might create a situation where appropriate decisions on pastoral provision would be made at the most appropriate level, which would often, but not always, be the local. Such a move would take some of the very best customs and arrangements of the past (prior to the standardisation of housing and stipends), and blend them with the demands of the present and future, with the need for reflexivity and imagination in a new economic and ecclesial climate. It is precisely this kind of *phronesis* (practical wisdom) that the Church of England may need to urgently contemplate, if the priest-like task is to be adequately funded and supported in the future. The alternative is less palatable:

> when great institutions decline they do not suddenly fall over a precipice; they simply slide down the slope, a little further each year, in a genteel way, making do in their reduced circumstances, like a spinster in an Edwardian novel.[26]

26 Lord [Kenneth] Baker, from a speech in the House of Lords, and quoted in *The Economist*, 16 November 2002, p. 11.

Some might see the proposals advanced on money in this chapter as overly capitalist. But to do so will miss the deeper intentions that lie at the base of these proposals, namely to re-empower parishes and the laity, and see appropriate subsidiarity redistribute power from episcopacy and central management. The power and potential of the Church of England will undoubtedly lie in ever-deeper local partnerships. There will need to be a marked shift away from the quasi-socialist paternalism of diocesan and central structures, which presently deprive local churches of the pleasure, desire and incentive in giving, precisely because congregations are conferred with almost no authority in how their gifts are to be reified and deployed. In short, more say for local congregations in how their money is spent might lead to more gifts being offered. But until a relationship of trust – rather than a system of taxation – is established as the true basis for funding the ministry of the church, we won't really find out what the future could be like. We will be condemned to struggle forever in the creeping penury of the present – fewer and fewer, paying more and more, for less and less.

Not in S.E.
Where do clergy live?
Who pays Rent / mortgage?

5   Spartacus
Modelling rebellion in the church

The film *Spartacus* (1960; directed by Stanley Kubrick) needs little introduction. Starring Kirk Douglas as the rebellious slave, it is based on a historical novel by Howard Fast – and inspired by the real life of a Thracian slave who led the revolt in the Third Servile War of 73–71 BCE. A small band of former gladiators and slaves, perhaps no more than 80 in number, and led by Spartacus, grew to an army of around 125,000, to challenge the might of the Roman Empire. Kubrick's film starred Laurence Olivier as Marcus Licinius Crassus, the Roman general-politician, alongside Jean Simmons and Tony Curtis. Among its four Oscars, Peter Ustinov won an Academy Award for best supporting actor as Batiatus, a slave trader.

Less well-known is the film's own story of rebellion. The screenwriter Dalton Trumbo, along with several other Hollywood writers, had been blacklisted for his political beliefs, and associations with movements seeking equality for coloured and black people, as well as with members of the American Communist Party, some of whom were jailed. Even though the age of McCarthyism was crumbling, it still took a young aspirational Senator – John F. Kennedy – crossing the picket lines to see the film, to help end Trumbo's blacklisting. Howard Fast had also been blacklisted, and originally self-published his novel.

Looking back, we can see why Trumbo's script should perhaps have caused audiences to ponder some potential for subversive political messages. But there were more obvious, overt challenges to the establishment in the film. Much of America was still colour-segregated in 1960. But we are introduced to Draba, a heroic black slave, first overpowering the white Spartacus in gladiatorial combat – and then sacrificing his own life in protest at the oppression of slaves. Equally unusual, for a Hollywood film of that era, was an ending that was both realistic and tragic – seemingly without hope.

The film also explores different kinds of love between men: rare for the time. There is the relationship between Spartacus (Kirk Douglas) and Antoninus (Tony Curtis) – made to fight to the death by their Roman captors. The final words between them are 'Forgive me, Antoninus' (Spartacus), to which the dying Antoninus replies, 'I love you, Spartacus . . .'. Earlier in the film, we find Crassus (Olivier), and his then slave, Antoninus (Curtis) in a bathing scene – with the slave gently sponging and washing his master.

The 'gay subtext' is pretty clear, Crassus declaring his passion for both 'oysters and snails':

Crassus:	Do you eat oysters?
Antoninus:	When I have them, master.
Crassus:	Do you eat snails?
Antoninus:	No, master.
Crassus:	Do you consider the eating of oysters to be moral and the eating of snails to be immoral?
Antoninus:	No, master.
Crassus:	Of course not. It is all a matter of taste, isn't it?
Antoninus:	Yes, master.
Crassus:	And taste is not the same as appetite, and therefore not a question of morals.
Antoninus:	It could be argued so, master.
Crassus:	My robe, Antoninus. My taste includes both snails and oysters.

Here, Trumbo's screenplay gives us an interesting excursion into moral philosophy. There is nothing wrong with taste (or orientation) according to Crassus; the ethical issue is the sating, or control, of appetite. Crassus' bi-sexuality in this scene – like others – carries subtle, seditious subtexts. The viewer of the film is being challenged on many levels: issues of race, sexuality, political hierarchy and slavery are all strongly featured in the screenplay. Yet most cinema-goers at the time would have missed these themes, explicitly. But they would have perhaps sensed them, implicitly. It was Kierkegaard who opined that 'life is lived forward, but understood backwards'. So it is unlikely that cinema-goers in the early 1960s picked up any subversive sublimation in the sub-plots. But looking back, we can understand what Trumbo may have wanted to say at the dawn of a new decade, in a repressive social and political climate that was about to become progressively liberal.

So what has Spartacus got to do with the Church of England, perplexed as it currently is (once again) by questions of sexuality? We will return to the subject of sexuality in the third part of this book, and in particular the most recent attempts to resolve the crisis this has posed in global Anglicanism (once again). So in this chapter, we set out the background main issues as a prelude to later discussion.

We begin by noting the social changes over the last decade, which have caught the church off guard, and on the defensive. It is only just over 25 years ago that Section 28 (of the Local Government Act, 1988) stated that a local authority should not intentionally promote homosexuality, or 'promote the teaching in any maintained school of the acceptability of homosexuality as a pretended family relationship'. Tony Blair's Labour Government attempted to repeal this in 2000. But the House of Lords resisted for three years, until Section 28 was finally defeated in 2003 – by a comfortable two-thirds majority.

In the summer of 2013, the Archbishop of Canterbury warned that allowing gay couples to marry would 'diminish' Christian marriage, and 'damage the fabric of society'. In the ensuing debate, the House of Lords vote was sobering: 390 Peers were in favour of the same-sex marriage bill, with only 148 against. A substantial majority of people in our country are now in favour of affirming the love, and rights, of same-sex couples seeking publicly-recognised and legal life-long union.

This change has been well-tracked by sociologists such as Professor Linda Woodhead.[1] Her recent research project shows that attitudes amongst churchgoers have now shifted significantly towards a more liberal and tolerant mindset. This contrasts starkly with our current church leadership.

Woodhead's research shows that the country is becoming progressively more tolerant and liberal. Statistical surveys repeatedly show growing toleration for same-sex unions in congregations and amongst clergy, across the theological spectra. Recent studies carried out by Gallup (USA) confirm the cultural shifts.[2] In 1977, 56 per cent of Americans thought that homosexual people should have equal rights in the workplace; the figure now exceeds 90 per cent. One can begin to see why the church's withholding of a licence to officiate from a clergyman who has recently married his same-sex partner looks like petty discrimination to the wider world.

But whilst the nation has turned its face towards justice, integrity and equality, our senior church leaders have turned the other way. The confident national church of the 1960s and 1970s – often producing senior clergy at the forefront of progressive social change on decriminalising homosexuality or divorce laws, for example – gave way to a more circumspect church in the closing years of the twentieth century. As our culture quickly changed, the Church of England busied itself with *Issues in Human Sexuality* (1991), or keeping elements of the Communion onside with Resolution 1.10 at the 1998 Lambeth Conference. Meanwhile, our nation offered sanctuary to people, persecuted for their sexuality, seeking asylum from overseas.

We are now witnessing what I term the 'Soaking-Ceiling-Syndrome'. Everyone can see the sagging bulge; some puddles are forming on the floor below. No-one dares to prod. Some hope it will all dry out, and the problem go away. It won't. Change is here to stay. Many evangelicals now also understand this, and are quietly adapting.

Yet despite this, the early years of the twenty-first century have seen our senior church leaders arguing (in the House of Lords) for more exemptions on equality legislation, and taking a continued hard line against homosexual practice and gay marriage. In the twenty-first century the senior leadership of the Church of England have slowly kettled the church into behaving like a wary sect on the subject of sexuality.

---

1 Woodhead, 'What People Really Believe About Same-Sex Marriage'.
2 Field and Clements, 'Public Opinion Toward Homosexuality and Gay Rights in Great Britain', also confirm these trends.

It's ironic that this 'leadership' largely consists of nervous silence. Underlying this has been enormous confusion in the church concerning the relationship between secularism and liberalism. But they are quite different. Secularism marginalises religion. Liberalism, however, has deep and profound roots in progressive, orthodox Christianity, which are found in the teachings of Jesus and his disciples – equality, justice and liberation being just some of the values that the early church embodied, and sought to extend to wider society.

The incapacity of our church leaders to grasp the opportunities in society today – for renewed mission and ministry in the context of complex changes within our culture – has meant that these opportunities have been egregiously spurned. Our crusading conservatism has left the church looking self-righteous, sour, mean-spirited and isolated.

In his prescient *Refounding the Church*,[3] Gerry Arbuckle argues that dissenters in society not only have rights, but also duties. He notes with care how Jesus, as a principled dissenter, challenged the status quo with patience, tolerance and love. He also argues that dissent is an essential component in mission – a mission that witnesses to the world, and also converts the church.

So, is this a kairos moment, or a crisis time for our church? It's hard to say, but this may be a good Spartacus-inspired opportunity for some of our gay bishops to become more courageous – to stand publicly, with others, alongside those clergy currently bearing the brunt for having married their same-sex partners. No point in cowering in the closet, hoping not to be 'outed' by a Tatchell or a tabloid. Anyway, the populace almost certainly regards an openly-declared marriage between two people of the same sex as better and healthier than any secretive praxis. Morally, the public are ahead of the church on this; marriage is an estate to be honoured.

Returning to *Spartacus*, as the film closes, and Crassus tries to identify his nemesis amidst the slaughtered remains and remnants of the crushed slave rebellion, the surviving comrades of Spartacus stand as one to proclaim, 'I am Spartacus'. We all are now.

The human spirit will not be crushed. Tyranny will not triumph. There is beautiful, loving solidarity abiding in our shared, deepest dissent. Surely it is better to die free than live enslaved? Yet some will point to how the film finishes. The hero is cruelly forced to take the life of his dearest companion in a hastily-organised duel-to-the-death. For the 'victor', only crucifixion awaits – with thousands of others along the Appian Way. And there the rebellion ends; as might the story.

But Kubrick's epic has one more scene. The slave-woman Varinia (played by Jean Simmonds), the lover of Spartacus, and with whom she has now borne a son, escapes from the clutches of Crassus through the intervention of Batiatus, the former slave trader. Leaving Rome in disguise, they pass Spartacus, dying on his cross. Varinia holds up their son to his face, and

3 Arbuckle, *Refounding the Church*.

simply proclaims, 'he is free, Spartacus; he is free'. The rebellion, it would seem, is vindicated. As the film hints, you only truly live by looking forward. As a church, we'll only understand how far we have travelled when we look back. But live forward, we must.

Living in the present

Living forward, however, is not easy if you think the answer to any present crisis always lies in a clear and resolved past. To an extent, theology is all about discernment. What God has revealed (past tense) has to be interpreted in each new age; and in a spirit of coherent faithfulness. Meanwhile, Anglican polity struggles on, trying to orientate itself in the challenging currents of contemporary culture. Anglicans in the Church of England perhaps forget too quickly how far culture has travelled on sexuality in recent decades.

In the United Kingdom, we have moved from Section 28 in 1988 – which in turn was founded on an ill-conceived AIDS and HIV campaign developed by the then Conservative government – to same-sex marriage (and a bill sponsored by a Conservative government) in 25 years. The change has been phenomenal. Similar cultural shockwaves were experienced by the Roman Catholic Church in Ireland. It urged the people to vote against the legalisation of same-sex marriage in 2015. Two-thirds of the country ignored the advice of their bishops, and voted in favour.

Here, I cast my mind back 20 years, to a lecture given by a publisher to a group of new writers, asking what Christians and theologians should be writing about in the future. A young scholar stuck up his hand, and suggested that homosexuality was likely to be a key issue for the churches in the twenty-first century. Several older scholars immediately rubbished the idea. And the rest, as they say, is history. I have an entire shelf of such books in my study.[4] Two recent offerings represent the bookends of the debate, so to speak.

---

4 A representative sample includes Vasey-Saunders, *The Scandal of Evangelicals and Homosexuality: English Evangelical Texts 1960-2010*, Farnham, Surrey: Ashgate, 2015; Groves (ed.) *The Anglican Communion and Homosexuality – A resource to enable listening and dialogue*, London: SPCK, 2008; Linzey and Kirker (eds), *The Gays and the Future of Anglicanism – Responses to the Windsor Report*, Winchester, Hampshire: O Books, 2005; Groves and Parry Jones, *Living Reconciliation*, London: SPCK, 2014; O'Donovan, *Church in Crisis: The Gay Controversy and the Anglican Communion*, Eugene, OR: Cascade Books, 2008; Allberry, *Is God Anti-Gay? And Other Questions About Homosexuality, the Bible and Same-Sex Attraction*, Epsom, Surrey: Good Book Company, 2013; Wilson, *More Perfect Union? Understanding Same-Sex Marriage*, London: DLT, 2014; Bates, *A Church at War – Anglicans and Homosexuality*, London: I.B. Tauris, 2004; DeRogatis, *Saving Sex – Sexuality and Salvation in American Evangelicalism*, Oxford: Oxford University Press, 2015; Sachs, *Homosexuality and the Crisis of Anglicanism*, Cambridge University Press, 2009; Cornwall, *Theology and Sexuality*, London: SCM, 2013; and Kaoma, "An African or Un-African Sexual Identity? Religion, Globalisation and Sexual Politics in sub-Saharan Africa," In *Public Religion and Politics of Homosexuality in Africa*, (eds) Adriaan Van Klinken and Ezra Chitando, London: Ashgate, forthcoming 2016.

First, Alan Wilson's *More Perfect Union?*[5] is a passionate, pacey and persuasive book. But it is also careful, nuanced and rich, with a great deal of scholarship underpinning the text – yet all worn lightly. For congregations and churches – of any kind, and any persuasion – this is a book that should be read and engaged with. It is a careful and considered polemic. Such a blend does not usually work, but Alan Wilson manages this with consummate ease, and the book opens up the issues with wisdom and insight.

Second, Sam Allberry's *Is God Anti-Gay?* is more like an extended tract; less of a discussion starter, and more of a discussion closer. Sam writes with firmness and conviction, but the closing down of scriptures and the narrowing of their meanings will leave many readers – conservative and liberal alike – puzzled and frustrated. For example, we are told that[6] Jesus doesn't mention homosexuality in his prohibitions anywhere – 'but he does include it'. It's an odd sort of argument, really – retrospectively co-opting current behaviour patterns and identities that Jesus said not a word about, but deciding nonetheless that he would have condemned them, and surely meant to? (Incidentally, the subject that Jesus spends most time moralising on is wealth – but we don't hear many sermons on this, of course.)

For several centuries of course, it was exactly this kind of double-thinking that led the churches to accept slavery as either 'natural', or perhaps even God-given. Jesus chatted to slaves, and had nothing especially bad to say about most slave-owners. Slaves were a normal part of the world that Jesus inhabited. How are we to read his silence on the subject? There are good answers to this question, and some of them would form part of an answer on the vexed question of human sexuality. But you'll need more than a tract to explore that kind of complex territory.

I mention slavery and sexuality in the same breath, because they are related. We know that in the eighteenth and nineteenth centuries, the churches were unable to resolve the tension between what the Bible seemed to say and condone specifically (i.e. slavery is not really condemned in either the OT or NT), and the broader principles that the Bible promotes unequivocally, namely equality, justice, fairness, compassion and love. Hundreds of Bible commentaries were produced that argued for the positions of both the slavery and the anti-slavery lobbies.

Slavery lobbyists included active Christian missionaries, who argued that their missionary work, albeit rooted in (exploitative) trades, nonetheless advanced civilisation, and so improved the lot of the countries and peoples who were enslaved. The anti-slavery lobbyists argued for the dignity and equality of every human being, irrespective of race.

What changed the course of history on slavery was not, interestingly, a new breakthrough book or Bible commentary. It was, rather, the experience of the churches in meeting people from other countries who had been slaves,

---

5 Wilson, *More Perfect Union?*
6 Allberry, *Is God Anti-Gay?* p. 41.

but were now liberated. When former slaves started to speak and teach, others realised that 'they were just like us'. Slowly, the argument turned.

How then, will the Sexuality Church Wars end? Not with a bang, I think; but with a whimper. There will be no knock-out blow from any new Bible commentary or book. And there will be no decisive battle in the 'what-the-Bible-really-says-and-means-debate'. Even churches claiming to be ruled by the Bible know that they are actually governed by the interpreters. And this is the point. The meanings of the Bible, even when apparently clear, sometimes point us in different ways. Not for nothing did Jesus speak in parables.

So how will change come? Gradually, Christians are coming to see that far from being a threat to churches – and perhaps even civilisation itself – gay people are ordinary, normal folk, with plenty of good things to contribute to faith communities and to the wider world. Moreover, they are not a distant group somewhere 'out there'. They are, rather, our friends, neighbours, relatives, sons, brothers, sisters, daughters: our kith and kin. And so the only questions to ask, I think, are these: how did Jesus treat the strangers, aliens, outcasts and foreigners in his own ministry? And what should we do, as churches, in the light of Jesus' ministry? Increasingly, this is a debate about the kingdom of God that Jesus both preached and practised; and whether the church can ever come close to embodying the unequivocal love of God for all humanity, which Jesus so richly and fully expressed.

Context and catholicity

The contrast between the Lambeth conferences of 1998 and 2008 could hardly be more marked for Anglicans. The 1998 Conference ended on a sour, divisive note, with some feeling that Anglicanism had passed resolutions that institutionalised homophobia in order to preserve unity. The 2008 Conference, with an emphasis on conversation and mutual discovery and reciprocity, had been 'resolution-light', in contrast, and had been less contentious. But equally, fewer had attended. That said, Anglicans could look back at the 2008 Lambeth Conference with some degree of satisfaction. In general, the verdict seems to be that for the most part, it passed off peaceably.

Of course, much ink was spilled in the run-up to the 2008 Conference, writing off Anglicanism, attacking the leadership of the Archbishop of Canterbury, and pointing to the gathering forces of conservatism in movements such as GAFCON (Global Anglican Futures conference) and FOCA (Fellowship of Confessing Anglicans). These may be new groups, but they are symptoms of an old malaise. The post-war years have seen an unholy and viral trinity of individualism, impatience and intolerance unleashed within Anglican polity. This has rapidly spread to very different quarters of the Anglican Communion, yet with unsurprisingly similar results. So now, each part of the worldwide church, whether liberal or conservative, white or black, can claim to be true and right, whilst expressing their individuality, irritation and annoyance with all those they disagree with.

I suspect the only antidote to this plague of rashness is an old Anglican remedy: the recovery and infusion of those qualities that are embedded in the gospels, and in deeper forms of ecclesial polity. Namely ones that are formed out of patience, forbearance, catholicity, moderation – and a genuine love for the reticulate blend of diversity and unity that forms so much of the richness of Anglican life. But in the warp and weft of the church, these virtues have been lost – or rather mislaid – in a miscibility of debates that are marked by increasing levels of tension and stress.

So if Anglicans could settle for a little less clarity and simplicity, and embrace complexity and catholicity, would all be well? Yes and no. Part of the problem for Anglicans, at the moment, lies in our inability to discern the underlying issues that are causing tensions, and squabbling about the presenting issues. Or, put another way, dealing with symptoms, not causes. Sexuality is a classic example of the dilemma that Anglican polity faces at present, and I want to suggest that finding a new conciliation and peace in the Communion will rest with discovering and addressing some of the deeper cultural pulses that are causing similar kinds of problems for other denominations, institutions and societies. Some perspective and composure is called for here. The story of Anglican dioceses and provinces in the post-war era merely reflects the travails (and triumphs) of the wider Christian family. Paul Avis' counsel is instructive:

> This is not necessarily unhealthy, a sign of ecclesial pathology. In some ways, the "normal" state of the Christian Church is to be seething with argument and controversy. Conflict is endemic in Christianity and Anglicanism is not a special case.[7]

There are some encouraging signs that other Anglican commentators and scholars have also perceived this, and Bill Sachs' is one such.[8] True, many Anglicans could be forgiven for the almost audible inward groan that emanates at the mere mention of homosexuality and Anglicanism in the same sentence. Surely Anglicans have had quite enough of the issue? Worn out by the divisive debates and debacles, is it not time for the Anglican Communion to move on, and perhaps tackle something a little less contentious – such as mission and ministry, or justice and peace?

The answer to these questions is, of course, 'yes'. But that should take nothing away from Bill Sachs' remarkable, indeed peerless, book which surveys the terrain of one of the knottier problems to have arisen in Anglican polity for many-a-year. His thesis will repay careful reading, and is well worth the time one might invest to ponder how a crisis such as this

---

7 Avis, 'Anglican Ecclesiology'. Elsewhere I have discussed the necessity, at times, for 'conflictual dialogue', drawing upon the work of Gregory Baum, cf. Mannion, *Ecclesiology and Postmodernity*, pp. 142–145.

8 Sachs, *Homosexuality and the Crisis of Anglicanism*.

assumed the proportions it did, and where any hope for the future of the church might lie.

There cannot be many Anglicans who don't hold an opinion on the subject in question. But as Sachs points out, eloquently, Anglicans across the globe, whether liberal or conservative, traditional or progressive, are often caught between their biblical, doctrinal, ecclesial and legalistic frameworks on the one hand, and their experiential, contextual and pastoral concerns on the other. Indeed, one of the great strengths of this book is the lucid articulation of emerging contextual theologies and the ways in which they compete with hitherto unarticulated but assumed notions of catholicity, homogeneity and more complex forms of global belonging. The local, indeed, is one of the strengths of Anglican identity, but also a potential source of weakness when attempting to speak and act on a global scale. Sachs articulates this potentially problematic dynamic beautifully and clearly, and without recourse to party-based sniping. There is no siding with liberal or conservative slants. Sachs knows too well that the Anglican Communion and its somewhat patchwork polity is far more complex than it seems. Anglicans all agree on what the Bible says; we are just spending quite a bit of time – and acrimoniously, on occasions – figuring out what it means, and where, why and when to apply texts in the twenty-first century.

Sachs' first chapter sets the scene – the defining moments of the debates, as it were – which brought an issue that was bubbling below the skin of Anglican polity and identity boiling right to the surface. As Sachs suggests, even with regard to the elevation of Gene Robinson, and the proposed elevation of Jeffrey John to the episcopate, the ensuing divisions in the church were in fact already emerging. Tensions on sexuality existed long before 2003, and caused significant difficulties at the Lambeth Conference of 1998, and had already coloured and clouded the arch-episcopacy of George Carey.

Sachs, as a contextual theologian, then locates these difficulties and disagreements in the wider milieu of ecclesial polity. Tensions, for example, have always existed in the contention for the shaping of early Christian unity. Ideals and realities can also be conflictual, as are the concentrations of power (in the centre or on the periphery, and between local and catholic) in the formation of a global polity. Sachs contends that the key to understanding the debate is the realisation that indigenous Anglicanism is both the foundation of its global polity, as well as its nemesis. Drawing on writers such as Michael Sandel and John Tomasi towards the end of his thesis, Sachs shows that the kind of activism which promotes rights – vindication through political processes – rather than seeking tangible social and communal harmony as a whole, and for the greater good of all, is bound to be deficient for a church, where there are higher goals to reach for.

Sachs is in no doubt that there are difficult days ahead for the Anglican Communion. One way of resolving its future would be to plot a more assertive course; to chart a pathway, in effect, that is directive and hierarchical. This would have its champions, to be sure. Another way forward

is to capitulate to despair, or simply to 'walk apart' – in effect, to cave in to endemic consumerist individualism. But there is another way, and Sachs carefully expounds this in his conclusion.

Taking respectful issue with Philip Turner's and Ephraim Radner's recent book, *The Fate of the Communion,*[9] Sachs suggests that unity will need to continue to be progressed through careful listening and speaking, and recognition of the blend between interdependence, intra-dependence, independence and dependence. All Anglicans dwell within this framework, and have to work through the consequences of practising 'contextual reliance on the authority of Spirit without the balance of a wider collegiality'.[10] Sachs believes that the future of the Communion lies in recognition of multiple contexts that partially form ecclesial polity, even though these same realities may need challenging and addressing from time to time. Many Americans, for example, operate quite happily and unconsciously within a 'spiritual marketplace', leading to an individualist and consumerist mindset that picks a tradition or combination of traditions that suits lives at particular points in time. The result is that the local congregation tends to express and interpret the wider tradition for individuals, but at the expense of the broader and deeper adherence to a given denomination. Local congregational life, therefore, and for the purposes of constructing meaning, value and concepts of wider belonging and catholicity, is now far more dominant than it used to be.

That said, the 'Communion' of the future must entail a readiness to be in fellowship with one another, but without this necessarily meaning 'agreement' on all things, or ceding authority to one another. As Sachs points out, 'no position on homosexuality could embody the whole of (the) Anglican tradition'.[11] I am sure that this is right. However, the argument for the future of Anglican polity doesn't necessarily hinge on dissenting from this kind of view. It might rest, ironically, on accepting that some positions – amongst traditionalists, progressives, conservatives and liberals – whilst being faithful expressions of a localised contextual theology, are nonetheless not easily able to fully commune within a body that is seeking to rediscover its catholicity.

Resolving the crisis?

The cultural and contextual difficulties currently plaguing Anglican polity need deeper and richer attention than they currently receive. Colin Podmore, in his discussion of American culture and ecclesial polity,[12] explores how decisions are taken in the Church; the roles of synods, bishops and primates; how the Archbishop of Canterbury's ministry should develop; what being 'in communion' and 'out of communion' means; and how significant diocesan

9 Radner and Turner, *The Fate of the Communion.*
10 Ibid., p. 247.
11 Sachs, p. 249.
12 Podmore, *Aspects of Anglican Identity.*

boundaries in an age of globalisation are? Flowing from Podmore's study, we can see that sexuality is clearly an important issue here. But it is also an unnecessary distraction – exactly not the issue that the church and the wider Communion should be focusing on. Yet that Anglicans have become so hopelessly and helplessly distracted in recent years is hardly surprising, for it is also part of the wider cultural milieu and malaise.

The play writer David Hare has characterised the last decade as a decade of distraction – something to which we alluded in the introduction to this book. Instead of looking at the issues and situations that truly need examination, many Christians have looked away and focused on other matters, allowing ourselves to be distracted by simple pursuits rather than wrestling with complexity, (Hare, 2009, pp. 5–7). A parallel case might be the distraction of the general public through heaping blame on the wrong culprit for the Twin Towers disaster, so that the ultimate response was to invade Iraq when in fact the attackers mostly originated from Saudi Arabia. In just the same way Christians in the church can be directed to the wrong target, if you identify the wrong target, you are likely to end up with the wrong solution.

In the church, with much angst and anxiety about declining church attendance, the response is interestingly not to reinforce the front line of mission (parish and established sector ministry), but rather to pour millions of pounds and resources into specious missiological schema that go under the nomenclature of 'fresh expressions' or 'emerging church'. Which, ironically, simply turn out to be ways of manouvering faithful Christians into lighter forms of spiritual organisation that do not carry heavy institutional responsibilities or broader-based ministerial burdens. The Christian consumer entering the new world of 'fresh expressions' or 'emerging church' can enjoy all the fruits of bespoke spiritual engagement and stimulation, but with almost none of the tariffs incurred through belonging to an ordinary parish church.

As the oft-quoted saying goes, 'if you don't want to know the result, look away now'. Alas, many Christians do. Unwilling to do their sums and calculate the cost of weaning a new generation of Christian consumers on light, carefully targeted spirituality, the churches simply end up losing some of their brightest and best potential leaders, who otherwise could bring much needed energy and effort into helping shape the broader institution, to projects that are essentially a form of distraction. Distraction is endemic: fed by consumerism, choice and the need to keep people engaged, fulfilled and happy, it is rife in the churches – to the left and right, amongst conservatives and liberals, traditionalists and progressives. It is a tough time to be an ordinary church member; but happy the person who has found their cultural and contextual home in niche 'fresh expressions' or a new form of 'emerging church'.

This may seem harsh. Yet a good deal of the presenting issues that seem to be de-stabilising Anglicans (and other denominations) at present are in

fact symptomatic rather than underlying and causal. To be sure, many of the attempts to return polity to its truer or truest state are full of sincerely held beliefs and worthy goals. But the common denominator is the lack of deeper ecclesial comprehension here, resulting in a real failure to read the cultural and contextual forces that are shaping polity at deep and profound levels. The consequence of this is that the churches tend to miss the moment.

Christianity does indeed face dangers in the developed world. But they are not, I think, secularisation or industrialisation. Plenty of people will turn aside from such things to embrace faith and meaning if that is all society can offer. The real threat comes from both within and without. Within, it is the uncritical absorption of individualist, consumerist assumptions that corrode catholicity and bonds of belonging. This moves the church, effortlessly, from being an established institution or body that faithfully replicates and transmits trustworthy and historic values, to being a series of attenuated organisations that have more short-term and utilitarian goals, including competing with each other for numbers, truth and vindication.

The threat from without is also one of comprehension. Christianity is intrinsically 'foreign' in any context. Every believer is a citizen of somewhere, but also of heaven. We are in the world, but not of it. Yet the foreign-ness of Christianity in the modern world has now begun to assume a new identity: alien. Whereas foreigners may speak other languages, learn yours, and otherwise mingle, aliens are unwelcome, treated with suspicion, and often repelled. Seen as invasive and intrusive, they are frozen out rather than welcomed in.

To some extent, 'fresh expressions' or 'emerging church' movements have tried to stem this tide. But all too often, and in so doing, many have sold the pass, culturally. By becoming too relevant they have lost the necessary otherness religion brings to society. Fearful of being alien, the foreigner has gone native. In the same way, liberals have sometimes been guilty of treading the same path. Many conservatives, on the other hand, have disengaged, and whilst succeeding in protecting their own identity, have only made an enclave for themselves, from which to make occasional and specious forays into the wider body politic. Each time this happens, the foreigners take one more step down the road to becoming aliens.

So, what's to be done? The risk of un-policed and uncritical enculturation has always been absorption – into one's self and into the society one is supposed to be transforming. And there is every sign at present that on issues of sexuality – secondary and symptomatic – the Anglican Communion, like all churches, needs to engage in two simple tasks. First, to figure out the constraints and opportunities afforded by balancing local contexts with catholicity. Second, to discern the potential for a higher vision of cultural transformation, that theology and mission might rightly seek. Third, to accept that many people who vote for, or strongly support same-sex marriage, do so because they are *pro-marriage*. That such a stance can still regard marriage as a gift of God in creation, such that we may become one flesh, and so no longer alone.

In all this, Anglican polity – globally and locally – might a have significant role to play, if it can but move the agenda on from sexuality to a theology of marriage. In Anglican liturgy, it is clear that understandings and rites of marriage have moved from a place where the wife submitted to the husband (1662 *Book of Common Prayer*), to one of equality (almost any modern liturgy). The equality has taken well over a century to emerge, but it is now the dominant and publicly accepted template for understanding a union between two people in the Church of England. It was not always so, of course. But to not make mutual, equal and consensual pledges to one another would, to most witnesses today, seem strange, and perhaps even perverse. The issue here is the extent to which marriage, as an institution, and both humanly and divinely inspired, has a continuing capacity to adapt. There is an operant theology to explore here. How did Anglicans renegotiate the reception of divorced women in the Mother's Union? What were the factors that allowed churches to consider and then offer re-marriage after a divorce? Far from being a marginal issue for the church, this debate could be, potentially, a life-giving debate in public life for the population as a whole, on the place, meaning and value of marriage in the twenty-first century – in the cultures in which we are emerged, and for the people we serve.[13]

Furthermore, we should not rule out ecclesial transformation coming from within. Evangelicalism, for example, has traditionally opposed same-sex relationships, and it has been something of a taboo subject amongst conservative evangelicals. But as culture shifts in the developing world, and an anti-gay stance becomes an inhibitor of mission and evangelism, there are signs that evangelicals are beginning to soften and broaden. It should also be said that part of this broadening and softening is also rooted in some of their own signed-up members 'coming out' – Michael Vasey, Roy Clements and Vaughan Roberts, to name but three – are all respected British evangelical church leaders who have changed their minds, and expressed this in writing.[14] Many more have done so publicly and in sermons; and countless others quietly, and in silence. Because churches, like their ministers, are rooted and grounded in their own distinctive cultures, it is likely (as well as it might be desirable) that social and cultural factors play a part. Recent studies carried out by Gallup in the USA show to what extent the cultural shifts on issues such as sexuality become, in the end, a force for change within the churches. For example, as mentioned earlier in this chapter, in 1977, 56 per cent of Americans thought that homosexual people should have equal rights in the workplace; the figure for 2004 is 89 per cent. Support for gay clergy has moved in the same period from 27 per cent to 56 per cent. Some 60 per cent of Americans in the 18–29 age-bracket now support same-sex 'marriage',

13 See Henwood, 'Is Equal Marriage an Anglican Ideal?'; see also Coontz and Thatcher, *God, Sex and Gender*.
14 See Vasey, *Strangers and Friends*; Clements, *Exchanging the Truth of God for a Lie*; Roberts, *True Friendship*.

compared to only 25 per cent of those who are over the age of 65. Regular polling and interview-based surveys consistently show that there is increasing support for same-sex unions in churches, whether liberal, conservative, traditional or progressive, evangelical or catholic.. All of which suggests the churches – beginning in the developed world – will adapt and evolve in relation to their context.[15]

There is nothing especially surprising about the idea that religions move with the times. Theodore Roszak, in *The Making of a Counter-Culture*, suggests that the agenda before those who seek to transform society is not centred on organising, managing or repairing reality. It is, rather, about asking 'how shall we live?':

> The primary aim of counter-culture is to proclaim a new heaven and a new earth . . . so marvellous, so wonderful, that the claims of technical expertise must of necessity withdraw to a subordinate and marginal status.[16]

In a similar vein, T.S. Eliot's vision for a Christian culture is not one where right has triumphed over left, liberals have achieved ascendancy over conservatives, or traditionalists and progressives have battled to a creditable stalemate. It is, rather,

> a society in which the natural end of man – virtue and well-being in community – is acknowledged for all, and the supernatural end – beatitude – for those who have the eyes to see it.[17]

If Anglicans could find the grace and humility to conduct their debates with this kind of higher vision in mind, we might be able to see that the present difficulties and differences are also our opportunity. For if we can find a way forward to live with diversity, and yet in unity, we shall have held up to the world such an example of polity that the wider public sphere and body politic might itself seek the renewal of its mind and heart, as surely as Anglicans earnestly seek this for themselves.

15 Myers and Scanzoni, *What God Has Joined Together?*, pp. 140ff.
16 Roszak, *The Making of a Counter Culture*, p. 122.
17 Eliot, *The Idea of a Christian Society*, p. 34.

6 Power in the church?
Congregations, churches and the Anglican Communion

Generally, one problem that faces many theological colleges is the unspoken assumption that most of the churches in which clergy will serve are essentially similar in character, and only different in form. Thus, principles, ideas and visions are taught and offered as though what might work in one place can be easily transferred to another context. Formulae for church growth particularly come to mind. Yet as one educationalist cautions,

> the 'church' so talked about in seminary is neat, tidy, and generally civilised. A particular congregation is never neat, sometimes barely Christian and only rarely civilised. Part of the 'culture shock' is due to the changed status of the student. There is a world of difference between being a member of a congregation, and carrying the weight of its symbolic meaning in the institutionalised role of 'priest', whether that word is understood in a high or low sense. In addition, the student emerging from theological college is a different person from the one who entered.

> Again what appears to be the case upon the surface is not necessarily the case. In one parish a prolonged conflict occurred over the practice of the ladies' guild of placing a vase of flowers on the communion table. The new minister on the basis of sound theological principles and an impeccable liturgical viewpoint well supported in theological college, made strenuous efforts to remove them.

> The conflict proved to be an illustration of two world views passing each other. The practice had arisen in the particular congregation positively as a confession of God's grace in renewing the world daily, and negatively because of the attempt of a former minister to close the women's group down. A vase of flowers was to the women's group, symbol both of their identity as a group and a confession of their faith as Christians. The new minister saw only a custom he could not affirm with integrity. That was all he saw, and before his outlook had become informed much damage had been done to the life of the parish. Similar stories can be told about attempts to remove national flags from churches, or to change the arrangement of

church furniture bearing brass plates in honour of deceased parents and grandparents.[1]

Power in religious institutions can be as inevitable and ubiquitous as anywhere else. It can be the power of virtue or vice. Equally, it can be a power that drives a morally ambiguous potency, or the naked assertion of a particular fecundity. Power can be seen gorgeously vested, splendidly arrayed in ritual, material and organisation. But it can also be disguised in the apparently ordinary and insignificant, only erupting as problematic when a synergy of events causes the hidden face of power to be revealed.

An understanding of power, then, is a crucial hermeneutical key for arriving at an understanding of the local church, and in specific congregations. To understand the nature of power in churches, it is not necessary to be engaged in a reductive sociological or psychological task. It is, rather, to recognise that any social body (and this includes churches) can benefit from a form of 'deep literacy' (to coin a phrase of Paulo Freire)[2] that readily faces up to the myriad of ways in which power is present, distributed, wielded and transformative. Furthermore, and perhaps inevitably, attention to the phenomenon of power as a primary motif within congregations can provide a degree of illumination that leads to transformative self-critical praxis within a congregation. In seeking to understand the local church, attention to the dynamics of power can go some considerable way to providing some causal explanations related to organisation, mission, identity and worship.

Because the nature of power is essentially contested – either within any one individual discipline, or in dialogue between the disciplines – there is no common analytic or explanatory language that uniquely commends itself to the study of congregations or the local church. Theologically, it is commonplace to speak of the power of God. In turn, most denominations will have a conceptualisation of how that power typically is expressed or reified (i.e. materially manifested) in the midst of a congregation. Put another way, the 'pure' power of God is known through particular and given 'agents' which (or who) are deemed to most faithfully express that power, and the nature of the giver (God). Thus, for some denominations, the power of God is made known in the celebration of the Mass; in a particular individual; in the exposition of an inerrant Bible; in the faithful gathering that witnesses miracles, signs and wonders; or in debate and dialogue, where fresh vistas of perception are reached through new patterns of communion.

What is interesting about 'mapping' theological conceptualisations of power in this way, is noting how conflated the giver and the gift become. Critics of the traditions mentioned above will often remark upon how the Mass is raised to a level of apotheosis; how the Bible is almost worshipped; comment upon the exalted status given to ministers who are gifted

---

1 Grierson, *Transforming a People of God*, p. 18.
2 Freire, *Pedagogy of the Oppressed*; Freire, *Education for Critical Consciousness*.

in thaumaturgy; or on how democracy can sometimes be paraded as the eleventh commandment. These preliminary critiques are all linked, insofar as they have identified one of the most pressing problems in expressions of theological and ecclesiological power: it is the problem of conflation. In other words, the inability to distinguish between the power of God, and then again, on the other hand, the power of the agencies or channels through which such power is deemed to flow. This is an acute issue in the study of congregations, and in coming to terms with implicit and explicit theologies in churches.

Until recently, sociologists have perhaps been more alert to these issues than theologians. Writers such as Max Weber,[3] developing theories of charisma, have been able to point to dynamics of power that explain the functioning of complex organisations such as local churches. For Weber, charisma is a mysterious and extraordinary quality that can confer authority upon a person, movement or situation. Charismatic authority governs through a combination of mystique, sublime quality and ultimate efficiency (i.e. there are 'results' from this leadership). Thus, the advent of a charismatic leader within a church typically inspires new patterns of believing and belonging, which inevitably tend to be more demanding. In order to witness or receive greater power (sociologists explain, especially in exchange theory), adherents are likely to be schooled into greater acts of submission and sacrifice. This, in turn, can make intense charismatic situations highly volatile, since the most exciting religious leaders will normally tend to be the most demanding. This leads to a form of power exchange, in which those hoping to receive greater power or spiritual fulfilment will, most likely, have given their self even more fully to the situation or person.

Typically, attention to power in local congregations focuses on abuse and the problematic. High profile cases are often reported in the media: clergy who sexually abuse adults or minors; arguments over money and trust; and disputes about promises made, and then broken. But it is a pity to become fixated on the pitfalls of power and to overly problematise it, since a deeper appreciation of the dynamics of power can reveal the hidden governance, resources and untapped potential in a congregation. Too often, it is the fear of power and its potential for harm that prevents many congregations from coming to a more assured appreciation of how they (as a body) might symbolise that power to the wider community. Understanding power is essential for mission, organisation and transformation; its dynamics need ownership, not shunning.

Conventional thoughts on power

In paying attention to the reality of power in the local church, it is virtually inevitable that a whole set of social and material relations will become

---

3 Weber, *Charisma and Institution Building*.

subject to scrutiny. In turn, some of the theological rationales that support those relations will also need to be assessed. For example, the defence of a particular tradition or custom is not 'simply' a group of people protecting what they know to be the truth. It is also a statement about a way of being; a preference for one type of tradition over another; a formula that affirms one pattern of behaviour, but at the same time resists others. Power, therefore, is not one 'thing' to be discovered and studied. It is, rather, a more general term that covers a range of ideas and behaviour that constitute the fundamental life of the local church.[4]

To help us think a little more about the study of power in the local church, it can be helpful to begin by focusing on different types of leadership, which in turn tend to embody different views of power. Consider, for example, three different caricatures of how Church of England bishops might operate within a diocese. One may see their role and task as primarily *executive*: being a hands-on manager, making key strategic decisions on a day-to-day basis. This view of pastoral power thrusts the bishops into the contentious realm of management, efficiency and rationalisation, where they operate as a kind of chief executive officer in a large organisation. This is a form of *rationalised* authority, and it will typically empathise with reviews, strategies and appraisals.

Another may take a different approach, and see their power in primarily *monarchical* terms. There are two faces to monarchical power. One is to rule by divine right: like a monarch, the bishop's word is law. But the second and more common manifestation of monarchical law is manifested in aloofness. Like most monarchs, bishops seldom intervene in any dispute decisively, and choose to remain 'neutral' and 'above' any divisive opinions or decisions. This is not an abrogation of power. Rather, the adoption of the second type of monarchical model proceeds from an understanding that others ('subjects') invest mystique and meaning in the power of the ruler, which in turn leads many monarchs and bishops to be 'officially silent' on most issues that have any immediacy, or are potentially divisive. Their symbolic power is maintained through mystique, and ultimately reticence. This is a form of *traditional* authority, where the power is primarily constituted in the office rather than in the individual charisms of the person holding it.

Another model is more *distributive*, and is concerned with facilitation and amplification. In this vision for embodying power in any office, the bishop becomes an enabler, helping to generate various kinds of powers (i.e. independent, related, etc.) within an organisation. He or she will simply see to it that the growth of power is directed towards common goals, and is ultimately for the common good. But in this case, power is valued for its enabling capacities and its generative reticulation (i.e. the energy derived from and through networking, making connections, etc.); it is primarily verified through its connecting and non-directional capacities. To a point, such

4 Percy, *Power in the Church*.

leadership requires a degree of *charismatic* authority, since the organisation constantly requires a form of leadership that is connectional and innovative.

To be sure, most bishops will move between these models of power (and their associated types of authority) according to each case, and with each situation dictating which mode of power is deployed. But most bishops will naturally favour one kind of model over another. The advantage of looking at power through models of leadership, though, is that it illuminates other issues. For example, how is power 'conceptualised' in this situation or place? Who is said to have any ownership of power? How is power shared or dispersed in a congregation or denomination?

These issues are important when one considers the perpetual puzzling that often persists in relation to the status of charismatic leaders. For power is at its most obvious when it is at its most concentrated, and is intensely experienced. For this reason, an understanding of the complexities of power in relation to the local church is an essential element within the study of congregations. There are at last three ways of 'mapping' the power as it is encountered.

In one sense, (as theorists of power in organisations argue),[5] power can be understood as *dispositional*. This refers to the habits and worldview of a congregation, and will closely correspond to their normative 'grammar of assent'. Appeals to an almighty God and Lord will have direct social consequences in terms of the expectations set upon obedience and compliance. On the other hand, *facilitative* power describes the agents or points of access through which such power is accessed. Here, the status of those agencies will normally match the power that they are connected to. Then again, *episodic* power, however, refers to those events or moments in the life of a congregation that produce surges of energy, challenge or opportunity.

Putting this together – with a charismatic congregation serving as an example – one could say that the worship is dispositional, the leaders are facilitative, and the invocation of the Holy Spirit a cue for episodic manifestations of power that are unleashed. This sequence, of course, quickly becomes a dynamic cycle: the episodic confirms the validity of the facilitative and dispositional, and in so doing, creates further expectations of episodic manifestations of power, and the strengthening of other kinds. There is a real sense in which the local church is a 'circuit of power', replete with connections, adaptors, converters and charges of energy. The local church is a complex ecology of power, where energy of various types can flow in different ways, be subject to increase and decrease, and be converted and adapted for a variety of purposes.

Closely related to power is the question of authority. All Christian denominations evolve over time, and their patterning of power and arrangements for agreeing on normative sources of authority are also subject to change. Again, given proper scrutiny, excavating models of authority and power

---

5 See Percy, *Power in the Church*; Percy, *Engaging with Contemporary Culture*.

can reveal much about the structure of a church or congregation. Following Paula Nesbitt's sociological observations, we might note that in the first evolutionary phase of denominationalism, or in specific congregational evolution, (which can currently be seen in the early history of new house churches), institutional relations usually can be governed through obedience and, if necessary, punishment. We might describe this as the exercise of *traditional* authority, where power over another can be nakedly asserted.

However, in the second phase, interpersonal contracts emerge between congregations, regions and individuals. Here 'ecclesial citizenship' is born, and law and order develop into agreed rather than imposed rule. We might call this *rational* authority: it has to be argued for and defended in the face of disputes and questioning. Again, a number of new churches are now at the point where their power and authority needs explaining in relation to their context and other relations. In the third phase (post-modern, etc.), more complex social contracts emerge between parties, which require a deeper articulation of a shared ethos and an agreement about the nature of a shared moral community. To retain unity and cohesive power, authority must be *negotiated*. It is here that the denomination effectively crosses the bridge from childhood to adulthood. Congregations learn to live with the differences between themselves.

Finally, there is *symbolic* authority. This states that authority and power are constituted in ways of being or dogma that are not easily apprehensible. Networks of congregations may choose a particular office ('chief pastor') or event ('synod') or artefact of tradition ('Bible'), and position as having supreme governance. However, the weakness of symbolic authority is often comparable to the dilemma faced by those who prefer monarchical power. By positing power in an office that seldom intervenes in a decisive way, symbolic authority normally has to justify its substance. If it can't, it loses its power and authority. And no amount of assertion can make up for the imprecision which people vest in symbolic or monarchical power. Attempts to compensate for this dilemma often end with accusations of capriciousness.

Unconventional thoughts on power

Locating instances of power and abuse is a fairly obvious way of studying the shape and cadence of a congregation. However, some attention to apparently 'neutral' phenomena is also useful when trying to sketch or map the power dynamics of the local church. At least one of Paulo Freire's aspirations was to help people achieve 'deep literacy' – to be aware of the far from innocent forces which can shape lives and institutions. Freire[6] argued that deep literacy came through dialogue. It is in conversation and reflection that we become aware of how we are *determined* by our cultural inheritance and the powers within it. For example, the power of a building, and the

6 Freire, *Pedagogy of the Oppressed.*

mystique invested in its capacity to mould and inspire, is a form of power that may operate restrictively in a certain context.

Equally, one must also pay attention to numerous instances and dispositional behavioural patterns that continually construct and reconstruct power relations in a congregation. Silence on the part of individuals or groups within a congregation, and in the midst of a dispute or debate, can be interpreted in a variety of ways: as defeat – they have nothing more to say in this argument; as withdrawal – a refusal to participate; as 'wisdom' – they are waiting for you to see their point of view; as an act of defiance, or disapproval; and as a spiritual rejoinder to too much discussion. Silence, then – even in its informal guise – is seldom innocent. It is a form of power that needs to be 'read', understood and interpreted.

Another example of what educationalists term the 'hidden curriculum' in relation to power can also be detected in apparently ordinary phenomena, such as dress codes and manners. I have often remarked that an important hermeneutical key for understanding Anglican congregations is to appreciate that, at a deeper level, Anglicanism could be said to be a sacralised system of manners. In other words, any disagreements must be moderated by a quality of civility. The means usually matter more than the ends: better to chair a good, but ultimately inconclusive discussion, than to arrive prematurely at a (correct) decision.

Similarly, codes of dress in church can also carry theological meaning that is related to dynamics of power. For some, dressing in a relaxed style connotes disrespect, a lack of formality and is ultimately unacceptable. It is not that a congregation will necessarily have any hard or written rules about how to dress (e.g., gentlemen must wear ties and jackets, etc.). The codes and expectations evolve over a period of time, and in their own way, act as a sieve within the congregation. Conformity in uniformity indicates a degree of acquiescence in the pattern of belonging. To 'not dress right' is to not only rebel against the prevailing code; it is also to question the formal or informal ascriptions of God that are symbolised in those dress codes. Thus, in the relaxed gathering of a house church, where God is deemed to be immediate, friendly, and even neighbourly, relaxed dress codes will tend to 'fit' and symbolise the theological outlook. Where God is deemed to be more formal and distant, with worship to compliment this, it is likely that, like the worship itself, the dress code will be much more 'buttoned up'.

To be sure, one would have to exercise considerable caution in pushing these observations too far. But my point is that by paying simple and close attention to what the laity chooses to wear when they come to church, one can begin to gain some understanding of how power relations and expectations are constructed locally, and how they, in turn, reflect upon the congregation's (often unarticulated) theological priorities. Furthermore, this is an area that can be rich with conflict.

For example, in a North American church that I was briefly involved with some years ago, the pastor presented the following problem. One of the newest additions to the team of 12 elders, elected by the congregation, was refusing to wear a suit and tie for Sunday worship as the others did. (The elders were all male by custom rather than rule.) The new elder was also late for weekly meetings, and sometimes failed to turn up at all. The 11 other elders petitioned their pastor to have the errant elder removed or 'brought into line', claiming that the casual mode of dress signified disrespect (to God), and was mirrored in 'sloppy attendance habits'. The pastor made enquiries of the dissenter, and discovered that he had his reasons for 'dressing down'. He wanted the church to be more relaxed and less stuffy; he thought that formal attire inhibited worship, and also suggested a stern, somewhat formal God. The dissenting elder added that he thought that God was more mellow and relaxed, and he was merely expressing this. It was to this God that he was committed – or at least thinking about being committed to. So he did not miss meetings to be rude, or to make an obvious point; he simply didn't think that it mattered that much, *theologically*, and in the wider scheme of things. And that, of course, is itself theologically significant.

This story leads me to conclude this brief section by underlining the importance of reflecting on stories. James Hopewell, in his alert and prescient study of congregations, discusses the extent to which congregations are 'storied dwellings'. By this, Hopewell means that congregations are frequently in the grip of myths and narratives that reflect world-views, which in turn determine theological priorities. Congregations seldom understand that they are often owned or 'performed' by these 'dramatic scripts', but the stories do shape a congregation, nonetheless. His book is too rich and complex to be discussed further here, but the agenda he sets is a teasing one for the subject that we are concerned with. More often than not, what makes a congregation are the powerful narratives and stories it collects, that then go on to construct and constitute its inner life. These may be heroic stories, or they may be tales of triumph over adversity. Equally, however, the preferred stories can be centred on struggle, or on the value of coping.

But in focusing on stories, Hopewell has understood that power in the local church is more than a matter of studying the obvious or official lines of authority, or the authorised power constructions and relations. True, there is value in paying proper attention to what we might term 'formal' religious structures and apparatus. Who is pastor or vicar, and how does their style mediate their authority and power? In what ways do people regard the clergy? And how do the laity perceive themselves – as passive receptors of power, or as generators of empowerment? This is important, to be sure.

But there is also value in paying attention to the less formal and 'operant' faith of a congregation. What is the scale of the gap between the 'official' teaching of a church, and the actual 'concrete' discipleship of a congregation and its individuals? What does that gap tell us about power relations between the macro denomination and the micro congregation? Quite independent of what congregations are supposed to affirm, what kinds of stories of faith do they commonly tell? Where does the congregation think power lies? With the clergyperson? With a committee or governing body? Or perhaps with named individuals who wield different kinds of power such as 'a pillar of the church' – perhaps through patronage, age, skill, charisma or experience? Or with an individual who has an alternative theological and spiritual agenda that attracts a significant part of the congregation?

Ultimately, stories have power because they give us a kind of knowledge that abstract reasoning usually cannot deliver. One of the advantages of 'story knowledge,' as a conveyor of power, lies in its sheer concreteness and specificity. Stories give us individualised people in specific times and places doing actual things: so they speak to congregations with a force and a power that dogma sometimes lacks. Rationality and theological formulae can tend to sidestep the messy particulars of life; stories, however, immerse us in life. So, if Hopewell is right, it is the narratives we tell each other that build and make the church what it is, and determine its sense of power. In imagining that the local church is a 'storied dwelling', to borrow a memorable phrase from Jim Hopewell,[7] we are invited to contemplate the many different ways in which we become what we speak, as churches. It is the stories that churches tell – much like personal testimonies – that turn out to be reliable reservoirs of power and authority. Such vignettes can be midrash: creeds-in-waiting.[8]

So, whilst it is commonplace to pay attention to abuses or collapses of power in churches, the purpose of this section has been to show that there are deeper reasons why a focus on power is important for the study of the local church. First, the contested nature of power means that its study is essential if one is to clarify the culture, theology or anatomy of the local church. Second, there are conventional understandings of power that can illuminate ecclesiological analysis. Third, there are unconventional ways of understanding the identity and location of power that also merit attention. To simply study 'official' authority in the church is to only undertake half the task, since there are hundreds of subtle and unofficial forms of power and authority that are no less significant. Ultimately, it is only by immersing oneself in a local church that one can begin to understand the complex range of implicit dynamics that make and shape a congregation. And in the act of immersion, the scholar needs to develop a deeper literacy that is attentive to the multifarious dynamics of power.[9]

A balance of power?

For many faiths, balance is merely finding the mid-point between liberalism and conservatism, or perhaps traditionalist and progressive. Faiths

7 Hopewell, *Congregation*.
8 On this, see Scharen (ed.), *Explorations in Ecclesiology and Ethnography*.
9 For an especially illuminating account, see Pickard, *Seeking the Church*.

of all kinds strive to find a way of being, living and moving forward that keeps together a tense synthesis of values, priorities, symbols and beliefs. Anglicanism is not unique in this regard. Indeed, it is, in some respects, a fairly typical expression of faith in the modern world, trying to mediate between past and present, or perhaps dissenters and conformists. As a faith, it is a fusion of tensions; and as such, it often expresses itself best not in uniformity, but in a unity that is rooted in discussion, debate, and sometimes disagreement. So 'balance' – which can sometimes become something of an apotheosis in ecclesial culture – is not necessarily a life-giving charism, even though many churches and denominations crave it. As Bruce Reed puts it, 'biologically, life is not maintenance or restoration of equilibrium, but is essentially the maintenance of dis-equilibrium, as the doctrine of open systems reveals. Reaching equilibrium means death and decay'.[10]

The point of balance, for Anglicans, is often elusive. It does not lie in a static, compromised middle ground, or in some (fondly imagined?) 'broad church' of yesteryear. The point of balance, for Anglicans, lies in the mutual and respectful comprehension of otherness. In other words, in an intentional breadth that embraces diversity. As such, the broad, middle ground of Anglicanism is often, perhaps surprisingly, the front-line or cutting edge; it is the radical, difficult place to be. It is arguably easy to belong to one of the many enclaves or tribal proclivities that make up the rich diversity of Anglican life. Being a conservative evangelical or conservative catholic delivers a world-view replete with real clarity on allies and enemies. But to hold on to and occupy a place of mediation that retains the poise and composure of the whole body – as do many in positions of oversight, whether ecclesial or governmental – is never easy. Maintaining balance is, of course, not an end in itself. It is, rather, that method and ethos that enables all of the life forces of the body – in their intra-competitiveness and complementarity – to empower and shape the whole body. The point of balance is that it enables diversity; it permits opposites to contribute, dialogue, debate, disagree and unite – but in a tense range of spectra. It moves a body from shallow uniformity to a distractive and rich unity. It enables different weights to co-exist in tension. Crucially, the point of balance is often *not* the mid-point, but rather the point at which all the different weights can be held and suspended to perform a deeper task.

It is something of a caricature of Anglicanism to describe it in 'middling terms'. Anglican polity as neither hot nor cold: just warm. The classic *via media*; Laodicean, tepid – and proud of it. Anglicanism is born of England, and like its climate, it is often a temperate polity: cloudy, occasional sunny spells and the odd shower – but no extremes. But the English like to discuss the weather, which is most akin to our polity. We complain if it is too hot . . . and too cold. Goldilocks has it right – we look for the warm middle. Anglicans are not alone in this. Even Wesley, as a good Anglican, only had

10 Reed, *The Dynamics of Religion*.

his heart 'strangely warmed' – not hot, then. Indeed, Methodists often celebrate their temperateness.

But what happens in congregations and denominations when things get a bit too heated? Some churches, of course, like intensity and heat; it is a sign of vibrant life and feisty faith. But others who are of a more temperate hue find this disturbing; heated exchanges, anger and passions seem to dismay more than they comfort. Anglicanism is a *via media* – what Archbishop Robert Runcie once described as 'passionate coolness'. This is a typically Anglican phrase – the framing of ecclesial identity within an apparent paradox. But you could say that what currently afflicts Anglicanism is not this or that issue – but the heat and intensity that often accompany the debates – because Anglicans are used to temperate, cool debates. We don't tend to do anger well; we don't cope well with excess. So the churches that are used to heat both climatologically and theologically can conflict with the more traditionally temperate culture. And when heat meets coolness, a storm can brew.

The worldwide Anglican Communion contains a great many varieties of tensions. On the surface, some of the most manifest difficulties appear to be centred on issues such as sexuality, gender, the right use of the Bible, and the appropriate interpretation of scripture. It is therefore possible to narrate the schismatic tendencies in Anglicanism with reference to authority, theology and ecclesial power. But on its own, as a thesis, this is clearly inadequate, as such tensions have existed within Anglicanism from the outset. There has not been a single century in which Anglicanism has not wrestled with its identity; it is by nature a polity that draws on a variety of competing theological traditions. Its very appeal lies in its own distinctive hybridity. Indeed, hybridity is an important key in understanding the wisdom of God – in Christ, his incarnate son – who chooses to work through miscibility rather than purity. Anglicans are born of compromise; it is where we found and find God.

Indeed, we can go further here, and suggest that all Christian history, generally, is a history of progression through *tense meetings*. The great councils of Nicea and Chalcedon, or the debates at Worms, the Reformations in Europe, right the way through to the First and Second Vatican Councils, are gatherings of opposites. These are places where ideas clash, are discerned and distilled, before slowly forming into a rich harmony infused with tension and agreement. As any parish priest knows, it is no different in the local church. Christians work through differences to find common ground. Debates, dissent and disagreement are never indicators of denominations in their early death-throes. These dynamics are rather, as Bruce Reed suggests, signs of life that point to vitality. The point of balance then, is the space and place where sufficient degree of unity is achieved to enable the body to regain the poise it needs to hold its diversities together. Balance is born of wisdom and maturity. Balance is not a political position that simply acts to sedate endless vacillation. Rather, it is the place that allows competitive and tense life forces in the body to continue contributing to the total well-being of that body, and to our wider social polity.

Balance, then, is something that enables unity, but does not confuse it with uniformity. Yeats' famous poem mourned that 'things fall apart – the centre cannot hold'. But the centre was always contested, not settled. So what is to be done? No single solution presents itself. Recognising that there are cultural factors in shaping and individuating churches is important. Valuing diversity alongside unity will always be vital. And praying fervently with Jesus 'that we may all be one' will also be crucial – although we might perhaps mutter in the same breath: 'but thank God we are all different'. As this collection of essays suggests, we as Anglicans should perhaps celebrate our diversity a little more. It is evidence of strength, not weakness.

But does that mean anything goes, as long as it can be balanced? Clearly not. Affirming diversity need not be a 'counsel of despair'. Far from it. There *is* a homogenous faith polity that Anglicans can identify and celebrate. But it is important to understand the ecclesial nature of that body. The first Lambeth Conference gathered because of disunity, not unity. In 1867, as now, a number of bishops refused to come. But it was not a disaster. Conflict is not a bad thing in itself; it can be creative and point to maturity in polity that is the envy of narrower ecclesiological frames of reference. Conflict can challenge commitment and breathe life into the connections that configure communion. Church is, after all, a long-term community composed out of committed relationships. It is not a short-term project or relationship that depends on agreement in the present; let alone an immediacy of rapport. In Communion – just like a good marriage – Anglicans work *through* conflict and difficulty; our faithfulness to God and one another sees to it that we find enrichment rather than weakness in our apparent tiffs and tantrums.

That said, we must also reckon that the heat and immediacy of our disputes does not help the gentle and temperate spirit of our polity. It is too easy – through e-mail and other modes of electronic communication – to respond immediately to our neighbour. And not, as the marriage service has it, after serious, considered and sober thought. This is a pity, because as many Anglicans know – or at least come to understand – much of our identity is better understood as implicit, not explicit. Moreover, we only reflect on our identity when under pressure, or in difficulty. And by then, it is often too late to rediscover the *via media*, because lines have already been drawn. This is unfortunate, because godly compromise and inclusiveness is part of our polity's soul. Our problems begin, as a church, when we try to be too overly defined; our genius, as a church, lies in our incompleteness and contestability. We are a humble church – still being formed. This is why resolutions and articles still feel alien to our soul. We are a church that is on the *viaticum* – still becoming.

Conclusion

It is perhaps no accident that when Jesus turned his metaphorically-disposed mind to the subject of the church, he reached for a rather riveting analogy: 'I am the vine, you are the branches' (John 15: 5). It is a suggestive, economic phrase, where one suspects that the use of the plural [branches] is quite deliberate. Even for an apparently homogenous organisation like the Church of England (let alone the Anglican Communion), 'branches' offers a better descriptive fit than most of the labels on offer. It suggests intra-dependence yet difference; unity and diversity; commonality yet independence; continuity and change; pruning, yet fruitfulness.

In other words, the analogy sets up a correlation between particularity and catholicity. This is, of course, a struggle that Anglicans are all too familiar with. There is a constant wrestling for the 'true' identity of Anglicanism; a struggle to reach a point where its soul ceases to be restless, and becomes more fully self-conscious. But in the meantime, the church finds itself easy prey to a variety of interest-led groups (from the theological left and right) that continually assert their freedoms over any uneasy consensus. The assumption made here is that any one branch is 'free' from the others. Technically, this is correct. But the illusion of independence threatens to impoverish a profound catholic aspect of Anglicanism. The right to express and practise particularity is too often preferred to the self-imposed restraint that is hinted at by a deeper catholicity.

Thus, one branch will exercise its assumed privilege of freedom – whether that is fiscal, political, theological or moral – over the others. The consequence of this is all too obvious. The branches attempt to define the vine. But this won't do. Which is why issues of gender, sexuality and polity quickly become the primary foci that distinguish one branch from another, rather than secondary indicators of emphasis that are subjugated to an innate connectedness to the true vine. There seems to be little understanding that an unfettered claim to act freely can actually become anti-social, or even unethical. With great freedom comes even greater responsibility.

Interestingly, this is why bishops may have a vital role here in presiding over diversity whilst maintaining unity. Indeed, this is why the key to some of the current divisive Anglican dilemmas may lie in dioceses and provinces becoming more consciously expressive of their catholic identity, and celebrating their coherence amidst their diversity. A diocese is more than an arbitrary piece of territory. It is a part of a larger, living, organic whole. It is a branch of the vine. Therefore, exercising its freedom and expressing its particularity is less important than maintaining its connectedness. The trouble starts when any specific branch purports to speak and act for the whole, but without sufficient humility. Naturally, such restraint need not impose limits on diversity. It merely asks that the consequences of exercising one's freedom be more fully weighed.

The key to the future, dare one say it, may lie in balance – and in learning to walk together, even with differences. As Anglicans anticipate the possibility of another Lambeth Conference (indeed, 2020 has now been mooted), there will be much to contemplate. How to hold together in the midst of tense, even bitter diversity? How to be one, yet many? How to be faithfully catholic, yet authentically local? Indeed, in finding the point of balance, we might discover that not all balancing points lie in the centre. In some balancing, the weights are always unequal, and the balancing point will be far to the left or the right of any equation. But finding that point is crucial, and is normally motivated out of a deep sense of catholicity, rather than perhaps any slightly weaker sense of equitable fairness.

Wisdom, then, is more than mere reasonableness; wisdom is not only having our rights vindicated, or merely balanced. It is also about finding a point of balance, within an ecology of breadth and diversity, in which much may be ceded, or much may be gained. It will depend on the weight of the matters in hand; and on the weight of glory we can discern together. Some of these issues will be explored again in the third and concluding part of this book. All that can be said now, therefore, is that in all of this, and in striving for the true balance of koinonia, Anglicans may well discover that an ethic of *shared restraint* – borne out of a deep catholicity – may have much to offer the Anglican Communion in the present and future. Without this, Anglicans risk being painfully lost in the issues that beset the church – unable to see the wood for the trees. Or perhaps, as Jesus might have said, unable to see the vine for the branches?

Part III
Maps and forecasts

7   Future directions of travel

Media accolades for church leaders are usually double-edged. So a recent acclamation by one journalist, that the Archbishop of Canterbury might be considered to be 'God's management consultant',[1] is arguably both constructive and critical. Constructive, in the sense that the accolade paints a picture of a person who gets things done. Critical, perhaps, when inferring that consultants rarely come up with deep wisdom and long-term solutions for institutions. They have a tendency to be quite faddish, and operate in a climate in which their counsel and services are dispensable. To be sure, the Archbishop has set about reforming and renewing the Church of England with a zeal and zest more usually encountered amongst secular management consultants. Yet the American contextual theologian James Hopewell has some sage counsel for clergy – at any level – embarking on a new role in the church. Rather than begin by trying to improve the church, he argued, the minister should first make an effort to understand it.[2]

The *Reform and Renewal* agenda[3] from the Archbishops' Council (to which we referred in Chapter 2) is currently working its way through the Church of England. The reforms are, in one sense, a kind of manifesto from the new team at the top. Their agenda is packed full of proposed improvements for the church, ranging from theological education and ministerial training and selecting and training leaders, to changes in church law, governance and regulations.

To be sure, there is scope for improving all of these. Yet the primary problem with the proposed agenda is that the reformers don't seem to understand the subtle nature of the church they seek to improve. They have set about proposals for alteration and transformation, yet with little evidence of having a deep and rich comprehension of the body they propose to reform – an absence of ecclesiology.

Of particular concern is how the church is to be read as a body. Is it a failing member-based organisation, which essentially needs a new business

1 Taylor, *The Tablet*, p. 28; Greaves, 'God's Management Consultants: The Church of England Turns to Bankers for Salvation', p. 20.
2 Hopewell, *Congregation*, 1987.
3 https://www.churchofengland.org/renewal-reform.aspx.

plan, led by a confident CEO, with the workforce re-trained? Or, is the church a support-based institution mainly composed of volunteers, that needs its community connections nourishing and deepening, with those called to serve affirming and supporting in this role?

Moreover, perhaps this kind of institution is less like an organisation, and more like a family, led by a parent-figure? Hopewell offers some more counsel here. Too much reform in the church and denomination – high-handedly imposed and hastily implemented – has the potential to cause significant and lasting damage to structures and morale. Try and understand the value of the past, he argues, before you usher in a new future.

There is some sense in which the current motto of what could be termed 'the new leadership regime' – an alloy of executive and episcopal executive managers – is 'out with the old, in with the new'. The justifying narrative for promoting the new is that the old has consummately failed. Bishops seem to be working with a scripted mantra: 'the Church of England only has a few years left – a generation at most'. Those who question this are deemed to be in denial. Those querying the wisdom of colluding in a collective anxiety about the future, together with the ensuing 'panic attack' consuming the resources of this body, are held to be dissenters or deviants. (In all seriousness, I wonder if some of the panic is being generated deliberately – 'establishing a sense of urgency' is one of Kotter's stages in his eight-stage change process, and it is clear that those creating and narrating the sense of panic are primary beneficiaries.)[4]

In the spirit of ethnographic theology, this helps explain, in part, a recent conversation I had with a clergywoman, whose bishop had spent a day in her rural parishes. One of her churches had an electoral roll of 25, in a village of 400. 'This will all be gone in a decade, unless something radical is done', he opined – both bleakly and critically. The same bishop conducted a ministerial development review just a few weeks later, for a clergyman running a 'fresh expression' – a new congregation of young people in their twenties and thirties. The congregation had enjoyed stable-but-flat numbers of two dozen. Apparently, these statistics were fine for the bishop, and the clergyman's ministry was duly affirmed.

Both forms of ministry are of course fine within a mixed economy. But only one contributes significantly to the diocesan coffers. Only one connects with several hundred people every week through baptisms, weddings, funerals, other services, and numerous village events. Only one preserves and fosters a rich heritage of buildings and practices, cherished over many generations. My hunch is that the village church will be active and alive for many years to come. 'Out with the old, in with the new' is a strangely dissonant motto at this juncture. Indeed, I observe that it is becoming increasingly difficult to hear bishops affirm, unequivocally, the core priority of standard patterns of parochial ministry. Clergy are experiencing increasing demoralisation at

4 Kotter, *Leading Change*.

the hands of bishops, who affirm and apotheosise all that is *new* (everything from 'Messy Church' to 'Fresh Expressions'), but are somehow unable to speak of parishes – and the ministry to them – except in terms of these being 'units', being both a contribution towards and cost borne by the diocese. It is becoming increasingly rare to hear of a bishop who simply affirms, values and champions ordinary, front-line parish ministry.[5]

The manifesto of the new leadership frequently claims to be rooted in research. But all-too-often, this research rests on assertion rather than argument; it arises from imposition rather than consultation. There is a growing conviction that under the new leadership, the thesis directs the facts, and the use of research amounts to 'driven evidence' rather than being evidence-driven. Good independent research from academic sectors is dismissed, for fear it will slow, dilute or deflect the reform and renewal agenda.

The recent *Green Report* – on selecting and training senior leaders in the church – offered an insight into the DNA of the Archbishops' Council reform initiatives. It emerged from a conspicuous lack of wider academic consultation. So, likewise, did the *Report on Resourcing Ministerial Education*[6] – steadfastly refusing to consult key staff in theological education institutions. Similarly, a group of lawyers from the Ecclesiastical Law Society have complained about the lack of basic comprehension of the place and function of canon law in the church to be found in the new 'Simplification' proposals. It is far too easy to claim you are 'cutting through red tape'; only to discover far too late that what you actually sliced through were crucial nerves and tissues in a delicate body-politic.

The *From Anecdote to Evidence* report was spun to promote the idea that 'fresh expressions' of church were equally as successful as parish ministry. But the data does not establish this. Good, broad parish ministry has a huge and extensive impact, connecting widely with communities. A 'fresh expression', with a narrower intensity, cannot match this. Suggesting the two paradigms are of equal value is a misuse of the data.

Much of the research that underpins the *Reform and Renewal* agenda has been narrowly conceived, and not open to wider academic scrutiny. Some of this work lacks appropriate robustness, and is then being 'spun' for particular ends. This does cross a line – an ethical line – which is eroding belief in the proposed reforms and their trajectories and confidence in those driving them, and is ultimately leading to a lack of trust in our leadership as whole.

Sometimes the art of leadership is engaging with the scepticism and dissent in the very body you are called to lead. Dissonant voices are often loyal, and contain essential truths that a culture of uncritical consent misses. The concern here is that the *Reform and Renewal* agenda is driven by executive

---

5 A reason, I suspect, for many clergy moving into chaplaincy, where value and affirmation are more apparent, and numbers – 'headcounts in pews' – not normally meaningful.
6 https://www.churchofengland.org/renewal-reform.aspx, accessed 9 August 2016.

managers who wish to transform a broad institution into a manageable organisation. In this coup, gentle though it may be, it still remains essential that the culture of compliance dominates, and critical voices are distanced or silenced.

What is perhaps extraordinary in all of this is the refusal to root the agenda for change in any kind of theological vision or narratives. When pressed on this point, the leaders and drivers of change will often be defensive, and proclaim 'but we don't have time to hold a theological commission – and no-one will read a report that begins with twenty-five pages of theology'. Maybe, maybe not. But there is no reason to think that several dozen pages of meagre managerial reflections will be any better. Indeed, they will be duller, and more prone to being faddish and expendable. Theology might, at least, be able to rely on materials that have some permanence about them. If the church cannot begin its new enterprises in robust and rich theological work, then our journey down the road to perdition is already well underway.

In a similar vein, I was struck by a recent high-level conversation with senior clergy and lay leaders, in which the *Green Report* was strongly defended with the line that 'we asked the bishops what they wanted, they told us, and so we delivered that'.[7] The comment simply assumes that this kind of consumerist approach was inherently practical and indisputably good. Yet the lack of critical self-reflection here is stark. Would a group of patients, I wonder, sitting in the waiting room at their local GP's surgery, be the *right* group to explain their symptoms to one another, to then not bother to consult the doctor (we don't really have enough time for this – all the patients are in a rush), and so diagnose, prescribe and self-medicate as a group – and all this without the aid of the medical and professional expertise just behind the door? Probably not.

But apparently, the bishops can manage this. They can all describe their ecclesial and missional symptoms to one another, diagnose the problem, prescribe – and then fix it all. So the *Green Report* does not engage with theologians or any other academics. It doesn't need to. The bishops apparently know what is wrong with the church in contemporary society, and know how to resolve the problems. There is a kind of epistemological Pelagianism at work here (i.e. we can sort this out. Who needs a God that might speak through theology, wisdom, or the wider academy? We have former executive managers to guide us now . . .). The hubris of this is entirely unintended, of course – but lamentable and breath-taking, nonetheless.[8]

---

7 This meeting took place on 4 January 2016, at Church House, Westminster.

8 The problem is caused, to some extent, by the Church of England's heavy over-dependence on the expertise of executive managers from secular or commercial contexts. Similar recent attempts by universities and hospitals to use 'business models' (and executive managers) from the private sector to lead such institutions have mostly ended unhappily – if not disastrously. Sometimes the best people to run hospitals are actually doctors, or those with medical training. The best people to run universities or colleges are often (but not always)

So, propagating a new quadrilateral – of impassioned fervour and spiritual zeal, linked together with secular reasoning and business-think – is an alienating and divisive platform from which to pursue an agenda for reform and renewal in the church. Camouflaging all of this under the controlling meta-trope of 'crisis' (cue: ensuing panic), and then claiming to be the sole purveyor of the necessary redemptive counter-tropes – 'the urgency of mission', 'the need for strong, decisive leadership', the necessity of (everyone who is a 'serious Christian') adopting the nomenclature of 'discipleship', the non-negotiable strategies and vision that apotheosise management, organisation and growth – is, to be sure, an effective piece of politicking. As a narrative counter-coup, this is clearly successful – at least initially. But it amounts to little more than manipulative rhetoric, whose sole purpose is to assertively lead and exclusively direct.

The *Reform and Renewal* programme lacks academic depth, scholarly wisdom, ecclesial extensity and emotional empathy. It has a dearth of *compassion* for the whole body of Christ. It lacks a theological point of origin. As such, the programme scatters, but does not gather; it repels more people than it can ever draw in. It believes itself to be omni-competent and self-sufficient. It is arrogant, rude, and insists on its own way (cf., 1 Cor. 13). Correspondingly, faithful resistors and questioners are branded as being in denial, as deviants or as dissidents, and they are quickly allotted a negative value.

As such, the *Reform and Renewal* programme is a rather grace-less enterprise. It lacks charity. A leadership without love, humility, vulnerability and broader collaboration is merely a bullying dictatorship. Unwholesome, it further alienates those who believe themselves to be part of the church, but don't self-identify with unsubtly coded nomenclature (i.e. 'committed disciples', 'vision', etc.) that aspires to divide believers either qualitatively, or by ecclesial ethos, and apotheosises the new leadership with their 'core priorities' and 'vision' – all scripted by an exclusive power-elite.

One is reminded of Yeats' poem: the centre cannot hold; the best lack conviction; 'the worst are full of passionate intensity'. Things will fall apart if the leadership continue to impose an un-spiritual and non-theological agenda on the church. Where there is no theological vision, the people perish (Prov. 29: 18). It is not hard to foresee, therefore, another kind of growth emerging in the light of the reforms led by the new leadership: one of widespread ennui, disenchantment, disengagement and lack of trust. Indeed, the

---

academics. The church is best-run by people with a strong, broad theological education, and some (professional) experience either of ministry, or of relevant charitable or social enterprises, or of educational institutions (NB: so such a person can obviously be laity). The *Reform and Renewal* agenda, and its resistance to theological roots and conversations, is reminiscent of the ill-fated attempts by one Health Secretary to conduct a wholesale reform of the National Health Service during the 1980s. It prompted an advertisement campaign sponsored by the General Medical Council. The advertisement ran with a teaser question: What do you call a man who ignores the advice of his doctors? The answer was: Kenneth Clark – the Minister for Health.

reforms are likely to lead to reluctant compliance in the short-term, and deep demoralisation in the longer-term.

A further concern is the worrying lack of emotional intelligence in those driving the reforms. In business idiom, the *Reform and Renewal* programme is a 'push', not a 'pull' strategy or agenda. That is to say, the programme has been pushed from the outset on to the groups and people in the arenas it seeks to reform; it is an imposed 'vision'. It has not pulled people together: either in well-convened theological conversations or in warming and enticing spiritual visions, that would gather and draw people in. At times the *Reform and Renewal* agenda has been driven by pushy politicking, bordering on bullying. The drivers of the programme have refused to recognise that, as the people holding all the power and authority in the equation, any resistance offered to the agenda must come from a position of comparative weakness.

James Hopewell's prescient work argued that attention should be paid not just to what is apparent and observable in the church, but also to what is not evident or immediately visible. So Hopewell might have been intrigued by a morning I spent in a nearby local village hall on the August Bank Holiday. I know the village well. It was a soggy wet day, but the coffee morning was in full swing, the sole purpose being to raise money for the parish church. Cake stall and plant stands mixed easily with tables selling second-hand books. Parishioners and pensioners shuffled around in damp coats, whilst children and dogs weaved in and out around them, gaining momentary affirming pats, strokes and greetings from the adults. A raffle that recycled unwanted Christmas bottles and boxes of biscuits did a roaring trade. Most of the people who donated books, cakes and plants looked on approvingly as their near-neighbours perused and purchased. They would take their turn to buy soon; for this is a virtuous cycle that all participate in. You can't just give something away; you have to take something back too. One's fulfilment of the offering-receiving relationship makes this all sacramentally valid. A huge tea urn steamed away in the corner – that reassuring secular thurible so beloved of the Women's Institute. The room may have been damp (it was *very* wet outside); but the mood wasn't.

Out of a population of 400, there were around 80 attendees – so a 20 per cent turnout. The 80 attendees could be sub-divided into four roughly equal groups. First, those who come to church frequently. Second, those who come regularly (e.g., Christmas, Easter, harvest, etc.). Third, those who come very occasionally (e.g., funerals, etc.). Fourth, those who never come to church, but nonetheless care enough to help sustain it. But unless you knew these individuals personally, you could not tell them apart.[9]

The mood is relaxed, but resilient, with notes of cheerfulness. Some, in their haste to organisationally rationalise the church, will undoubtedly be calling for Beeching-style cuts to rural churches. Yet one striking and stark fact about village churches is that they are remarkably resilient, and despite

9 cf., Goodall, 'How to Relish the Parish Church', p. 7.

their resources, continue to persist and flourish.[10] A village church is a support-based institution to which many subscribe. It is not a member-based organisation, in which it is obvious who belongs and who doesn't. Indeed, those who habitually attend would be resistant to such demarcations. The church is a body with a soul – a mystery; more than the sum of its parts. It is a social-transcendent reality, occupied with God, virtue and values. So, as Hopewell counsels, before you try to reorganise and transform the church, first take steps to try and understand it – and deeply. Because if you don't comprehend this body, those proposed reforms may do more harm than good. As Mary Douglas helpfully counsels,

> [i]nstitutions systematically direct individual memory and channel perceptions into forms compatible with the relations they authorise. They fix processes that are essentially dynamic, they hide their influence, and rouse our emotions to a standardised pitch . . . Add to all this that they endow themselves with rightness and send their mutual corroboration cascading through all levels of our information system. No wonder they easily recruit us into joining their narcissistic self-contemplation. Any problems we try to think about are automatically transformed into their own organisational problems. The solutions they proffer only come from the limited range of their experience. If the institution is one that depends on participation, it will reply to our frantic question: 'More participation!' If it is one that depends on authority, it will only reply 'More authority!' Institutions have the pathetic megalomania of the computer whose whole vision of the world is its own programme.[11]

Some will respond to all of this by reiterating the need for urgent action. Indeed, there may be chastisement for not participating in the panic – a trope and state of being that already demarcates those who have 'seen the light' from those who 'still sit in darkness'. When it comes to times of crisis, or perhaps addressing challenging changes, there is one picture that is all-too-familiar: beware that we are not just rearranging the deckchairs on *The Titanic*? The image is immediately captivating. The gaping hole in the hull means the liner will soon sink: panic stations. The time for action is now, and urgent. So what is the point of a better view of the iceberg from a deckchair?

Yet *The Titanic* sank, not because it hit an iceberg, but because it was going too fast in difficult conditions, and there was no sentinel in the crow's nest to keep watch for danger some way ahead. On the bridge, inexperienced hands took the wrong kind of aversive, panic-led action, swerving to avoid what they could see, but failing to comprehend what they could not sense below the water-line – thereby ripping an even bigger hole in the starboard

---

10 cf., Duggan, 'The Salt and the Sweetness', pp. 15–17.
11 Douglas, *How Institutions Think*.

hull. Had the bridge simply stopped the liner, it would have hit the iceberg head-on, bow-first. There would have been a serious accident, to be sure; but probably only resulting in injuries, not fatalities – with not enough damage to cause the ship to finally sink. *The Titanic* disaster was caused by cascading human errors.

The lesson hardly needs spelling out. The *Reform and Renewal* programme needed to stop, pause and reflect; not simply plough on. It needed to re-engage with theology, and find appropriate theological points of origin for its work, and be guided and shaped theologically. This needed to be inclusive, collaborative and collegial. Reform cannot be led by a small number of largely unaccountable executive-managers, with compliant episcopal acolytes, deciding on the vision for and priorities of the church, and then finding a convenient theological gloss. Or those same leaders deciding that they have no real time for theology – at all. The leaders of *Reform and Renewal* could also have made some significant gestures of reconciliation. They could have repented of their over-confident hubris; the imposition of the *Reform and Renewal* portfolio and programmes had been characterised by a high-handed, arrogant and rather dismissive approach to the rest of the church.

The new power elite, of course, will have none of it. The emergent 'ecclesiocracy', which in turn promotes the new 'ecclesionomics', has no need for theology. Business and management is the new Gold Standard by which to measure the effectiveness and impact of the church. Yet the executive-managers' *New Quadrilateral* – secular reasoning, business-think, spiritual zeal and passionate intensity – can never compensate for its own unfathomable lack of ecclesial comprehension, spiritual vision and theological depth. In *Reform and Renewal*, the church becomes a body without a soul. This will only serve to create an emergent 'Zombie Church' – animation, but not true life: it will never be a body to inspire or cherish. The new reformist agenda does not feed the soul. And a leadership that can't feed us won't easily be able to lead us – for very much longer.

Sex, sense and non-sense for Anglicans

And so to return to that subject, again. And yes, for one group of Christians, at least, sex has become really rather boring: Anglicans. Not for individuals, necessarily. But rather, for the worldwide Anglican Communion. It is weary of the topic, and dog-tired of debating sex and sexuality – continuously wracked by insoluble disagreement and divisive dialogues it cannot seem to resolve.

To be sure, Anglicanism is not the only denomination trying to find a way through the mire and myriad conversations on sexuality. But as a global church, Anglicans would quite like to change the subject, please. The Anglican Communion knows that its public mission and ministry is perpetually blighted by the issue, and will remain so until it can draw a line under this debate, and finally move on.

The Anglican Primates from around the world gathered in January 2016 at the behest of the Archbishop of Canterbury. This was, we were told, a last-ditch attempt to stop the Communion either imploding or exploding – a steady, solid, prominent planet in the ecclesial universe, that might be about to morph into a burning star. Brightly shining, but nonetheless burning – frictionally breaking apart.

Yet other churches had already faced the divisive issue of sexuality with a bit more nuance. The Church of Scotland (Kirk), for example, deemed that same-sex relationships were a 'matter of liberty of conscience, guaranteed by the Church, on matters that do not enter into the substance of faith'. Here, the question of same-sex relationships was left to the liberty of conscience of individuals, congregations and their ministers.

Thus, a few might say that they cannot support same-sex relationships, and never will. But a quieter majority of others might think otherwise, and therefore affirm such relationships. The liberty of conscience applied here is still a matter of beliefs and practice, but not one that ultimately divides members of the church, who are all mutually affirmed as still ascribing to the core substance of Christian faith.

That carefully worded phrase, which was supposed to bring peace to the Church of Scotland, almost succeeded. Almost. The intention in the drafting of the 'liberty of conscience' clause was to accommodate revisionists and traditionalists alike, liberals and conservatives. In many ways, it aped that beloved Anglican ideal – an 'ecclesial DNA' of inclusive dynamic conservatism that characterises the polity of the church.

Unfortunately for the Kirk, however, when the debate on sexuality took place at the General Assembly in 2014, the 'traditionalist' line was reaffirmed as the normative-default position. Although the Kirk subsequently permitted congregations and ministers to opt out if they wanted to affirm civil partnerships. This was done to 'keep the peace of the church', of course – and avoid an unholy row.

That was a pity, because there were two problems with this compromise, and they are ones that the Archbishop of Canterbury, and the Anglican Primates, could avoid. First, the concession maintains discrimination and perpetuates an injustice against gay and lesbian people, and so runs contrary to the spirit of the 2010 Equality Act in the UK. Second, and despite initial appearances, the two interpretations of 'liberty of conscience' are not in fact symmetrical. They appear to be chiral, so to speak; but there is one crucial difference to note.

And here, an allegory may be helpful. There is a world of difference between going to an ordinary restaurant and requesting a vegetarian option, and going to a vegetarian restaurant and asking for a steak, medium-rare. The first scenario is fine and has sense – no decent restaurant menu is without vegetarian options. But we would rightly regard the second scenario as non-sense. Indeed, potentially rather offensive to vegetarians – and entirely against the spirit of the restaurant. Yet by making heterosexual relationships the exclusive and traditional default position, the Kirk effectively chose this second scenario. The relatively small numbers of traditionalists and conservatives who reject same-sex unions and gay marriage in churches, are, in effect, dictating the menu for everyone else.

In this allegory gay people are fully part of the mainstream of the population. The majority are usually quite happy to eat vegetarian food; just not all the time. But that same majority would not think of insisting vegetarians occasionally ate meat. That would be non-sense. One key ecclesial question flows simply from this allegory: how might churches manage to live well with constrained differences and minorities? Moreover, in a way that does not stigmatise minorities, and caters for them in a non-discriminatory way?

Is this a recipe for diversity of practice that inexorably leads to irreparable disunity? Not really. The Church of England already knows how to live with this kind of reality. Some of the more catholic-inclined clergy and congregations already exercise their liberty of conscience on women priests and women bishops. They've opted out, and reasonable (some would say overly generous) provision is made for them. Some of the more evangelically-inclined clergy and congregations don't always hold services that technically conform to stricter interpretations of canon law on robing or liturgy; they also exercise a liberty of conscience. In neither case are these clergy or congregations cast out. They are catered for; or even permitted to self-cater. And although both these groups might claim to hold more firmly to the truth than others, no-one is asked to dine elsewhere, so to speak.

No established church can afford to de-nationalise itself on an issue that is now treated as a matter of equality and justice by the state. Civil partnerships and same-sex marriages, and those entering into these unions, enjoy the full protection of the law, and majority affirmation by the population as a whole. For any national church to turn its face away from those who are full and equal citizens, and have their unions and marriages recognised as such, effectively augments a process of de-nationalisation and privatisation. It is a route-march towards a tribal church.

The church becomes, in effect, a sad and unwelcoming restaurant with a rationed menu, where the diners who tried to order a meat dish were made to feel terribly guilty. Or more likely, quietly asked by the sullen owner, or embarrassed waiter, to take their custom elsewhere. The diners duly leave. (Lesbian, gay and bisexual church members are weary of being treated as second-class Christians, and of being patronised, pathologised and problematised.) In effect, this is the position adopted for the Church of England by the current Archbishop. But a national church must cater for the whole palate of the population. That is what a broad church does.

So, what about the rest of the Anglican Communion? And what of the future? Here, it might be time for some home truths. In 41 of the 53 countries within the British Commonwealth, homosexual conduct is still regarded as a serious crime. This categorisation and legal stigmatisation of homosexuality was largely 'made in England' in the nineteenth century, and imposed on cultures and emerging countries that had not been, hitherto, homophobic. This is one of England's less wholesome exports. The Archbishop of Canterbury could begin the Primates' meeting by accepting responsibility for the part the Church of England has played in perpetrating this discrimination and the subsequent injustices – and publicly repenting of them.

There is also widespread myth in the Anglican Communion, that the dioceses and congregations of the global south now form the majority, and are the only ones growing numerically. Moreover, this myth has some leverage. It prompts reactionary post-colonial guilt in Anglican churches, and those in the USA, Canada and New Zealand. So when it comes to divisive debates, more moral ground is ceded to African churches, amongst others, than might be judicious. But as we noted in the introduction, the evidence claimed for the number of Anglicans is questionable. The numbers are unreliable – perhaps deliberately exaggerated to acquire leverage in debates.[12] The actual claimed 'core membership' of Anglicans in many African countries may be no more dependable than it is for the Church of England. In contrast, figures for the USA and Canada may be more robust. So the received wisdom – that the future lies with the majority, growing, surging churches of the global south – may not be as reliable as many assume.

The Communion might therefore want to think harder about poise, proportionality and perspective in relation to its moral reasoning, geographies, membership and guilt-tinged post-colonial identity. The Primates cannot simply align themselves with those proffering inflated claims to represent the largest, growing churches. The right treatment of homosexual people is not a conditional concern to put to a vote of argumentative Archbishops. This is a fundamental issue of truth and justice.

Nor should postcolonial guilt be allowed to be converted into spiritual capital that then becomes a tool of oppression. And who, exactly, are the oppressed? Not the surging, strident churches of the global south. Those needing protection and care are still gay and lesbian Christians; and women in violent, abusive relationships. The reconciliation required is between, note, *inequalities of power*. Conservatives are not oppressed or criminalised for their opposition to gays – ever, anywhere.

For some Christians, the issue will continue to be non-negotiable. Conservative Christians argue that relationships between the sexes are prescribed and proscribed in the Bible. God has willed heterosexual union as a natural given, and any deviation from this is to be regarded as an illness or other form of disorder (e.g., a fall), or a wilful act of disobedience (i.e. a sin). But if equal rights for LGBT Christians seeking to have faithful and life-long blessing of their relationship recognised and blessed are seen as matter of justice and equality, then we have a different Christian perspective to contemplate. At the heart of this is a debate over what is 'natural' and

---

12 Munoz, 'North to South: A Reappraisal of Anglican Communion Membership Figures', pp. 1–25.

'normal', and therefore part of God's created order. Sinful and intentionally disobedient humans are not hard to imagine.

Yet as any zoologist will confirm – and this is awkward for some Christians to face up to – same-sex unions and acts do seem to be, in fact, quite normal and natural, and commonly occur across the mammalian genus. What exactly are we to say about same-sex acts between apes and llamas? Or Oliver Reed's opening line as the character Proximo in *Gladiator*: 'those giraffes you sold me were queer'. Are these giraffes sinful, fallen, or just dumb animals? Or normal, but just a minority?

So what can we look forward to? What does the future hold, and what might the map of Anglican polity look like on issues of human sexuality? What no Archbishop must do, I think, is continue to affirm dissonant voices from the global south, in order to uphold an oppressive conservative coalition that is determined to denigrate those of a more liberal persuasion. It may be important for the Archbishop to remember that the Scottish, Welsh and Irish Anglican churches have all been far more positive and open-minded on the issue of same-sex marriage and civil partnerships. Meanwhile, the Church of England – alone in Britain – has continued to travel in the opposite direction. This puts the Church of England in an alliance with developing nations, but is out of kilter with the rest of the UK.

The Archbishop knows full well that this is a problem, and here he is caught between a rock and hard place. The Church of England's stance on sexuality is deeply alienating and quite incomprehensible for most young people in the UK. It confirms their view of religion as being backward-looking and bigoted. +Justin Welby knows that he won't make much headway on evangelism and mission with a church that saddles him with an inherently homophobic polity. A non-inclusive church is an evangelistic dead-duck.

The recent employment tribunal finding for Jeremy Pemberton – a priest who has married his male partner – gave the Church of England the worst kind of pyrrhic victory. The Tribunal ruled that the Church of England was allowed to discriminate against Pemberton, because the church had exempted itself from the government's equality legislation of 2010. But the tribunal case – brought as a result of a Suffragan Bishop denying Pemberton a licence, and so stymieing his promotion to being a senior healthcare chaplain in the NHS – highlights the farce that the Church of England finds itself in on the same-sex marriage issue. Other clergy in the Church of England have married their same-sex partners, and have not been deprived of their licence. Some have experienced the opposite – as in the case of the Archbishop of York, removing a licence from a lay Reader, who married his partner of more than 20 years. So it seems that Bishops may *choose* to discriminate against gay clergy or licensed ministers in same-sex partnerships and marriages. But most Bishops choose not to discriminate. The anomaly grows ever more ridiculous – with each and every same same-sex wedding for ministers.

To add to the problems, the Church of England recently decided that it can lawfully discriminate against those being considered for future high office in the church. So a selection panel may now take into account the content and manner of any statements previously made by a candidate on same-sex relations. The Church of England is, in other words, not only enshrining, but also perpetuating its own discrimination.

Whilst this may be depressing news for many, the pace of cultural change on issues of human sexuality is now noticeably quicker in churches – partly due to advances in media and communication. As we noted in Chapter 5, studies carried out in the USA highlight the extent of the social, moral and cultural shifts on sexuality. Surveys of churchgoers repeatedly show that there is growing toleration for same-sex unions in congregations and amongst clergy, across the ecclesial and theological spectra. All of which suggests a church that will adapt and evolve in relation to its changing cultural context.[13] The world only spins in one direction. It doesn't stand still. And it doesn't spin backwards.

So, can the Bible help the churches resolve their differences on the matter of human sexuality? To some extent, perhaps; but not as easily as some suppose. It is important to remember that as the churches divided over the issue of slavery, the remarriage of divorcees and the role of women – all on the basis of sound or literal interpretations of scripture – so the churches are here again on the issue of sexuality. Some Christians claimed that the Bible is pro-slavery, against the remarriage of divorcees and not especially happy about women in leadership roles – at least in the church. Many more Christians have dissented, and have worked over the centuries for a different interpretative framework, cast in a different, more generous light.

The Primates will still need to grasp that LGBT Christians are now an inescapable part of the Anglican Communion. In many countries across the Communion, they enjoy full and equal citizenship under the law. So, the Primates will now need to turn their critical attention to those countries in which they have influence, where this is not yet so. Gay and lesbian Christians will not suffer discrimination in heaven. In the Kingdom of God, as faithful Christians, all will enjoy a full and equal citizenship.

Exploring what liberty of conscience means for the global Anglican Communion will therefore be a fruitful pathway for the Primates to explore in the coming years. Liberty of conscience recognises that that there will be some disagreement on some practices. But that such diversity is not part of the substance of faith that ultimately unites Anglicans. Anglicans have always varied in their practices; but they remain as one on the creeds, doctrine and the essentials of faith. They always have.

The January 2016 gathering of Primates was not a straightforward meeting, and could not have expected to be so. Yet no matter what his fellow Archbishops thought or now think about the right way to talk about homosexuality, there is no case for continuing to persecute gay and lesbian people under criminal law. In any country, anywhere. The church needs to get past

13 Myers and Scanzoni, *What God Has Joined Together?*, pp. 140ff.

its judgemental and nonsensical mantra, 'love the sinner, hate the sin'. This simply won't do. As the head of the Anglican Communion, and with many Commonwealth countries still criminalising sexuality, the Archbishop could take a simple moral lead, call his fellow-Primates to repent, and in so doing remind them that people of different sexualities should neither be persecuted nor criminalised. Nor should they be unwelcome in our churches. As fellow believers, they should be received as such in Anglican churches across the globe.

Conclusion

So how will these next few years pan out for the Primates and our Anglican Provinces? I hope and pray there will be much poise, prayer, patience, perspective – and poetry. Yes, poetry. One of the key problems the church currently faces is our lack of poets, and those prophetic theologians who often accompany them. Our lexis on the 'issues of human sexuality' debate is far too shallow; the words and phrases to hand simply lack requisite depth.

It was the spiritual writer Bill Vanstone who once remarked that the Church of England is like a swimming pool – all the noise comes from the shallow end. On any issue of gravity, the commotion tends to come from shrill reactionary voices that crave attention. Fathomless profundity goes unheard; depth-words that need to be received and discerned are drowned out by all the splashing and shouting.

If diversity of belief and practice in the church could be so easily managed, we might have expected the New Testament to say so. It doesn't. It is the vanity of our age to suppose the Church is just like an organisation in which diversity can be smoothed over; the faithful warily kettled into some false compliance manufactured by its leaders; difficulties managed and controlled; and the Church pasteurised so as to become a body of utterly consistent clarity. All for the benefit of some imagined public relations exercise.

But the church is, in contrast, a contested place of ideas; a civilised community of differences in opinion and practices. It is a body that seeks deep, profound unity in the midst of much diversity. Anglicanism badly needs its poets just now – people who understand how simple words can take Anglicans to new places as a Communion. Poems are just words, of course. But words so woven that they express a truth more compactly and subtly than if the words were left to their own devices.

Poetry takes a word, term or expression – like 'sex', 'gay', 'issues in sexuality', or even 'church' – and turns this into a quite different language of desire: of longing, lament and laughter. Poetry transforms ordinary words into new shapes and ideas that enhance our existence. It creates something new out of seemingly nothing.

Just like a Communion, a poem is greater than the sum of the parts. So as Primates gather, may God grant them – and the church that I love and long to see swell and intensify – exactly what it needs right now: the true non-sense of poetry.

8 Re-charting the church

Much of my work in ecclesiology draws on anthropological frames of reference, and has tended to imagine Anglicanism in spatial terms – essentially as a series of complex relations between church and world.[1] Like any cartographer, more is attempted here than mere sketching. The map-maker aspires to link signs and symbols that represent the seen and unseen, the explicit and the implicit. This kind of ecclesiology makes 'suggestive guesses' on the links between culture and ecclesial life. How, for example, do prevailing socio-economic 'plausibility structures' shape our expectations of ecclesial life?

As Natalie Wigg-Stevenson suggests, and drawing on the work on reflexive sociology of Pierre Bourdieu and the cultural theology of Katherine Tanner,[2] theologians dig and excavate; they look for meanings below the obvious surfaces we encounter; they look for hidden linkages, and the underlying body of rules or patterned order which may exist. (I sometimes refer to this as 'ecclesial DNA' – the hidden codes that programme behaviour, reflexes, bodily identity and overall healthfulness.) Theology and anthropology are not 'pure' empirical disciplines. Both disciplines involve tactics, guesswork, hunches and preliminary findings – all of which are gradually refined as more material is unearthed, discerned and interpreted.

Theology, like anthropology, is not a matter of locating singular agreement, but rather of finding meaningful interpretations that are faithful to their subject. Both anthropology and theology practise engagement: they are inherently relational discourses and practices, born of hybridity, not purity.[3] Some would see this as 'theological reflection' or 'ethnographic theology'; some might call it 'congregational studies' – more in the qualitative-interpretative tradition of Jim Hopewell, I think, than in the quantitative-descriptive tradition favoured by others. To some extent, I am happy to own any of these nomenclatures, provided it is understood that the heart of this labour is

---

1 See Coleman, 'Locating the Church: On Corridors and Shadows in the Study of Anglicanism' in Day, *Contemporary Issues in the Worldwide Anglican Communion: Powers and Pieties*, Farnham, Surrey: Ashgate, 2015, pp. 213–226. Coleman discusses my 'spatial' approach to Anglican identity and the field of ecclesiology.
2 See Wigg-Stevenson, *Ethnographic Theology*, London: Palgrave-Macmillan, 2014, p. 11.
3 cf., Wigg-Stevenson, 2014, p. 24.

deeply infused with sociological and anthropological lenses. This 'binocular' approach to studying the church has much to commend it. But it has to be modest and circumspect in order to construct meaningful accounts of ordinary ecclesial life, rather than to inhibit the church or denomination through the use of theological or social-science metanarratives.

I have tended to refer to this as 'implicit theology' – the idea that strong, hidden theological tropes or ideologies lie deeply buried and unseen in the very foundations of ecclesial life, and shape the expectations, mood and behaviour of a given congregation or denomination. The word 'implicit' is suggestive. Normally used as an antonym with 'explicit', the terms have a complex etymological history. 'Implicit' is derived from the Latin *implicitus*, meaning to implicate – a term, in turn, that suggests involvement, interweaving, and entanglement. The Latin word *implicatus,* expresses this, with *plicare* conveying the notion of 'folding' – in the sense of mixing and combining, rather as one might expect to 'fold' an ingredient into a recipe. Thus, 'implicit' means the meaningful folding together and close connecting of a variety of strands. Correspondingly, 'explicit' is the un-folding, un-ravelling or explaining of the miscible; order from apparent chaos, and clarity from complexity.

It is my contention that what currently shapes the missional priorities of much of ecclesial life – especially in the Church of England – is not, in fact, a well-thought-through theology of mission. Nor is it confident conviction in the Kingdom of God. It is, rather, deep-seated panic, fear and a deficiency of wisdom – primarily linked to a lack of spiritual perspective and poise, and an inability to read contemporary culture. The consequence of this is, unfortunately, a church that easily becomes (manically, rapidly, repeatedly) culturally-relative or culturally-resistant, when in fact it is only seeking to become culturally-resonant. But in its disorientation, it loses both its identity and moorings, and further compounds its problems by making deficient maps and charts of the very territories and seas that it seeks to navigate. Moreover, the more one examines the attempts of the Church of England to transform itself, the more it becomes apparent just how lost this body actually is within the very culture it seeks to comprehend and transform. So in what follows in this chapter, therefore, I offer a binocular approach to the some of the issues facing the Church of England at present, drawing on both theology and social sciences in order to help read the signs of the times.

Church and contemporary culture: accommodation and resistance

In the introduction to this book, we touched on how the church both sought to shape culture, yet is also shaped by it. This is evident in attitudes to leadership, and to the formation of ecclesial polity. The Church of England often finds itself shaped by currents and contours that it barely notices, let alone reads. And sometimes only dimly discerns long after the currents and contours have ceased to matter. A church shaped and led by the forces and ideologies of managerialism is not developed and shaped by ideas that are necessarily secular, and is certainly not neutral. Like all ideologies, they contain nascent political DNA that only later emerges in patterns of polity, praxis and proclivities. Here, I hold that the Church of England, and Anglicanism more generally, needs to recover its capacity to read culture more deeply, in order to understand the impact this has on its own mission and ministry. Only from here, I think, can the re-charting of the church be done.

This is perhaps a contentious note to be ending on, but I think that many of the currents shaping the contours of the Church of England lie in the modelling of the mind-sets and moral horizons of those who witnessed the collapse of socialism in the 1970s, and the resurgence of late capitalism in the 1980s. These factors, put together with the disintegration of communism (1989) and the eventual birth of New Labour (1997), which was distinctly capitalist-friendly, have meant that our whole sense of what institutions are has been changed – and this now includes the Church of England.

In this discussion, of course, Mrs Thatcher needs no introduction. She was a woman demonised by the left and sanctified by the right, and arguably the most divisive British politician of the post-war era. Yet, as Eliza Filby acknowledges, there has always been a certain religious undercurrent to discussions of Margaret Thatcher.[4] As someone who lived for seven years in Sheffield – long after she left office as Prime Minister – it was striking how much Thatcherism remained a focal point of the socialist struggle in South Yorkshire. However, whilst her Methodist roots are well known, the impact of her faith on her politics is generally overlooked by most commentators. Yet Filby's thesis leaves us in no doubt that Thatcher was on a religious and moral crusade, as much as it was one of economic and social reform. As Thatcher was to say in an interview with *The Times* in 1981, 'economics is the method; the object is to change the soul'.

In an attempt to source the origins of Margaret Thatcher's 'conviction politics', Filby explores how Thatcher's worldview was shaped and guided by the lessons of piety, thrift and the Protestant work ethic learnt at the Finkin Street Methodist Church, Grantham, from her lay-preacher father. In doing so, she tells the story of how a Prime Minister steeped in the Nonconformist teachings of her childhood entered Downing Street determined to reinvigorate the nation with these religious values.

However, Filby concludes that this was ultimately a failed crusade. In the end, Thatcher created a country that was not more Christian, but more secular; and not more devout, but entirely consumed by a new faith: capitalism. The consumerism of the early 1980s created a culture of aspiration that celebrated individualism and militated against the communal. In upholding the sanctity of the individual (for economically liberal, yet socially conservative ends – an odd combination), Thatcherism inadvertently signed a death

4 Filby, *God and Mrs Thatcher.*

warrant for Christian Britain. The country created by Thatcher destroyed – almost at a stroke – local communities of all kinds, with their intimate bonds of affinity and deep-rooted values. And in the longer term, even the economic 'method' seems to have had uneconomic results.

Whilst training for ordination in the late 1980s, I spent a year on placement at the former steel town of Consett. The steel and railways had all been swept away by the 'economic miracle' promised by Thatcher. The Trade Unions had been faced-down and seen off; and unprofitable 'state industries' sold or privatised, or just closed. Consett had lived through this. True, new light industry and retail parks had sprung up. But the employment that many of the new businesses now offered was lighter and more flexible (i.e. part-time), and certainly less fulfilling. So yes, the old, costly industries were despatched. But the queues at the Department of Health and Social Security (DHSS), and at the doctors – for prescriptions to deal with stress and depression – grew exponentially. The result? Industry costs were slashed; but social care costs soared. Inevitably, the next target would be these new, emerging cost-centres: 'benefits culture' and the National Health Service (NHS).

Thatcher's political, moral and religious vision lacked a deep social polity. Although she was widely misunderstood to have said 'there is no such thing as society, only individuals', there was more than a grain of truth in this imagined opinion. True, it was arguably a headline for her politics, and not the real content. But what she actually said is this – and it is worth quoting in full – in an interview for *Woman's Own* magazine, 31 October 1987:

> We've been through a period where too many people have been given to understand that if they have a problem, it's the government's job to cope with it. 'I have a problem, I'll get a grant.' 'I'm homeless, the government must house me.' They're casting their problem on society. And, you know, there is no such thing as society. There are individual men and women, and there are families. And no government can do anything except through people, and people must look to themselves first. It's our duty to look after ourselves and then, also to look after our neighbour. People have got entitlements too much in mind, without the obligations. There's no such thing as entitlement, unless someone has first met an obligation.

Closer to home, the individualism of the 1980s created a culture of aspirants – ambitious, driven and focused. But nothing stands still, and it is often said that Thatcher's children, in the end, grew to know what they wanted to *acquire* (i.e. property, cars, holidays, etc.), without knowing what they wanted to *become* – and in relation to whom. Her legacy was that she set out to create a country in the image of her father – an age of thrift, discipline and conservative values. But she ended up creating a country in the image of her son. Our present 'celebrity culture' is just the endgame of this; our gawping media fawning at (so-called) 'personalities' who have great wealth, and seem merely to pass the time indulging in conspicuous consumption. These 'heroes' of our age are not what Thatcherism intended. But this is what a culture of unrestrained economic liberalism and anti-social(ism) ultimately spawns. A secular grace in regular use from Mansfield College Oxford sounds a note of warning here: *Nullius boni possessio est iucunda sine socio* (No good thing is worth having unless you have someone to share it with).

The Church of England that had the calibre of leaders to produce something as theologically rich, nuanced, daring and prophetic as *Faith in the City* (1985) seems like an age ago. Thatcher's revolution turned Britain to the right, and away from the left. Tony Blair's achievement with New Labour was to be the first party that was Red Tory/Blue Labour, and at least return the country to some kind of centre ground. But the Church of England, meanwhile, has continued to drift rightwards. Our present preoccupation with numbers, mission, management and any apparent 'metrics of success' simply shows how pervasive Thatcherism has become, even in the church.

Filby's book examines how the rise of Thatcher was echoed by the rebirth of the Christian right in Britain, both of which were initially and forcefully opposed by the Church of England. Yet the Church of England that bravely and prophetically produced *Faith in the City* (1985) was, in the end, to meekly capitulate to the right-wing revolution orchestrated by Thatcherism. The reaction of the right was furious and strong. By November 1987, the General Synod was embroiled in a debate initiated by the Revd Tony Higton on human sexuality. *Faith in the City* had been condemned by the Tory press as 'Marxist'. And so it was, only five years after *Faith in the City*, that the National Theatre staged David Hare's excoriating play, *Racing Demon* (1990). Part of a trio of plays about British institutions, it focuses on the Church of England, and tackles the torment of the church over issues such as the ordination of gay people, and the role of evangelism in inner-city communities. And it was in *Racing Demon* that we met Lionel, the exhausted clergyman in a poor south London parish, who essentially represented the demise of Anglican social, catholic and incarnational ministry, and the emerging power of the new Christian right.

It is a pity that Hare has not returned to the subject of the church in his subsequent plays. But his *The Power of Yes* (2009) gave us a gripping narrative of a dramatist seeking to understand the devastating financial crisis of 2007–2008, which sounded the death-knell for over-hyped economic Thatcherism – the endgame of deregulation in our banking systems and financial services. Similar epitaphs have come from writers such as Graham Stewart and his *Bang! A History of Britain in the 1980s* (2013).

In all this, it's perhaps all too easy to talk about and demonise the new Christian right. But we perhaps forget that as the story of the Ethiopian famine broke into our homes through our televisions in the early 1980s, a large number of our evangelical churches were off somewhere else, captivated by the healing ministry of the Californian John Wimber, and his 'signs, wonders and church growth' agenda. In face of the most dreadful starvation on another continent, charismatic evangelicals mostly looked away for personal and ecclesial spiritual revival. Churches such as Holy Trinity Brompton, London and St. Andrew's, Chorleywood, amongst others, already prosperous and well-resourced by their congregations, became the hubs for the new revivalism. In all this, somehow, the 'wilful blindness of the age' – a phrase coined by Margaret Hefferman[5] – allowed many of these same Christians to forget that almost all disease and illness, whilst experienced as an individual problem, is caused by stubborn, shared social conditions, and most especially by poverty. Most sick people can't do much about the primary *causes* of their illness; they are rooted in their challenging and poverty-stricken social contexts.

According to the World Health Organisation, well over 90 per cent of the illnesses and diseases on this planet have a single cause: poverty. In Africa, a child dies every minute from perfectly preventable malaria-related fever. Clean the nearby water supply and you eradicate the breeding grounds for the mosquitos that spread the disease. I have sat through many healing meetings that described individuals recovering miraculously from a fever, whilst inside I would be protesting, all the while, that even if true, it was pointless when the causes of fever were not addressed. In our own country, obesity is now one of our biggest threats to health, and one of our biggest killers. It is not a disease of the rich; but the poor. One can look at maps of the United Kingdom that spell out the demographics of obesity plainly. The concentrations of obesity lie in our poorest and most disadvantaged communities. And the related consequences – cancers, heart conditions and diabetes – follow in their wake. I have been to many healing meetings that have been beautiful, pastoral and powerful. But never to one in which people went home several stone lighter.

In the 1980s, I too listened to many an eloquent sermon and testimony from Christian healers, who would tell you Jesus could heal anyone and anything. And I would then watch them take off their spectacles, put them carefully in their top pocket, and invite people for ministry. I would puzzle over how illnesses were described, and addressed. Some of the things I saw and heard were profoundly moving. But what made me struggle was the refusal of most speakers and preachers to really acknowledge the relationship between cause and effect in illness, unless it could be tied to something personal and moral. Most diseases and illnesses in the world are caused by poverty and malnutrition. I never once saw these issues addressed as causes of illness, and as either individual or social concerns – let alone 'healed'.

But the appearance of a new culture of healing movements in the churches – promising instant numerical revival, huge growth, power, prosperity (blessing)

---

5 Hefferman, *Wilful Blindness: Why We Ignore the Obvious at Our Peril*, London: Simon & Schuster, 2012.

and personal fulfilment – was part of the same tide of euphoric late capitalism that Thatcher was riding in the 1980s, and wholly unsurprising. Christian books on healing in this decade sold in their millions – mainly to middle-class consumers who already enjoyed pretty good health and wealth. Tackling social poverty was, the Tory press assured us, an out-of-date agenda for batty left-wing clerics and cranky Marxists. So, Bishop David Sheppard's powerful and popular riposte to early Thatcherite culture, *Bias to the Poor* (1984), was greeted by a chorus of dismay and disapproval by the new Christian right and the Tory press. Redemption and healing, for the Christian right, was primarily a matter of *individual choice* – and not a shared social problem for clergy and politicians to go meddling and moralising in.

As Julie Burchill once remarked on Thatcher, it wasn't for pleasure or profit that she kicked away the crutches of the poor. Thatcher genuinely believed everyone *could* walk without them – and that the best way to help people was to take the crutches away. She was doing you a favour, really. As Norman Tebbitt famously suggested, once the crutches were gone, a bicycle could help. In the aftermath of the devastating 1981 riots in Handsworth (Birmingham) and Brixton (London), Tebbit responded to a suggestion (from a youth member of his own party, actually) that rioting might be a natural reaction to unemployment: 'I grew up in the '30s with an unemployed father. He didn't riot. He got on his bike and looked for work, and he kept looking till he found it'. As Alan Bennett has remarked of England, and I might echo of the church, 'there's been so little since the 1980s that I have been happy about or felt able to endorse, you've only had to stand still to become a radical'.[6]

So Filby might have added that, where the Wesley brothers failed in reforming the Church of England, Mrs Thatcher might have unexpectedly succeeded. We now have a Church of England that prizes individual salvation through numerous individualistically-centred apologetic courses, frets forever about its statistics, subjects its own clergy to relentless performance appraisals under the guise of 'mission action plans', and follows them up with ministerial development reviews. Meanwhile, poorer dioceses find their central subsidy is slowly squeezed, and replaced by a culture of competitive and incentivising financial bids made to 'the centre' for resources and grants that prioritise numerical growth. Instead of valuing ordinary front-line parish clergy and their solid ministries, the leaders of today's church prefer to praise bespoke forms of 'privatised mission' (it must be 'new', not old), and elite forms of evangelical activism – an investment of high energy for quick returns. This church is now largely run by Thatcher's cast-offs – ex-bankers, former city executives and middle managers. You reap what you sow.

Filby ends her book with these words: 'In her crusade to raise Albion from the ashes, Thatcher ended up destroying all that was familiar. The future was not to be conservative, but consumerist; not English, but cosmopolitan; not Christian, but secular'. As the Church of England currently wrestles with its

6 Higgins, quoting Bennett in 'The Armchair Revolutionary', p. 25.

latest *Reform and Renewal* programme – a true progeny of Thatcher, if ever there was one – and with its agenda of simplification and financial rationalisation, one hopes that some wiser heads may yet still emerge in our time.

Thus, the matter in hand – and one of the main problems that needs to be addressed by the Church of England – can now be simply stated. The central issue in the current style of leadership is trust. The new regime is offering business-led, management-led and even growth-led ideologies. The counter-claim, of course, will be that the reforms are mission-led, and that mission is inherently theological. That would be fine, if a true missiology sponsored the reforms. The reality is that the progenitors of the new emphasis on mission are a combination of anxiety, displaced nostalgia, false-memory syndrome, pragmatism, managerial hubris, and a desire for tangible signs of success. A theologically-led missiology would be rooted, in contrast, in wisdom, contemplation and conversation. So, there is currently no example of theology-led reform. Articulating an alternative theological vision is not possible if the ruling elite refuse to disclose their own, and rule out discussion of others as irrelevant or unnecessary.

Propagating a new quadrilateral of impassioned fervour and spiritual zeal, linked together with secular reasoning and business-think, is an alienating and divisive platform from which to pursue an agenda for reform and renewal in the church. Camouflaging all of this under some meta-trope of 'crisis' (cue: ensuing panic), and then claiming to be the sole purveyor of the necessary counter-tropes – 'the urgency of mission', 'the need for strong, decisive leaders', the necessity of (everyone who is serious) adopting the nomenclature of 'discipleship', the non-negotiable strategies and vision that apotheosise management, organisation and growth – is, to be sure, an effective piece of politicking, and as a narrative-coup, clearly successful – at least initially. But it amounts to little more than manipulative rhetoric, whose sole purpose is to assertively lead and direct.

The *Reform and Renewal* programme lacks academic depth, scholarly wisdom, ecclesial extensity and emotional empathy. It has a dearth of compassion for the whole body of Christ. It lacks a theological point of origin. As such, the programme scatters, but does not gather; it repels many more people than it can ever draw in. It believes itself to be omni-competent and self-sufficient. Faithful resistors and questioners are branded as being in denial, as deviants or as dissidents, and they are quickly allotted a negative value. Compliant followers, however, are welcomed and rewarded. As such, the *Reform and Renewal* programme is a rather grace-less enterprise. It lacks the virtue of charity. A leadership without love, humility, vulnerability and broader collaboration is merely a bullying dictatorship. Unwholesome, it further alienates those who believe themselves to be part of the church, but won't self-identify with unsubtly coded nomenclature (i.e. 'committed disciples', 'vision', etc.) that aspires to divide believers either qualitatively, or by ecclesial ethos, and apotheosises the new leadership with their 'core priorities' and 'vision', all scripted by an exclusive power-elite.

To many people now, the Church of England and the worldwide Anglican Communion feel dislocated and somewhat lost. Buffeted by tempestuous and stormy debates on sexuality, gender, authority and power – to say nothing of priorities in management, mission and ministry, and the leadership of the church – a once confident Anglicanism appears to be anxious and vulnerable. Our purpose in this volume has been to offer a serious, constructive and critical engagement with the currents and contours that have brought the church to this point. We have attempted to sketch, assess and critique the forces currently shaping the church, and challenge them both culturally and theologically.

We have also offered something of a vision for reframing and renewal, and a way forward for the church that is simultaneously dissenting and loyal, as well as critical and constructive. In effect, arguing for a church that is rooted in vocation, theology, and seeking the Kingdom of God, rather than self-preservation or expansion. In the field of ecclesiology, many now study the Church of England and the wider Anglican Communion, and this thesis has made an attempt to offer some alternative charts and new maps for the present and future, and to act as a companion and guide to some of the key trends and forces that are currently shaping the church. Moreover, despite these challenges, I have sought to retain a hopeful vision of the church that is rooted in resilience and renewal.

Soundings and charts

So, in all of this, and as the church remains continually concerned with mission, we must be vigilant: success is not the purpose of the church. Nor is numerical growth an axiomatic certainty related to technique. We need a watchfulness; some careful husbandry – to step back, but also to be willing to plant. Not everything can grow all the time. To quote an older and much-loved text, 'we cannot persuade ourselves that the time is ripe for major works of theological construction or reconstruction . . . (but perhaps) it is a time for ploughing, not reaping'; 'it is a time for making soundings, not charts or maps'.[7] *Soundings* concludes with a startling essay from Alec Vidler, in which he questions whether the Church of England can be satisfactorily regarded as a 'religious organization'. He thinks not, and argues for a national church, in which public debate – and salient theological contributions to such debates – can make a real difference to humanity. Vidler believed that the Church of England remains well-qualified for, and less at peril of, becoming a mere 'religious denomination'. Even if its anomalous relation to the state looks quirky to some, the advantages to public life and social well-being, and to the church itself, remain substantial. The point is that the church – to be spiritually faithful to the vocation of incarnation – needs to heed the spirit of the age and the Holy Spirit, and to be engaged,

7 Vidler, *Soundings*, 1962, p. 3.

therefore, in public theology, not private church-speak. To fulfil its national vocation, it needs to be an institution.

This partly explains why, in the introduction to this book, we referred to that unusual phenomenon that sometimes occurs in significant institutions – namely some members experiencing an 'exile' within the body to which they still somehow belong. This book has been written for them, and for this time. The theme of exile is one of the great golden threads running all the way through the scriptures. The great beauty of exile is that God uses such times to chasten, to call the people to account, and to prepare them for a return. In all that, God never leaves or forsakes. In exile, the call is to wait, and be faithful. In exile, God still builds, even though the experience is often one of desolation and despair. God uses all our histories and tribulations; God does good things through exile. What the faithful need, then, is some simple re-charting – and understanding the currents that have shaped their cultural contours, before finding the map that takes them home.

Meanwhile, the sense of the dissonance of exile is set to continue. As one clergyman commented privately, 'it is as though the Christian Union have taken over the college chapel'. He added that he felt that the organisation of the church had been taken away from trusted colleagues with backgrounds in social policy and welfare, and handed over to businessmen and bankers. He concluded his elegiac musing by saying that he thought we were returning to a more conservative past – one of *Mere (Public School) Christianity* – in which the faithful were urged to talk evermore loudly about Jesus to the unconvinced and un-convicted, on the assumption that all you needed to do with people to get them to come to faith was *explain* it – again and again.

The recent report-based campaign by some evangelicals, urging Christians to talk more about Jesus,[8] rested on highly questionable assumptions, including the difference between (what the report terms) 'self-identified Christians' (this implies 'nominal'), 'non-practising Christians' (the report says 'they do not qualify as Christians' under the criteria put forward) and 'practising Christians' (whom, the report relays, are those who 'report regularly praying, reading the Bible', etc). The arrogance of these categories is somewhat extraordinary, especially since the definition of a Christian, though implied, is nowhere bluntly or clearly stated in the Bible – which is perhaps just as well, as the creeds would surely be unnecessary. Such differentiations between practising and non-practising do rather suggest that the Christian Union now runs the College Chapel. As Andrew Brown commented,[9]

> Oxbridge and public school (evangelical) Christians (did) not have any difficulty proselytising if they were doing volunteer social work on council estates at the weekends. (There, they were) outside the constraints of

8 See *Talking Jesus: Perceptions of Jesus, Christians and Evangelism in England.*
9 Brown, http://www.theguardian.com/commentisfree/2015/nov/04/christianity-evangelical-embarrassment-jesus-religion, accessed 9 August 2016.

their class. But in the hedge funds and City law firms where they work, they could not talk about their faith. It was just too embarrassing; not something people do . . . The trouble then is that very few people want to join (evangelicals) . . . The most reliable way to become an evangelical Christian, (a recent) survey found, is to be born into a family of them. Only 7% of the evangelicals surveyed had been converted in the past 11 years.

The relatively recent inward turn of the Church of England has led us into an organisational revolution characterised by an emphasis on growth and organisational development. This has, at the same time, inhibited our capacity to develop nuanced and sharp forms of public theology. Part of this organisational revolution has, in itself, led us unwittingly into the worship of growth – any apparently rationalised indices that suggest success or impact. This is prevalent in mission, of course.[10] But it has also led us into a kind of theological narcolepsy. Instead of being the church for the nation – in its broadest sense – we have developed more muted approaches to public life, or sometimes more culturally-relative ones (in the cause of mission), but lost sight of the larger goals. Indeed, growth has loomed as the only goal for some, and this is leading, I think, to some dangerous forms of cognitive dissonance in the Church of England. The church may be running serious risks in constantly talking up the prospects and possibilities for growth, and its alleged evidence. Whilst on the ground the situation is one of increasingly stretched resources, fewer stipendiary ministers, and greater pressure on clergy, churches and congregations. And the dissonance may become unbearable if the push towards the new goals continues to be asserted as non-negotiable, and in any case rooted in research.

In the meantime, the Church of England needs to develop a more thoughtful and robust account of why those outside the church don't come in. It may not be secularisation that is at fault here. Ironically, the fault may lie with those who push narrower, more tribal versions of faith.[11] The incremental increased emphasis on confessional subscription in pastoral offices – baptism, weddings and funerals – has already led to a haemorrhaging of casual adherents. We seem to have forgotten the value of familiar tradition. In our contemporary culture, which often seems to prize the 'new', and has little time for what is old or established, there are dangers for an institution such as the church. As John Templeton perceptively observed,[12] 'this time it's different' are usually the four most expensive words in the English language. A new Archbishop, borrowing heavily – tens of millions of pounds – from

---

10 See Platten, 'Stop the Bean Counters who are Meddling with our Mission', p. 27.
11 On this, see Martin, *On Secularization.*
12 cf., Bernstein, *The Four Pillars of Investing: Lessons for Building a Winning Portfolio,* Chicago, IL: McGraw-Hill Professional, 2002, p. 56.

the future, and from the Church Commissioners, to fund the 'new present', may be something the Church of England comes to reappraise in due course.

What we can say, meanwhile, is that the future is not what it used to be. It will be one that is leaner, sharper and more targeted. There will be winners and losers in the church, just like in the parable of the talents (Mt. 25: 14–30). In this parable, it was always clear that the master sought some kind of return from the servants' oversight of his original investment. The parable uses money as its vehicle for shaping our moral and visionary horizons, but to leave the interpretation of the parable as a sacral validation of some kind of savvy business dealings and entrepreneurship is to miss the parable's deeper pulse. The master does indeed reward each servant according to how each has handled their stewardship. He judges two servants as having been 'faithful', and gives them a positive reward. For the unfaithful servant who 'played it safe', however, there is chastisement and reduction. Yet the parable nowhere explains how the talents were multiplied, and we are left to guess at what might be investment born of faith, and what might constitute safety-led hording born out of fear, and simply depending on familiar behaviour patterns. Indeed, the parable asks questions about what constitutes a *good* investment?

The matter is far from straightforward. For example, Pope Francis (re-) invested the interest and commitment of the Roman Catholic Church in liberation theology – an oft-neglected branch of theology mostly eschewed by the church, especially since the surge of late capitalism in the 1980s and the rise of Reaganomics, Thatcherism and a succession of right-wing governments in South and Central America.[13] But the Pope's renewed attention to and investment in liberation theology, in the spirit of the gospels, and for the poor, is a serious venture and outlay. Who knows what reward this will yield, and when? What might the returns be for this investment?

Meanwhile, the Church of England is investing in rather tired late-capitalist tropes clustered around concepts of growth and numbers. The so-called 'talent pool' to which we referred in Part I of this book is, of course, capable of being read against the parable in several ways. But all the signs are that the Church of England is probably opting for safety, albeit clothed in the rhetoric of risk. It does not seem to be able to entertain, for example, a broader church, comprising more liberals and radicals to help shape the polity, mission and ministry of the church. It continues to marginalise lesbian, gay and transgendered individuals, for example, seeing them as a threat, not a gift (or asset) to rejoice over and invest in. Managers tend to be risk averse in a way that leaders are less inclined to be. And as we have seen, the Church of England is currently management-led. So the parable asks us, in every generation, who are the *faithful* servants here, and what might the good returns for investment eventually be? Who is *really* taking the risks in our risk-averse church, run by the new breed of ecclesial-executive managers?

13 See Yardley and Romero, 'Liberation Theology's Revival', p. 1.

It is as though the sponsors of *Reform and Renewal* have come up with a business blueprint for the church, and barring the mild forms of resistance they have so far encountered (and mostly dismissed), leading to slight modifications, they now seem set to impose their agenda. Yet the progenitors have not understood that what feeds the soul of the church, and whole the body of Christ, is *spiritual food*. Moreover, good spiritual food is something that pulls us in; it gathers us. And this is where *Reform and Renewal* fails so miserably. It is a sterile, imposed *recipe*; one that few find appetising. Yet it is being foisted on the church. In contrast, the church wants to be fed something that is rich and nourishing. It does not want a meal consisting of processed pre-packed secular-business fodder, no matter how much passionate intensity it is served with. The banquet of God's kingdom gathers us in. The Eucharist is God's grace; food for sharing. Is it really too much to ask for vision from our leadership that is robustly intellectual, theological and spiritual? And not, instead, a meagre morass of managerial pottage?

It will take some time in the Church of England to know what kind of investment in the future the Archbishop's latest *Reform and Renewal* programme really constitutes. Many will assume that as it both looks and claims to be 'new', and talks a language of gamble and risk, it must be of the faithful kind, described in the parable. But I wonder. Such interpretations look increasingly like safe and superficial readings of the parable. Because the language of *Reform and Renewal* currently in use sounds wholly reminiscent of the Thatcherite restructuring of the 1980s: blame the past, demonise any opposition, set targets, reduce core funding and replace with incentive-isation; and in all this, give due obeisance to the idol of growth. I suspect that the current alloy of passionate intensity, spiritual zeal and secular reasoning to be found in the new breed of ecclesial-executive managers is very far from being cutting edge; instead, it represents a retreat into pallid forms of neo-conservatism.

The future of the Church of England is, so it seems, lost somewhere in the past. Given that the current leadership of the church was so strongly shaped by the 1980s and its ideology, we should not be surprised. As Joseph Stiglitz argues, sometimes the drastic solutions proposed to deal with apparently drastic crises do more harm than good. And they were never drastic solutions; they were old ones, dressed in contemporary rhetoric; old wine in new wineskins (to reverse the metaphor of Mk. 2: 22 and Mt. 9: 17). Pleasing platitudes that make their mark today are no substitute for a deep, self-aware leadership that critiques contemporary culture, rather than merely being captivated by it.[14] The parable of the talents suggests that the unfaithful servant merely stuck to methods that were entirely familiar and predictable, and which he or she believed could not fail. I fear that the new *Reform and Renewal* programmes might be, after all, just another version of that same investment strategy. We shall see.

14 Stiglitz, *The Great Divide*.

In summary, the time may be ripe for the Church of England, and indeed the wider Anglican Communion, to recover its broad, public and institutional identity; and to engage more critically with the secular paradigms of organisational theory and practice that have shaped so much of its life in the modern era. To do this, the Anglican Communion and the Church of England will need to become more *mindful* – to become more patient and reflective, so that the breath of the body of Christ and that of the Holy Spirit flows through the whole to all its members. It needs to become less of the 'poor little talkative Christianity' (a jibe that comes from the character Mrs. Moore in E.M. Forster's 1924 novel, *A Passage to India*, in which she hears an echo in a cave and realises Christians believe this to be revelatory, whereas they are in fact only hearing their own voices). In contrast, Psalm 8 calls the church to a place of contemplation and awe; to sit in silence, and pause; less talk, more prayer.

9   Old maps for new territories?

Bill Bryson, in his *Notes From a Small Island*, offers the following observation about one of our most famous maps, which is also an iconic piece of design:

> the London Underground Map . . . what a piece of perfection it is, created in 1931 by a forgotten hero named Harry Beck, an out-of-work draughtsman who realised that when you are under ground, it doesn't matter where you are. Beck saw . . . that as long as the stations were presented in their right sequence with their interchanges clearly delineated, he could freely distort scale, indeed abandoning it altogether. He gave his map the orderly precision of an electrical wiring system, and in so doing created an entirely new, imaginary London that has very little to do with the disorderly geography of the city above.[1]

Beck, of course, was also a trained electrician. So it was no accident that he laid out his map like a circuit diagram. He knew that as long as the lines and junctions connected, the 'disorderly geography of the city above' need not be a problem to those who followed a simple circuit diagram. The map, in other words, is an attempt to confer intelligibility on what cannot be easily seen or understood. It is not simply about navigation. Rather, it is also about orientation, imagination and innovation. It is an aid to reflection and potential ways of seeing.

So, what does a future map for the Church of England and the wider Anglican Communion look like? Are there lines and junctions – to borrow from Beck's skilful cartography – that can be traced? We have seen some evidence of connections. Whether the presenting issue is the rise of managerial power and executive authority, the ascendancy of money, sex and power as problems, church-going and secularisation, or the apparent failure of catholic cohesion, the consistent thread that runs throughout is how churches relate to contemporary culture. This is an issue for Anglicans at every level.

For example, an empathetic, culturally-resonant stance on same-sex marriage in the USA will, on the whole, lead a majority of US Episcopalians to

---

1 Bryson, *Notes from a Small Island*, p. 54.

affirm and bless same-sex unions. This is becoming so in the United Kingdom too – though there is a dissonance here between what congregations will support, and what bishops will countenance. But because Anglicanism is global, the consequence of local decisions and actions is keenly felt across the world. Of course, no-one expects Anglicans in Uganda or Tanzania to practise their polity in the same way that Anglicans do in the USA or Canada. Most of the beliefs and behaviours are similar – recognisably a familial morphology – but there are regional variations. As we noted earlier, Terry Holmes reminds us that the local variables in Christian expression and witness should not obscure the shared, central core of our faith:

> There is an inevitable course to our religious profession . . . that course leads to living in the world as God sees the world. We can debate the trivial points, but the vision is largely clear. To love God is to relieve the burden of all who suffer. The rest is a question of tactics. [2]

What is intriguing about the early years of the twenty-first century, however, is how different faiths – and here I include Christianity – have retreated from public faith and full engagement with contemporary culture, to be superseded by smaller niche groups of believers who have become self-absorbed in creating their own micro-cultures. The older meaning of culture – associated with civility and the free exchange of ideas – has become compressed into potentially destructive zones such as nationalism or tribalism.

There are many downsides to the comforts of tribalism. The ensuing lack of catholicity means that the ecclesial and theological breadth of a global church turns, instead, into something far narrower and more insular. The capacity of the church to engage with the complexity of the challenges presented by contemporary culture is significantly reduced, which erodes its public appeal and identity. The tribalism cannot avoid favouritism, which in turn breeds suspicion and nepotism, which then go on to sponsor demoralisation.

Anglicans are perhaps unusual as a religious group. They are not tribal, in the sense that can sometimes describe nonconformist groups, such as Methodists or Jewish groups. They are not tribal and bounded, with borders, in the same way that English Catholics can be said to be. Anglicans have no distinctive culture – not in terms of mode of dress, or the like. They seem to span social classes, and their tastes are wide, deep and varied. But Anglicans have produced distinctive cultural artefacts – music, poetry, literature, architecture, etc. They also have a distinctive mode of behaviour. They orientate towards accommodation, and are of mild proclivity. They are instinctively inclusive rather than proactive and proclaiming any inclusivity. They are habitually open and generous. They struggle with creedal formulae that act as a barrier, or amount to a form of exclusion.

2 Holmes, *What is Anglicanism?*, p. 95.

It is my contention that the Church of England, and to an extent global Anglicanism, has developed into a much more tribal polity in recent years. The irony of an increasing accent appealing to mission and evangelism is that the language and supporting conceptualisation often tended towards being tribally-coded tropes which, far from being inclusive and uniting, tend to be alienating and divisive. The relatively recent appeal to the language of 'discipleship' is a case in point. On one level the concept of a disciple seems plainly biblical. The word appears in the gospels (often) and in the Book of Acts. But the word does not feature in the remainder of the New Testament. The current use of the term – in a plethora of new and draft documents from within the Church of England – gives a range of values and attributions to the word, some of which are intended, and some of which may be implicit. Zeal and activism are strongly implied, but this alienates many who once supported the church, but who may now feel they are not 'real' or 'proper' Christians. 'Going to church' and 'following Christ' – two 'traditional' tropes – have been quickly replaced by phrases such as 'becoming missionary disciples'. Those who (think they) understand this phrase are, de facto, members of the tribe (i.e. chosen); those who flinch from such phrases are left on the edge, or perhaps even outside the church. In all this, the church, ironically in the name of mission and evangelism, moves from being a broad institution to becoming a narrow organisation.

There are winners and losers in this development. The winners are those conservative elements of the church that have sought to leverage the anxieties of developing nations, in order to shore up their own agenda in the developed world. This has been most apparent on the issue of sexuality, where small fringe elements in the Anglican Communion – notably Sydney Anglicans and some conservatives in the USA and in the Church of England – have turned sexuality into a global issue of mission and identity, through amplifying their concerns through African Anglican Provinces. Forms of funding support have also strengthened this new alliance, which finds its expression in groups such as ACNA, GAFCON and the like.

But this era is, I suspect, temporary. Partly because, though the battles on sexuality continue to smoulder in the Church of England, the war is largely lost. Developed nations have largely embraced same-sex unions and marriages, and are now seeking a national church that will celebrate this. And this is where the strength of Anglicanism, oddly, comes into its own. The resilience of the Anglican tradition lies deep – in dispersed, extensive and localised contexts. Parishes pay little attention to the hierarchies that try to usher in a change of tempo and timbre. They move forward at their own speed, being the incarnate and enculturated expression of faith in their communities. The art, liturgy, poetry and aesthetics of Anglican polity continue to tower above new and vogueish innovations. History will judge the contemporary currents shaping the church. The Anglican tradition is not only resilient, but also constantly replenishing, and renewing. It can accommodate the present, as much as it also has the wisdom to discern and resist those forces that would undermine it. All this just takes its time.

There is also one further problem to note. Those that are the 'urgent voices that speak of crisis' are often the ones to gain from the sense of panic that they propagate. Those who proclaim a crisis are frequently the principal beneficiaries of the ensuing action. This dynamic is certainly apparent in the Church of England. The prioritising of mission over ministry, and evangelism as the pre-eminent form of mission, has led to a skewed leadership in the church. Moreover, this is a leadership that does not attend to the value of theological diversity and balance. The result is an assertive conservatism that constricts the identity of the church – causing, ironically, greater public disinvestment, making the evangelistic task that much harder as the church becomes narrower. So, the Anglican capacity to hold together different theological perspectives and intense, competing convictions within a pattern of common prayer needs to be retrieved and restored. The Anglican Communion also needs to read its local contexts more deeply and honestly, if it is to hold on to any kind of full, visible unity.[3] 'Crisis', when written in Mandarin, is a character that represents both danger and opportunity: and Anglicanism faces both these possibilities.

Crisis? What crisis?

In terms of crisis, the worldwide Anglican Communion woke up in the autumn of 2015 to some new proposals on how it might imagine its collective life and identity, and address its crises. The invitation from the Archbishop of Canterbury to the Primates – to attend a gathering in January 2016 – looked straightforward, on one level. The gathering would be a discussion to explore common issues of concern (e.g., religiously-motivated violence, the protection of children and vulnerable adults and the environment), as well as, of course, to examine more divisive issues (e.g., human sexuality).[4] The media reported the proposed gathering in a relatively straightforward way. But the media also picked up on the more implied and refracted proposals from the Archbishop of Canterbury, namely suggesting that the ties in the Communion 'might be loosened' to preserve unity; 'all can go their own way a bit more'; and that the Communion might mean, in future, 'separate bedrooms, but not divorce'.[5] In effect, the suggestion appeared to be 'living apart together' – an attempt to allow western liberals and conservative Africans to cohabit, but not necessarily on agreeable, consensual terms.

3 See Kane, 'Tragedies of Communion: Seeking Reconciliation amid Colonial Legacies.'
4 See: http://www.archbishopofcanterbury.org/articles.php/5613/archbishop-of-canterbury-calls-for-primates-gathering, Wednesday 16 September 2015, accessed 9 August 2016. See also Bingham, 'Welby's Way'. Bingham suggests that a quasi 'Orthodox Model' of global Anglican polity was being tabled by Lambeth Palace, freeing individual provinces to disagree with one another, or not even to recognise it – but to still have a central focus of, with the role of the Archbishop of Canterbury effectively being reconfigured as a kind of Ecumenical Patriarch.
5 Orr, 'Comment', p. 23; see also Bates, 'Living Apart Together', pp. 8–9.

Put another way, claiming the same address, but living in different wings of the house. Possibly more than this, in fact: the same address, but separate flats within the same dwelling. (So, the proposal seemed to imply some kind of agreement on shared utilities and service agreements – but otherwise living separate lives.)

It will take time to process the implications of the gathering of the Anglican Primates from around the world that eventually took place in January 2016. Differences over women priests and bishops, sexuality, and more besides, have certainly exacerbated pronounced differences between those parts of the Anglican Communion found in the developing world, and those from the developed world. Yet to some of the more seasoned commentators on ecclesiastical matters, the adaptive ethos of Anglicanism has probably been, once again, undervalued. Anglicans have lived with crises-related issues that threatened unity in every century of their existence. Rather than wearying of such inner struggles, Anglicans appear to weather these storms rather well. As a church, its polity – irenic, mild, temperate – often wins through, and against passionate intensity.

That said, geographical boundaries mean rather less for churches today than they used to. Local and provincial forms of Christianity always, until recently, experienced a tension between being both moral and territorial communities. But the advent of easy travel and social media now means that moral communities can quickly form that pay little attention to territoriality. Congregations and churches are increasingly related by their shared affinities and agreed moral coherence. Interestingly, Anglicanism is not, and never has been, one vast, catholic continent. It is more like an *archipelago* – a connection of provincial islands that share doctrinal, liturgical and cultural ties. Might the Communion become a kind of Federation, in just the same way that the British Empire has become a Commonwealth? Anglicanism is undoubtedly global, but may now be too diverse to be centrally or collegially governed in a manner that guarantees unequivocal unity. So, overlapping or extended episcopal oversight *might* be possible in a church that has always valued a degree of pluralism. Some congregations (note, not parishes) that can't accept women priests or bishops in the Church of England already have this option.

So, if we have understood the Archbishop's proposal correctly, he invited his fellow Archbishops to quietly drop the chimera of 'Communion', with the future identity of Anglicanism becoming more like a 'family of churches'. The Anglican family name could, in future, be used rather like the Baptist family name – a shared essence continues, but the prefix (American, Southern, Reformed, Strict and Particular and so forth) indicates the flavouring. In more cartographical terms, the Anglican Communion could be visualised as a vast mansion, with the addition of Evangelical and Catholic wings. It remains a large stately home – albeit one in which the vast rooms are now being made into self-contained flats, like many grand houses today. Everyone still has the same official address and shares the imposing exterior and frontage, but different internal relations within the 'storied dwelling' mean the union is not as it once was.

That said, I have three concerns about the Archbishop's apparent proposals and the implied direction of travel. First, there was no sign of the Anglican Consultative Council being referred to. The Archbishop's initiative felt like it might be born out of impatience, frustration and exasperation, even though it was being marketed as potentially visionary. Holding complex tensions and competing convictions together is what Archbishops are supposed to do. We need them to model patience and wisdom, not terminate tensions through executive managerial short-cuts.

Second, the invitation from Lambeth Palace placed a stress on the Bible, when 'properly interpreted'.[6] This is a tetchy phrase, and begs questions about coded affirmations and denigrations being buried in the text. There is no explicit acknowledgement of the role of reason and tradition in shaping church polity (or the role of the Holy Spirit in these).

Third, the assumption in the 2015 Lambeth invitation was that distinctive cultures, though different from country-to-country and continent-to-continent, are homogeneous in their own local and regional contexts. They are not, of course, as many of our cities and towns support a highly variegated ecology of parish churches – some that are passionately conservative, others avowedly liberal, and others just mixed. In any parish, anywhere, some parishioners are happily married; some in civil partnerships; some straight, some LGBT; some ethnic, some white. You get the picture: parishes are just a microcosm of the wider Communion.

Anglicans will need, in the future, bishops and Archbishops who can hold these tensions together, not just allow divisions to grow, people to go their separate ways, and tribal enclaves to develop. We will need skilled ecclesial navigators; good episcopal leaders who can chart and re-chart ways forward. And these charts will vary from province-to-province, and even from diocese-to-diocese. Our aspiration is a United Kingdom of faith diversity, not a post-war Balkanisation of theological differences. Irrespective of the Primates' rather terse communique from January 2016,[7] my guess is that any further degrees of separation will not necessarily mean schism, let alone divorce. Those family members that want the space to individuate should perhaps be given some licence. Eighty-five million members, in 38 provinces, all living under one roof, might be a bit too stifling for the twenty-first century. But to be clear, a pan-territorial federation of churches is not the same – theologically or ontologically – as a worldwide Communion.[8]

---

6 http://www.archbishopofcanterbury.org/articles.php/5613/archbishop-of-canterbury-calls-for-primates-gathering, accessed 9 August 2016.

7 http://www.anglicannews.org/news/2016/01/statement-from-primates-2016.aspx, accessed 9 August 2016.

8 See Bates, 'Back from the Brink'.

'High, Broad and Low' – old maps for today's terrain

One way forward here might be to return to some old maps, and reckon with their value. The temporary triumph of neo-conservative Anglicanism has witnessed a remarkable change in the 'mental map' that the average Anglican carries around inside her or his head. It used to be a simple type of triptych: High, Broad or Low. The High Church party had a distinctive theology, vocabulary, liturgical aesthetic – and even, for clergy, modes of dress. The Low Church party was just as easy to identify, yet quite different. And in the middle, was the Broad Church – neither High nor Low, and capable of blending and infusing the best elements of either wing – it was, crucially, passionately committed to holding the centre ground. The Broad Church was, at its best, the primary vehicle of generous, orthodox, inclusive Anglicanism. It was not Laodicean – a tepid compromise of warm, balmy Catholicism with the chilly climes of Calvinism. The Broad Church was simply warm – but also reflective, cool and capacious. It was an embodiment of the faith in the church as an open, non-membership-based institution. It eschewed sectarianism, and sought, above all, to serve the mass of society. It was temperate and mild – and so perfectly suited to the pastoral climates it served.

The neo-conservative revolution of the last 50 years – the last three decades of the twentieth century, and the first two decades of the twenty-first century – have seen both the High and Low wings of Anglicanism entirely out-narrate the middle ground (i.e. Broad Church), and re-brand it as 'liberal'. And in turn, this has been followed swiftly by the term 'liberal' being allotted a consistently negative value in ecclesial climes. For Catholic conservatives, and a handful of conservative Evangelicals, this began with Gender Wars (i.e. the debate on the ordination of women). The vast majority of clergy and laity who desired (and eventually voted for) women priests found themselves re-positioned as 'liberals'. On sexuality, a gradual acceptance of lesbian and gay Christians, and an eventual (still growing) acceptance of same-sex marriages has also led to the Broad Church and middle ground being labelled, once again negatively, as 'liberal'.

What is intriguing in all of this is that this Broad Church element within Anglicanism merely holds sensible views on gender, and progressive (note, not radical) views on sexuality. The Broad Church, such as it is, tends to be entirely orthodox on creeds, doctrines (e.g., the physical resurrection of Jesus), articles of faith, liturgical proclivities, church polity, Christian practice and canon law. Broad Church elements within Anglicanism tend to be, if anything, theologically orthodox. And they view the High and Low elements of the church as rather more sectarian – and inclined towards 'membership-speak' – than the more inclusive, 'public' ministry that they would seek to embody and practice.

Maps, as we indicated earlier in this volume (cf., the introduction), can be deceptive social constructions of reality. And the shift from high-middle-low to a crude Liberal-Conservative dialectic has been one of the ecclesial great confidence tricks of the last 50 years within Anglican polity. But like all such tricks, it had a purpose. It has been an attempt to persuade people who inhabit the wings (whether high or low, catholic or evangelical) that the *true church* and *real faith* is only to be found in their own more intense, sectarian expression that they represent. And that the middle-ground – which is largely where the population as whole resides, with their innate spiritual proclivities – are in fact starved of 'real' religion and faith, and now need evangelising or catechising. Indeed, secularisation, and the failure of evangelisation or catechisation, is often (still) blamed on the centre ground of the Broad Church. But what in fact has happened, as a result of the inexorable momentum of this coup?

In her prescient and prophetic book,[9] the Dutch ecclesiologist Mady Thung suggests that national churches in northern Europe have come under increasing pressure in the post-war years to become 'organisations' – 'nervous activity and hectic programmes . . . constantly try(ing) to engage' members in an attempt to reach 'non-members'. She contrasts the 'organisational' model and its frenetic activism with the 'institutional' model of the church – the latter offering, instead, contemplative, aesthetic and liturgical frameworks that take longer to grow, are often latent for significant periods of time, but which, she argues, may be more culturally resilient and conducive than those of the activist-organisational model.

Thung draws on interlocutors within the realm of contextual studies that are rarely read and understood these days in theology or ecclesiology – Philip Selznick, Gibson Winter (his work critiquing the 'captivity' of the suburban church), for example – to name but two. But of particular interest to us here is Thung's assertion that the organisational-activist model of the church is, itself, a by-product and captive of a highly-secularised society. In her thinking, the organisational-activist model is a corruption of the true church.[10] It does not serve society, or the kingdom; but rather registers membership, growth and efficiency as tangible signs of productivity. Success – in entirely explicable worldly terms – becomes an apotheosis.

Thung's map-making drew on older chartings of how religion was to be mapped in society. Weber and Troeltsch's perception of 'church' versus 'sect' is, in one sense, all that Thung is developing here: 'organisational-activism' versus 'institutional-contemplative' dialectic. But there is more to Thung's work than this, since she sees that the quality of charisma (on which Weber had much more to say) is located differently in her two models. In the 'organisational-activist' model, charisma resides in the gathered congregation and the effectiveness of the pastor or priest. In contrast, charisma in the 'institutional-contemplative' model resides in the buildings, aesthetics

9 Thung, *The Precarious Organisation: Sociological Explorations of the Church's Mission and Structure.*
10 Ibid., p. 32.

and timeless rituals. The 'organisational-activist' model requires constant renewal; raising, indeed, newness and relevance to the level of apotheosis. The 'institutional-contemplative' model roots charisma in unchanging and eternal truths, which are reified in music, liturgy and architecture.

Now, the 'organisational-activist' model produces significant growth – and sometimes rapidly. But it does so at a cost. For it risks the gradual alienation of the population at large, who are seeking not activism and an endless series of new forms of engagement. But rather, solid, reliable institutions that echo with permanence and eternity. So the 'institutional-contemplative' model can invest in constancy; but it also risks complacency, as well as being ignored for significant periods of time by the same population – who simply take its presence and permanence for granted, but do very little about it.

Thung's thesis essentially speaks into the situations and contexts that the Church of England has been immersed in over the last 50 years. The Decade of Evangelism (proclaimed and championed in the 1990s by the then Archbishop of Canterbury, George Carey) arose out of an 'organisational-activist' mindset that assumed a clear division in society between church members and non-members. The activist programme for that decade, perhaps inevitably, resulted in far *fewer* people coming to church. (To paraphrase President Ronald Reagan, if you are explaining yourself, you are losing, not winning.) This correlates with Thung's thinking: it is not Jesus or the gospel that was in fact being rejected, but rather the explicit activism of the messengers (and granted, their much narrower 'take' on the message, and perhaps especially their *style* of belief and apologetics).[11]

Two more recent examples in the Church of England of this (evangelical) 'organisational-activist' mindset *widening* the gap between the church and the population it serves have included the 'Talking Jesus' campaign[12] and the 'Just Pray' cinema advertisement.[13] Both were roundly rejected by society, but produced high-levels of indignation from the church (e.g., 'the world is becoming more secular and anti-Christian'). Both examples highlight two of the three models of the church available in western Europe at present – Institutional, Gathered and Mystical – but the Church of England seems only to be able to invest in the gathered. It frequently complains about the cost of the institutional (and ignores its powerful contribution to mission through presence, engagement and pastoral practice). And the Church of England, despite its investment in vogueish forms of 'fresh expressions',

11 Recent research suggests that evangelical Christian Unions may in fact put more people off Christianity than they actually convert to faith. See Guest et al., *Christianity and the University Experience: Understanding Student Faith*. See also: https://www.dur.ac.uk/news/newsitem/?itemno=20988, accessed 9 August 2016.

12 http://www.theguardian.com/commentisfree/2015/nov/04/christianity-evangelical-embarrassment-jesus-religion, accessed 9 August 2016.

13 https://www.churchofengland.org/media-centre/news/2015/11/church-of-england-%E2%80%9Cbewildered%E2%80%9D-by-cinema-ban-on-lord%E2%80%99s-prayer.aspx, accessed 9 August 2016.

seems not to comprehend the aesthetic possibilities of the mystical church – despite clear signs of growth in cathedral congregations, where art, beauty and mystery are abundant.

So, Thung points to several paradoxes in mission here; and especially for national churches, such as the Church of England, that are seeking to be the national church for their country. First, that the more explicit evangelism and mission becomes, the *weaker* the church appears in the eyes of the public. Second, a non-member-based institution (it is there for everyone, independent of their affinity) will *narrow* its appeal if it tries to become too much like an organisational member-based body. Third, an institutional church that is there for everyone will *decline* if it moves towards being a highly delineated, differentiated and *gathered* community, rather than being a *broad*, dispersed community that supports multiple forms of affinity (e.g., patterns of belonging, attendance, ranges of belief, etc.). Fourth, the harder the gathered church tries to connect – through explicit mission, preaching, apologetics and evangelistic discourse – the further non-members *retreat* from the church. Moreover, there is a consequential *increase* in the number of actual committed members who then loosen their affinity to the church, or decide to leave.

As things stand at present in the Church of England, there is a bifurcation in ordained leadership. Virtually all the bishops are exponents of the 'organisational-activist' model of church – and much of this leadership is quite bipolar in character. They are, in turn, supported by laypeople from business and commercial backgrounds, for whom 'organisational-activism' is *obviously* what the church needs to adopt. Whilst in contrast, most cathedral Deans, the majority of parish clergy and chaplains, and the silent majority of laypeople, are exponents of the 'institutional-contemplative' model, and its variants. This bifurcation is now beginning to have significant implications for theology and for ministerial practice. Three brief examples will suffice to illustrate this.

First, the *Report of the Evangelism Task Force* to General Synod,[14] set up by the Archbishop of Canterbury, demonstrates high levels of anxiety-inspired activism, but little in the way of deeper theological reflection. The Report is laced with activist rhetoric, which in turn is wrapped in spiritually mawkish language – 'sharing the news of the beautiful shepherd is itself beautiful, a delicate, gentle and rich privilege' (p. 2). The preface continues (p. 5):

> Sharing Christ with others is a joyful, encouraging and empowering feature of being a Christian disciple. Ours is the privilege of pointing others to the glory of God in Christ. Most of us only know Jesus because someone took the trouble to bear witness to God's love revealed in Him. The moment of evangelism is the specific proclamation of the good news of Jesus Christ to another person or people. It is undertaken for God and

14 Report of the Evangelism Task Force, GS 2015.

with God, with news from God about God. There is no greater honour than bearing this Good News to another, no greater privilege than seeing others respond to the Good News, and no greater challenge than to be captivated by the urgency of this vocation. This urgency is apparent to us as we look around our families, our neighbourhoods, our places of work and our nation. So many, young and old, rich and poor, live without knowing the love of God in Jesus Christ.

There is nothing here to indicate that the church or Christians might meet God in the poor, the outcast, the stranger and the prisoner. The underlying assumptions in this revealing preface are that most people come to faith through an explicit proclamation. That Christ is not known outside the church, and faith and encounters with God not possible until this is actively engineered by activists ('the moment of evangelism is the specific proclamation . . .'). And finally that evangelism is the greatest challenge – and so both our premier and most urgent vocation. The Preface therefore rests on several heterodox misunderstandings of the nature of God and of the *Missio Dei* – but it is precisely what one would expect from an organisational-activist mindset that has already decided the institutional-contemplative model has no value.

Second, the Report on *Resourcing Ministerial Education*[15] largely depends on functionalist, corporate-business language for describing the church and its ministry, and is wholly lacking in a theology or spirituality of formation:

> The guiding vision of *Resourcing Ministerial Education* is of a growing Church . . .
>
> helping bishops and their leadership teams articulate and implement strategies for a hopeful future . . . helping create the conditions for dioceses to flourish . . . simplifying legal constraints and removing some of the barriers to change, creating additional financial resources to support activities intended to foster growth and developing major training programmes for current and future leaders within the church . . .
>
> (p. 3)

Intriguingly, there is no theology of formation for clergy or lay ministry; and as we have observed earlier in this book, no spiritual vision or theological point of origin for the work envisaged, other than some rather simplistic and eclectic appeals to a handful of scriptural verses. As a document of the church, it is, like the one briefly discussed above, shamefully inadequate and embarrassingly mawkish. The vision in the Report on *Resourcing Ministerial Education*, such as it is, merely proceeds out of its own self-declared agenda of haste and urgency, and assumes that

---

15 GS 2020 – Reform and Renewal: Resourcing Ministerial Education (https://www.churchofeng-land.org/media/2442565/gs_2020_-_resourcing_ministerial_education.pdf) accessed 9 August 2016.

the activism it prescribes for the church must be the answer. Anything of value in the institutional-contemplative model of ecclesiology is entirely ignored – if indeed, it was ever comprehended. Thus, both the *Report of the Evangelism Task Force* and *Resourcing Ministerial Education* assume that pastoral care and liturgy – primary callings and tasks for clergy – are in fact distractions from activist-led evangelism.

Third, the approach adopted by the Archbishop of Canterbury to resolve the pan-provincial differences on sexuality across the Anglican Communion is also developed out of this same uncritical 'organisational-activist' approach. The Archbishop attempted to resolve the differences through a combination of personal charm and charisma, pastoral intervention, political process and pragmatism. Of course, none of these on their own, or in any combination, was ever going to grapple with the deep theological and ecclesiological issues Anglicans face as a Communion. The final communique from the Primates gave very mixed messages.[16] The actual agreed text between the Primates does not mention or affirm lesbian or gay Christians (Addendum A). The text that introduces the agreed statement, however, does take some steps in addressing homophobia, and condemns the repression of people on the basis of their sexuality. However, it is not clear if this preface is an agreed text of the Primates, or intended as a more conciliatory retrospective. The media coverage of the January 2016 gathering made much of the 'remarkable' achievement of all the Primates staying together for the week. And on the face of it, this did look like a significant development. However, it later emerged that Archbishop Foley Beach (head of ACNA) and a number of other GAFCON Primates had left early, and so could not easily have been signatories to the agreed statement. This suggests that the claimed achievement of unity was in fact a 'spun' story from Lambeth, especially as Foley Beach claimed that a number of Primates left early when the Episcopal Church of America was not compelled to repent.[17]

So although the political and public relations skills of Lambeth Palace appear to have succeeded where others might have failed, it would seem that the gathering of the Primates was very far from being an unqualified success. Arguably, the Archbishop needed to resource the Primates' Gathering in January 2016 with a more binocular approach, developing a theology of the Communion out of an 'institutional-contemplative' approach to ecclesial life, and not just seeking to run the processes with organisational-activist methodologies. The failure to do this may, oddly, now lead to much deeper and more-lasting damage than is currently visible. Since the approach to the Communion was 'something to be fixed', (though undoubtedly well-intended), it showed that the body and its complexity was not truly comprehended from the outset. The Lambeth Palace staff needed to reflect for longer and more

16 http://www.primates2016.org/articles/2016/01/15/communique-primates/, accessed 9 August 2016.
17 http://www.anglicanchurch.net/?/main/page/1170, accessed 9 August 2016.

deeply, build new bridges, and engage in deeper wisdom, before embarking on a crusade of repair. Ultimately, this was another step backwards for the church, whilst many in the world continue to move forward. Indeed, it is hard to see how the meeting of 2016 was any better than the Lambeth Conference of 1998 – less acrimonious, to be sure, but no more progressive. As for some hope – and a message of justice and peace to LGBT Christians – this represented a dreadful missed opportunity in terms of national mission and international ecclesial credentials.

So, whilst the Archbishop of Canterbury made a personal apology, in the final press conference, for the way the church has treated LGBT people, the actual communique sent out by the Primates' meeting focussed on its decision to suspend the only part of the Anglican Communion which has been most supportive of LGBT people – the Episcopal Church of the USA. In fact, the communique didn't even speak of an apology. It only referred to 'expressing profound sorrow' – a self-justifying phrase that is resonant of 'sorry – but you made me do this to you'. Actions tend to speak much louder than words, and the Primates' actions completely undermined the Archbishop of Canterbury's verbal apology. The Primates, as a group, faced with their own disunity on sexuality, turned on the one scapegoat most of them could agree on – the Episcopal Church.

Turning, therefore, to the local church level, the continued investment in 'membership-speak' leads to incremental alienation. Several examples could be cited here, but branding a congregation 'the whole baptised people of God', and tasking them with mission and evangelism makes all kinds of assumptions about who is in the church, and who might reside outside. Such branding also rides roughshod over the multifarious motives that people may have for being in the church. Perhaps they did not join to become activists, or to be organised? Perhaps they simply joined out of a deep need that may take years to come to the surface, but which in the meantime is addressed by profound epiphanies, deep pastoral care and prayer? Not every person that comes to church wants to be dubbed an apprentice-evangelist, disciple or spiritual warrior. Some just come to feed, and be still. Some just come because there is nowhere else like church that just allows you to come and be, and sit in the presence of a people and a God that will love you – unconditionally. Such things may be possible in a restored and renewed model of the 'institutional-contemplative' church; but less so in the organisational-activist church.

But in the meantime, the grip of the organisational-activists over the last 50 years seems to have been inexorable. Nowhere has this been more sharply felt than in liturgy, and especially the 'occasional' or 'pastoral' offices – baptisms, weddings and funerals. In the Church of England, baptism of infants has declined sharply as organisational-activists have sought to control and limit access to this rite, turning it into a ritual reserved exclusively for 'members'. A once public, locally and familially resonant symbolic-spiritual act used to be done mainly at times that worked for the families and communities, the rituals bringing them together. But baptisms, or

Christenings, have been steadily 'privatised'. The ritual has been relocated and folded into longer liturgies within the context of church services, and that operate out of 'gathered' models of the church, rather than institutional ones. Thus the baptisms can often only take place on Sunday mornings when the regular congregation gathers. The reasoning for this is that it is necessary to *induct* all the baptism party into an *explicit* Christian narrative and experience – the baptism being deemed insufficient here, as it may just be 'custom' or 'folk religion' that non-believers and the half-committed avail themselves of. Thus, the nascent distrust of the church towards those seeking christenings is clearly, even intentionally, communicated – precisely what the activists propose. And with the christening ceremony now securely wrapped within a much, much longer liturgy, the seeds of alienation and sectarianism begin to germinate. Add to this the strangeness of the baptism taking place in front of dozens of witnesses who may not know the child or family, and the estrangement only grows. The forced induction often alienates the baptism party – with the result that the very opposite of induction is achieved.[18] Similar observations could be made of weddings and funerals, where the lack of flexibility by the Church of England, coupled to a lack of imagination, and a capped limit on any largesse in spiritual vision (too much induction in too short-a-time once again being attempted in the liturgies), has simply increased the sense of alienation between church and people.

As Thung observes, wryly, the organisational-activists often 'unwittingly become captive to mundane powers' and 'this religious language' (of theirs) only serves legitimising purposes. Moreover, the initiative and its trajectory may turn out to be worse than actually doing nothing. So, she continues:

> An organised church must be aware that the actual 'people of God' may reside outside its boundaries and it is a people whose names and numbers are unknown to (us). The point of correct organising is, that one tries to obtain as great a coincidence as possible of the 'manifest' and the 'latent' church.[19]

Thung suggests that the interests of a national church may be best served by a leadership that understands, articulates and practises the 'institutional-contemplative' model, but also makes space for the 'organisational-activist' approach. In terms of mission, this is the best blend or calibration of energy and gifts. But the weaker and more insecure a national church becomes, the more likely it is to forget its institutional identity. It will try and compensate

18 The post-war emphasis on moving baptisms from Sunday afternoons to a being part of a normal Sunday morning service must be partly responsible for the decline in baptisms overall. Moreover, it takes a long time to reverse this decline. In one parish I worked in for seven years, the parish priest conducted an average of 300 baptisms a year in 1940 – most of which were done on Sunday afternoons. The figure for 1990 was 30 – all conducted in the main Sunday service.

19 Thung, *The Precarious Organisation*, p. 325.

for this loss by increasing frenetic, activist reforms and initiatives – often clothed in missional language. But all this will do, suggests Thung, is drive more people further away, consolidate a tribal and sectarian identity, and increase the gap between church and world. The Church of England's journey down this road is already well advanced. There is little commendable public theology, and far too much spiritual 'in-talk'.

Conclusion

The implications of this for the Church of England will take time to absorb. If the church continues to be dominated and led by the organisational-activists, it will become more gathered, less institutional, and therefore narrower and smaller. The attempts to evangelise and organise will become ever more frenetic, resulting in a much wider gap opening up between the church and the population it serves. This, of course, may well suit those who espouse a dialectical liberal-conservative map. The 'liberals' – who of course don't really exist as a unified and coherent group, paradoxically – will always be the 'straw man' to blame for the failure of the neo-conservative agenda to progress and take root. All this means the church will become more tribal and sectarian, with those who believe in the 'middle ground' continuing to be allotted the negative value of 'liberal'.

For those who hold a different map for the future, however, and want to see a Broad Church flourish, and the institutional model renewed and re-energised, with confidence in Anglican aesthetics and the missional power and potential of pastoral presence in our communities rather than activism, there is a considerable challenge ahead. It is not at all clear that the Church of England, or the wider Anglican Communion, will see these old maps re-emerge to help us chart the new cultural challenges and contextual territories of the twenty-first century. Time will tell.

Conclusion

Mady Thung's thesis, discussed in the previous chapter, advances an argument that pivots on the shortcomings of the 'missionary church model'. Namely, a paradigm that risks becoming narrower and more sectarian; working harder, but failing faster, because it locates its energy and charisma in the leadership and the faithful. The institutional church, in contrast, understands that the charisma and energy (of God) lies in the church as a more aesthetic body – not simply with a small group of leaders and 'members'. And although the institutional church model may struggle with numbers sometimes, it can last longer, and is ultimately stronger.

There may already be some evidence for this, with urban and suburban churches arguably more precarious in their longevity than their more resilient rural church cousins. Indeed, the rural churches may be emerging as a new paradigm of resilience and adaptive strength – the 'implicit', 'latent' or 'broad' church that serves its community, and does not easily use nomenclature such

1 Advertisement posted by Church of England, 20 November 2011.

as 'member' and 'non-member'. The 'gathered', 'explicit' church models (or the 'manifest', in Thung's writing), and currently favoured by the Church of England's leadership, tend to ignore the high numbers of people present in more 'latent' expressions of ecclesial life – college and school chapels, prisons, other institutions, hospitals and hospices. Such contexts represent, to varying degrees, 'captive audiences', to be sure. But the church consists of far more people than its visible, obvious membership. There are supporters, friends, allies, advocates, defenders and exponents, none of whom are necessarily 'active members'.

So, as Albert Einstein once opined, not everything that counts can be counted; and not everything that is counted, counts. Counting 'members' or the hard, inner-core of congregational attendees does not tell the whole story; indeed, it does not even account for the half of it. A church – especially a rural one – may have many more supporters and followers, who are in more attenuated relationships with their church, than a congregation that is tightly defined and easily delineated. The mission of the church is a vocation to serve communities, not just convert individuals to countable membership. As Darrell Guder says,

> [t]here are examples of very successful Christendom maintenance, if the measure of success is numbers, budgets, well-attended programmes and satisfied members . . . however [this] focus effectively obstructs any movement toward continual conversion to missional calling . . . maintenance leaders rarely equip saints for missional vocation.[2]

The new emphasis on leadership in current missionary discourse, and in church management, is skewed. The New Testament lists some functions of leadership, to be sure; and sometimes leaders by name. But the calling of the church is to the whole community, not just a few. The emphasis is on the whole body of Christ, not just those deemed to be the chosen. It takes a wide range of gifted people – who need to be cherished and valued as members of the body – to build up the body. The authority of individual leaders is not so much conferred as emergent – and especially out of deep, long processes of discernment. It emerges not out of the essence of some function, but rather as an outworking of their calling, which they expound and exhibit in their lives. For this reason alone, perhaps, the church needs to be critically aware and cautious of recasting clerical and ministerial paradigms of leadership in apparently more successful secular moulds:

> What is happening to ministries that equip the saints for the work of service when we adopt the language and values of the corporate world and describe ministers as Chief Executive Officers, Heads of Staff, Executive Pastors, Directors of this and Directors of that? Why is it that ministers'

2 Guder, *Called to Witness: Doing Missional Theology*, p. 145.

studies have become offices? [This] may be superficial evidences of the problem . . . [but it is what happens] when the values of the corporate world join with the values of the market place in the church.[3]

Of course, the elevation of 'talent' as a concept in the Church of England hardly helps stem this tide. And there are further dangers that await the new culture that has now been born within the church. To be sure, the culture of clericalism has, in the past, allowed for all kinds of deference, and with the associated potential for abuse. The culture of clericalism sometimes created a flawed pyramid of respect: those with the titles or the offices were to be look up to, trusted, and sometimes treated with undue adulation. The church often colluded with this culture of hierarchy and deference, and other institutions have also succumbed to this temptation.

But when the clergy-laity gap is dissolved, and replaced with the leader-led dialectic, another danger lurks: the culture of deference switches from the office-holder or rank, and moves instead to 'talent' and 'charisma'. The worship of talent can then hide even greater abuses, since the institution becomes dependent on the 'talent' to maintain its creaking identity, and the 'charisma' to reassure followers that it still has some capacity for enchantment. 'Talent' is not a biblical concept, and for the church it risks a dangerous fraternisation with contemporary 'celebrity culture'. Instead of ministry being 'ontologically other' and sacred, 'talent' and charisma become the new measures by which we judge the individual performance of ministry in the church. The risks are enormous here, and whilst the culture of clericalism was arguably just as problematic, the secular worship of 'celebrity culture' – effectively the apotheosis of 'talent' – is something to be refused rather than regarded by the church. There are some worrying signs, moreover, that reputational concerns – archiepiscopal 'legacies' now paraded as indicators of talent – place achievement and success above faithfulness.[4]

It is, of course, no different when the church turns to consumerism or capitalism for its energies and ideologies:

> The partnership of church and state has been replaced by the partnership of church and marketplace, and the marketplace appears to be winning. What is going on when members are treated like customers . . .? What is the theology of mission that propagates mission statements intended to function like advertising slogans? What kinds of ecclesiology have we developed if our sense of ourselves is that we should be user-friendly, full-service consumer-sensitive churches? What shall we

---

3 Ibid., p. 157.
4 See Tim Wyatt, *Church Times*, 11 March 2016, p. 3: 'Welby looks at the church and sees signs of spring' – '[the archbishop said that] looking at the names of and deeds of his predecessors made him feel the weight of his position. As Augustine, Dunstan, Thomas Becket, Anselm and Thomas Cranmer had each left a legacy, so must he'.

make of the practical redefinition of the ordered ministries as a mixture of narrow-gauge behavioural therapist, organisational development expert and programme impresario?[5]

Missional activism, then, such as it is, must become rooted in a much deeper ecclesiology (as we saw in Chapter 1). The Church of England needs to stop talking about talent, numbers and mission, and start talking more about God. It's not difficult. As every leader of any political party knows, once you start talking about the need to increase membership, it usually decreases. But when you start talking about ideas and the fundamental things that matter, people tend to join. Dare one say it? The Church of England, as a body, currently risks sounding like it is out of theological vision, energy and ideas – but keen on new members and talent that secures new recruits. And so our leaders increasingly sound like managers trying to fix the numbers.

This is potentially quite serious for the national mission of the Church of England. The vast majority of the population remain well-disposed to the Church of England. What puts them off, however, is too much talk from inside the church of money, management and numerical growth. The church – in continuing to stress these concerns – may imagine it is being proactive. But these foci represent reactive responses to wider cultural concerns, which can occlude the deeper character of the church. Correspondingly, it is rare to see an advertisement at the back of a church newspaper seeking a vicar who will lead a church into deeper theological learning, or open up the riches of contemplative prayer to the wider parish. Our absorption with management and growth dominates our selection processes – from top to bottom.

Measuring quantity as an indicator of quality, and success as a gauge of faithfulness, carries challenges and risks. The Church of England will need some deeper discernment here, and some sharper critical reflection. In the end, the gap between our ideology and reality is too telling. As the philosopher Roger Scruton argued, Marxism became so cocooned in what Orwell once called 'Newspeak' that it could not be refuted. It meant that the communist parties wound up spouting meaningless slogans which they themselves knew made no sense. The same could be said of the Church of England's increasingly problematic 'membership-speak':

> facts no longer made contact with the theory, which had risen above the facts on clouds of nonsense, rather like a theological system. The point was not to believe the theory, but to repeat it ritualistically and in such a way that both belief and doubt became irrelevant . . . In this way the concept of truth disappeared from the intellectual landscape, and was replaced by that of power.[6]

5 Guder, *Called to Witness: Doing Missional Theology*, p. 158.
6 Anne Applebaum in conversation with Roger Scruton, 6 June 2012, and quoted in Applebaum, *The Iron Curtain*, p. 494.

Scruton adds that once people were unable to distinguish truth from ideological fiction, however, then they were also unable to solve or even describe the worsening social and economic problems of the societies they ruled. The more the church is treated as an organisation, the more its mission becomes focussed on mechanistic techniques designed to maximise output and to reify productivity. We become obsessed with quantity instead of quality and where we have a care for quality, it is only to serve the larger goal of increasing quantity. The church moves to being mechanistically driven; to becoming a managed machine, with its managers judging their performance by growth-related metrics. Invariably, the clergy and the congregations are made to collude with this – largely through the imposition of codes of compliance, in the name of 'missional excellence' or 'healthy churches'. This can rob clergy and parishes of their distinctive local autonomy, and can also override the value of local knowledge. It turns partnerships and soft forms of association rooted in trust into hard forms of organisation and corporation. As Alvesson and Spicer note,

> [p]rofessionals . . . value autonomy . . . [yet] there are many examples of professionals surrendering their autonomy in the face of managerial change agendas. It has happened in health care, as management systems have been imported from automobile manufacturing, to control the workflow of doctors. It has happened in the law as traditional partnerships have become corporations. Now even priests are being sent on management training courses in business schools.[7]

Back to the future? Bureaucracy, management and executive leadership

All that said, this is hardly a new problem for the Church of England. In 1995, the Church of England published *Working as One Body*, also known as *The Turnbull Report*.[8] At the time, I was critical of the centralising and bureaucratising forces at work in the report, dubbing the proposed reforms as 'consecrated pragmatism'.[9] So in what follows, I propose to revisit some of the problems in *Working as One Body*, and show how such 'future maps' have shaped the journey and identity of the Church of England over a period of more than two decades. There is a sense in which the current pattern of archiepiscopal leadership is entirely scoped – prefigured, in a way – by *Working as One Body*: centralisation and control, and dominated by singular forms of charismatic leadership.

One could say that *Working as One Body* not only predicts, but also plots the course from the 1990s to the present. Namely, a retreat from institutional

---

7 Alvesson and Spicer, '(Un)Conditional Surrender? Why Do Professionals Willingly Comply with Managerialism?'.
8 *Working as One Body*.
9 See Percy, *Power in the Church: Ecclesiology in an Age of Transition*.

identity to the organisational. And a move from a national, comprehensive church – a sort of 'spiritual National Health Service' – to becoming a suburban-sect. Certainly, the 'ecclesionomics' of the Church of England currently seem to be suggesting that rural ministry is expensive, and so has its services and resources continually trimmed. Whilst the gathered 'suburban church' model, which has clear delineations between members and non-members, appears to be the preferred ecclesial paradigm. In other words, the Church of England is retreating, under the current leadership, from being a national institutional institution to becoming a member-based organisation.

One of the oldest jokes about the Church of England asks 'how many Anglicans does it take to change a light bulb?' Answer: five – one to put in the new one and four to admire the old one. Typically, the joke is often used to lampoon almost any institution beholden to its past and is almost infinitely adaptable. For Anglicans however, there is an irony in the joke: admiration of the past is an important and necessary feature of their ecclesiology and theology. The past is how the church is shaped – and understanding the past is inherently a part of present identity. Without tradition, structure, history and liturgy, the Church of England would not be. Its rootedness in the past is part of its fabric and value. Consequently, anything that transforms the past or dispenses with it is bound to raise questions about identity for the Church of England.

As we have seen in this book, one of the issues for management techniques applied to the church is the emergence of a 'polity of oppression'. Two decades have now passed since the publication of the *Turnbull Report*, which was designed to concentrate, focus and intensify bureaucracy in the Church of England. The very existence of the *Turnbull Report* presupposed an older 'civil service' type bureaucracy that was now deemed in need of dismantling, in much the same way that Margaret Thatcher's government had attacked public services and turned them into private industries. Efficiency for the 'common good' was the aim of the agenda, and *Working as One Body* was the outcome of the Archbishops' Commission on the organisation of the Church of England.

The Commission was headed by Michael Turnbull, Bishop of Durham (1994–2003), and was intended to offer a 'blueprint' for ordering the governing and consultative bodies of the Church of England. The Report was, in its own words, 'a more comprehensive review of the national institutions of the Church than has ever before been undertaken . . . if implemented, it would radically change the ways in which the Church of England operates . . . [redefining] Episcopal leadership and synodical governance'. The Report consisted of 12 chapters, the first three of which outlined the main theological basis for advocating change. The remaining nine chapters covered areas such as finance, restructuring the church and the task of Episcopal leadership. It was a comprehensive review of spending, resources, leadership and centralisation, in all but name.

The proposals included swallowing up a variety of long-established committees that had very particular social and ecclesial tasks (e.g., the boards of social responsibility, education, and so forth), and 'streamlining' their breadth and diversity under one Board of Mission and Evangelism, presided over by a single Chairman.[10] Effectively, and in one fell swoop, mission and ecumenism were subjugated to the narrower and more explicit task of evangelism. The Report was 'noted' by the General Synod in November 1995. There was even a rationale for the haste and speed with which it might be adopted ('a time for swift action', pp. 44ff), which in a way justifies its own haste: 'Most of the changes outlined . . . are essential to an integrated package of reform . . . we do not believe they could be implemented piecemeal . . . they are urgent, and [failure to assent to them] will damage staff morale' (p. 43). The resonance with the 'Reform and Renewal' schema, two decades later, is both notable and chilling.

The current 'Reform and Renewal' agenda is, therefore, prefigured in the *Turnbull Report* – with a kind of 'back to the future' dynamic emerging. So, what were the principal problems with the *Turnbull Report*? Since 1995, it is clear that the concentration of power in the Archbishops' Council, and suggested by the *Turnbull Report*, has made the task of liaison and consultation with the wider church, and even the General Synod, more difficult, since the Council is largely accountable to no-one but itself. Three key problems flowed from this.

First, the way ecclesial power was handled as the basis for the report was at serious fault. The members of the Commission were almost entirely male and bourgeois (and so too, was the emerging Archbishops' Council – see pp. 118ff). As such, *Working As One Body* was not reflective of society, and signalled a retreat from the Anglican faith in comprehensiveness and its capacity to reflect the diversity of God's people, and for those same people to reflect God, and so help society transcend itself. *Working As One Body* also proposed the concentration of ecclesial power in the hands of the bishops (or just a few of them?) and a small bourgeois power elite (pp. 47ff) – or executive managers. Whilst this might have made the church 'sharper', it has also made it much narrower, since the guiding philosophy seemed to be 'let the managers manage'. There is an irony here for Anglicans: it is not quite congregational enough in its polity to 'let the people manage the people', because it is an Episcopal church. At the same time, however, it is not Episcopal enough to devolve power to just a few: the *via media* rules. Generally, Anglicanism may be said to have an endemically compromising ecclesial habit. Thus, one of the major problems for *Working As One Body* was that it posited power in the hands of an elite class: 'the executive leaders', or those with certain kinds of managerial skills. This has been successfully argued against by a number of Anglican theologians as being contrary to the true Anglican ethos, besides being an abuse of power.[11]

---

10 I do mean 'Chairman' here. The Report lacks any finesse in the direction of political correctness.

11 See for example Roberts, 'Lord, Bondsman and Churchman: Power, Integrity and Identity'.

Second, the vision for episcopacy could be said, in some sense, to be distorted. *Working As One Body* was littered with phrases such as 'the Bishop-in-Synod', 'leadership' and 'authority'. There are serious problems with the way the Episcopate is treated in the *Turnbull Report*. For example, by using Hooker in a selective manner, *Working As One Body* conflated 'Bishop' with the (biblical) metaphor 'Head' of the body, which is Christ. But Hooker used 'head' mainly to describe the supreme Governor of the Church of England (namely the King or Queen), which he then deliberately conflated with Christ.[12]

Students of late sixteenth and seventeenth century history will recall that the monarchs enjoyed the privilege of governing by 'divine right' and over-ruling an elected and representative Parliament when they saw fit, which partly led to the English Revolution of the 1640s. The Report's use of 'head' could easily lead to a form of 'divine right' being established in the contem-porary episcopate in a similar way to the Stuart monarchs. This may not have been the intention of *Working As One Body*, but it was always the likely result. In terms of ecclesiology, one could now begin to see a kind of papal authority being invested in the Archbishop of Canterbury, and the authority of the Curia being invested in the new Council. Sociologically speaking, *Working As One Body* unintentionally invested too much in the *charism* of the individual bishop. Concentrating power in the hands of a few requires a degree of charisma if the power is to be held responsibly (or authoritatively) and shared dynamically. If this does not happen, severe routinisation of charisma and over-management of people and resources can lead to fissure.

Third, there were some wider ecclesial perspectives that needed deeper consideration. Almost since its inception, Anglicanism has worked with a 'quadrilateral pattern' in its moral reasoning and for arriving at provisional theological truth claims.[13] The four-fold relationship between scripture, tradition, reason and experience (or culture) is sacred to the ecology of Anglican identity. *Working As One Body* disturbed the delicate balance of this ecology by adding a fifth dimension – namely enhanced Episcopal authority. Or, it unintentionally placed the bishops *over* the quadrilateral as its presiders. Ironically, either of these positions would now allow the Church to become hostage to congregational or ultra-catholic forces. It is a path that potentially leads to a capitulation to conservatism.

This, of course, is precisely what has happened in the two decades that followed, and is exactly the dynamic that Mady Thung's work is alive to. Furthermore, the erosion of clergy and laity rights implicit in *Working As One Body* – Bishops or Council as 'head', the rest the subservient body – now began to transform the Church of England into an Episcopalian

---

12 See Hooker, *Of the Laws of Ecclesiastical Polity*, pp. 158–176, 161–175.
13 See Evans and Wright, *The Anglican Tradition*, pp. 343, 355, 387 and 450. Of course, the actual Quadrilateral is Scripture, Creeds, Sacraments and the Historic Ministry.

denomination. More serious, however, is what the combination of marginalisation under the governance of that small power elite might bring.

So, as we noted in previous chapters with Mady Thung's work, the organisational-activist model of the church cannot conceive of the broader definitions of 'membership' in ecclesial polity that might be implicit in more institutional-contemplative expressions of the church. Thus, one of the ecclesial features that the *Turnbull Report* neglected was Hooker's much broader vision of the 'body of Christ', which extended beyond the gathered congregation. The 'commonwealth' model was his preferred mode of socially describing the mystical nature of the church.[14] *Working As One Body* worked with a limited notion of 'body', and a distorted notion of how the parts of the body or commonwealth relate to each other. Who defines the 'head', and in what sense is that part of the body superior to the others?

Thus, there is an inversion of Paul's vision in 1 Corinthians 12 in the *Turnbull Report* as a whole, which is very curious, given its appeal to the idea of 'one body'. It is essential to remember that Hooker and Paul agreed on the need for the body of Christ to be a *body of power*, not a passive association that only receives its power from or through the head: that is no *kind* of 'body'. Indeed, we can go further here and ask why 'body' and 'head' occurred as the choice metaphors to describe the church in the *Turnbull Report*? There are many other images and metaphors in the New Testament to choose from (bride, vine, etc). The notion of a 'body' always invites deferment to a 'head' in contemporary thinking, since we are used to imagining our personal 'centre' as somehow being cognitive – in the mind. Thus, a hegemony *naturally* arises when this image is overplayed or used exclusively: perhaps other metaphors might counteract this?

Another issue that the *Turnbull Report* appeared to miss is that management and efficiency are not at the 'heart' of leadership, as portrayed in the New Testament. Instead, service and sacrifice are presented as 'models', mirroring the *kenosis* of Christ on the Cross (Phil. 2: 5ff). The 'head' or 'manager' of the early disciples was the one who, according to the fourth evangelist, took a towel and washed his disciples' feet (John 13: 1–11). The Son of Man who came 'to serve' (diakonesai, Mark 10: 45) is the one who calls Christians to do likewise. In terms of leadership and a hegemony of power, Jesus rebukes his disciples thus: 'it shall not be so amongst you' (Mark 10: 43). What, in effect, seems to be the problem here is the use of biblical language and metaphors, yet in contexts and with meanings which have been detached from those in the New Testament's own self-understanding. 'Bishop', 'body', 'head', 'power' and 'authority' are indeed all words that occur in the New Testament, yet mostly in the context of service and suffering. Not so in the Report, where the words have been linked with management and efficiency.

14 Hooker, *Of the Laws of Ecclesiastical Polity*, pp. 129ff.

In short, *Working As One Body* attempted to offer a 'mechanistic' blue-print – 'the rationalisation of congregational process and the animation of social will to achieve results' that lacks a 'symbolic', 'organic' or 'contextual' vision.[15] The first three chapters did not actually inform the report, and in spite of their periodic genuflection to a symbolic and organic blueprint, they are surpassingly weak in their ecclesiology. The irony of *Working As One Body* was that its bold vision necessitated a restriction of ecclesial horizons in the interests of concentrating and managing resources.

The *Turnbull Report* was perhaps right to deconstruct the history of Synod (pp. 61ff), and question the working arrangements for Boards, Dioceses and Deaneries, but the basis of the document still, even now, feels aggressively dialectical, failing to comprehend the mystical, dispersed nature of Christ's body on earth. Thus, although a rationalising document, it is not a document of *faith*: this is no *Lumen Gentium*, but a bourgeois-management-led bid for the centralisation and control of power. In effect, we are left looking at a document that is pure ideology, with a theological *gloss*. And like all ideologies, some would be liberated by it, but many would be oppressed. The Report suffered by *beginning* with a capitalist-managerial ideology, and then attempting to fund that theologically. The consequence of this was that the ecclesiology looks thin, even alienating. The defence of a *nouveau* hegemony amounted to the creation of a *Kyriearchy*, in which feudal Lords, their leadership uncritically mapped and projected on to biblical concepts such as 'head', the serfs as the 'body', would rule and dominate in the name of the Lord. This would be done through a crude rationalising, efficiency-based and capitalist ideological dogma that oppressed the weak, powerless and (allegedly) inefficient, but rewarded the loyal. Laity, parish clergy and those beyond the 'body' (but who are served by it) were right to be deeply concerned about the implications of the Report.[16]

In *Working As One Body,* we witnessed the first decisive steps in a church moving away from being an institution and becoming a narrower organisation (following Selznick), moving from institutional-contemplative paradigms of polity to those of organisational-activism (Thung). All of this pointed towards a future that has now arrived: a collapse into systems of ecclesial management and narrow executive-led organisational models that borrow their ethos from a culture of privatisation, local (and often

15 See Hopewell, *Congregation*, for a *severe* critique of mechanistic approaches to ecclesiology. A sharper sociological critique of the dynamic I am describing can be found in Ritzer's *The McDonaldization of Society*.
16 For a discussion of *Kyriearchy*, see Nicholls, *Deity and Domination: Images of God in the Nineteenth and Twentieth Centuries*, p. 30. See also Hardy, *God's Ways with the World: Thinking and Practising Christian Faith*, p. 184: 'the (distorted) *monarche* of God is transferred to states and individuals . . . social structures (become) arbiters of social coherence . . . by contrast, the complexity, pluralism and changeability of society are regarded as alien . . . justice is seen as conformity'. In other words, ideology is dictating 'theology', blotting out appropriate diversity.

non-accountable) bodies, and a small, supreme central authority that could overrule at will.[17] Indeed, the Report actually proposed a regionalising scheme (p. 105) which implied a twin strategy of de-centring the people's power on the one hand, whilst at the same time consolidating central and ultimate power in the hands of a few.

The *Turnbull Report* can therefore be interpreted as an early attempt at a 'mechanistic blueprint' for the church because its focus is 'programme effectiveness'. James Hopewell, in his excellent analysis of different types of ecclesiology based on structural critiques of narrative, highlights how mechanistic approaches to the church occur when contextual visions are lost.[18] Typically, a contextual ecclesiology is concerned with how it relates to its environs. It sees the church, in relation to the world, as a woven fabric that share with the world a variety of strands, yet also has an obligation to somehow stand apart from society, but not in a way that removes it from its deep and implicit social inter-connections. Closely allied to this vision is the organic perspective, which is also concerned with 'style, grace and social cohesion'.

Hopewell notes that these institutional-incarnate visions have given way to mechanistic and image-led (symbolic) ecclesiological blueprints. This is partly due to the specialisation and particularity encouraged by consumerism and capitalism, and also because many religious responses to pluralism and secularisation are in fact quite pragmatic. (Indeed, as we have already noted, few are *genuinely* theological; most are ideological, with theology added for legitimisation). Of course, it is necessary to consecrate this pragmatism so the church can adopt it, but this often amounts to little more than the sacralisation of marketing, management or communicative techniques. Critically, the supporting philosophy of the agency or tool being used is left unaddressed.

Further considerations

It is important not to read this critique of the *Turnbull Report* as 'anti-management'. I fully recognise and affirm the need for good organisation and sound management. However, the pretexts for the *Turnbull Report* were predictable tropes: too many 'inefficient' parishes and clergy, for example, that 'management' would 'sort out'. The *Turnbull Report*, in concentrating greater powers in the hands of bishops, archdeacons and a new 'management class' imported into the church, would apparently solve this. But how many is 'too many'? Is it 5 per cent, for example, or perhaps 10 per cent; or maybe even 50 per cent? If it is only about 5 per cent or

17 See my 'The Churchgoers Charter', pp. 5–8. Indeed, the Synod has been warned about the link between the Turnbull Report and 'disestablishment . . . by stealth'. Michael Alison, MP, *The Independent*, 14 February 1996, p. 6.
18 Hopewell, *Congregation: Stories and Structures*, pp. 19ff.

10 per cent, then why reform all for the sake of a few? The rationale was highly reminiscent of Thatcher's demonising of 'inefficient state-owned industries'. Yet some of the smallest churches have the greatest community witness. Some of the largest, slickest and apparently 'successful' turn out to be the most sectarian and socially irrelevant.

Then again, some championed the *Turnbull Report* because they believed General Synod 'lacked competence' to deliberate and cogitate on issues of theological or liturgical merit. So it follows that the argument for the Holy Spirit at work within an institution *now* goes like this. First, the Spirit is clearly hampered by slow and deliberate democracy, even though the Anglican church witnesses to the broad and plural ways in which truth and discipleship are expressed. Second, the slow, fudgy deliberation and collegiality of Anglican polity should be replaced by a sharper, executive-managerial regime. Yet I would far rather have the Spirit struggle in the first model of ecclesiology, instead of being privatised and dominating in the second. I also suspect, that for all its frustrations, God speaks more through plurality than well-intentioned totalitarianism, infused with vacuous 'management-speak'.

What the *Turnbull Report* missed in 1995, and the current leadership of the Church of England fails to comprehend some two decades on, is that the Church of England is a slow, plural body, that often fails to be tidily defined or easily managed. In seeking to alter this, great caution always needs to be exercised. The indecent haste of the *Turnbull Report* smacked of an arrogance of power rather than Christ-like service, and an attempt to 'free the Spirit' within. Thus, even though many clergy and laity expressed deep reservations about the report in 1995, the timetable still intimidated opponents by stating when it would be implemented, irrespective of the wishes of Synod. Then – as now – I do not welcome this style or type of reform. It is too insistent, assertive, non-democratic, and theologically vacuous. I am all for organisation, but one of the tasks of the Spirit is to *listen* and *discern* before prompting – an agenda wholly absent from *Working as One Body*, just as it is from its successor agenda, 'Reform and Renewal', discussed in earlier chapters. The question remains: how is this working as one body?

There are some further issues to consider here. First, it is vital that the church considers the advantages and disadvantages of restructuring. Whilst restructuring may be *necessary*, swallowing the current organisational assumptions that are present in society may be unhelpful. The underlying symptoms and side-effects the *Turnbull Report* presents are left unaddressed. For example, the Church of England has experienced a (recent) shift in transforming its sense of mission from something relatively benign into something far more proactive. What was once an ecclesial habit became the focus of a decade – the Decade of Evangelism. There were some advantages in this focus of evangelism; yet in defining itself more sharply as a body to cope with contemporary culture, the church created an even bigger gap between itself and society. The function of this was to maintain distinctiveness, but it also risked alienation: social or established religion can quickly move from being public religion to private belief.[19]

Second, and correspondingly, the Church of England began to relinquish its sense of being a national church service, a role it exchanged for one as a body that offered spiritual commodities, but as an option alongside other goods or products. This is not a new situation in contemporary culture. Sociologists of religion such as Peter Berger and Thomas Luckmann have been describing and analysing 'the privatisation of religion' for many decades. Berger, in particular, is alive to the 'demonopolisation' that is occurring: the pluralistic situation creates a market situation, in which religions compete. Thus, 'the religious tradition which previously could be authoritatively imposed, now has to be marketed – "sold" to a clientele that is no longer constrained to "buy"'.[20]

Third, the old modernist response to this was ecumenicity – reducing competing units through amalgamation and cutting resources, dividing up the market between the larger units that remain, and engaging in a form of ecclesial cartelisation.[21] This can have definite benefits for the institution concerned, not least because the organisation itself benefits from the impetus of a sharper identity: ironically, the adjustments made, even if they are a 'scaling-down', convey a sense of relevance to the group. However, this approach probably has as much to do with a loss of nerve and identity, as it does with a desire to reform. Frequently, many people resent the shift, because they detect the distance that has been created between themselves and what was once *their* church, health service or public utility. This is what Sara Maitland described as 'the Church of England PLC . . . stress(ing) the "L" for limited'.[22] It is the logical end of all mechanistic blueprints.

Fourth, it follows that the perceptions of its employees might also change. *Working As One Body*, because it lacked an organic dimension to its interpretation of embodiment, effectively created a machinery in which decisions and people were now to be *processed* in the interests of efficiency. The lack of humane, alternative-symbolic and mystical visions of the church played into the hands of capitalist philosophies and rhetoric that have done so

---

19 The problem lies in the exaltation of the individual over the corporate as a 'market'. The most accessible discussion of this dynamic is Bellah's *Habits of the Heart: Individualism and Commitment in American Life*. Following McIntyre (*After Virtue*), Bellah makes helpful distinctions between expressive, ontological and utilitarian individualism, which each hold public religion to ransom for private gain in slightly different ways.

20 Berger, *The Sacred Canopy*, p. 138. In terms of the Church of England and mission, the most obvious area that this shift is located in is Baptismal policy. The rise of groups like MORIB – with their desire to restrict and delimit the availability of sacraments – implicitly embraces disestablishment and congregationalism.

21 Berger, 'A Market Model for the Analysis of Ecumenicity'.

22 Maitland, *A Big Enough God? Artful Theology*, p. 150. See also *Tomorrow is Another Country: Education in a Postmodern World*, pp. 58–9, for a distinction between 'Church of England and Son', 'Church of England plc' and 'Church of England Enterprises'. The Turnbull Report offers an ecclesial vision somewhere between those last two.

much to de-humanise our society.[23] The problem might be, as one writer puts it, something like this:

> in the Church of England this (problem) is reinforced by a whole raft of legislation from national government and from the Archbishops' Council. Child Protection, Disability Discrimination, Employment Law, Charities Law, Clergy Code of Conduct, Clergy Discipline Measure, Clergy Terms and Conditions of Service, Ministry Development Review and Continuing Ministerial Development requirements have all fuelled expectations that the clergy will routinely operate to professional standards of work, behaviour and accountability. There are good reasons why the Church should warmly welcome these developments. We definitely do not need less professionally aware clergy pastoring and leading the twenty-first-century Church in mission and ministry.[24]

Fifth, and in terms of mission, phrases such as 'audit', 'action-plan', 'effectiveness' (again!), 'strategy' 'target' and 'accountability' now riddle discussions about evangelism. The assumption is that the Church of England is engaged in some sort of evangelistic accountancy, always looking to numbers, being geared up to be sent out to the world, as though it wasn't there already. Yet Anglicans are not primarily called to be relocated as a church (even if we do feel profoundly dislocated), nor are we to draw people away from society into an exclusive church. In England at least, and certainly in the Church of England, Anglicanism affirms that all belong to the body unless they choose not to do so. To be sure, the price to pay for this is a profound lack of definition; a blurring of boundaries between church and world, which risks losing the public attention as much as it has rights in gaining it. This may seem a tangential point in respect of the report, but it is actually quite central. The 'body' of *Working As One Body* assumes a cultural and moral gap between the established church and the world. By definition, an established church has no right to create or assume such a gap; rather, it is constantly attempting to obviate it, knitting together heaven and earth, sacred and profane. The impoverished notion of mission that underlies the report provided a mirror to some of the other underlying assumptions that were uncritically inculcated. Sharper definitions may raise profiles and rationalise the ecclesial processes. Yet the same strategy also risks marginalisation by society, alienating constituents and sounding a general retreat from a comprehensive service.

Sixth, some further dangers lie in wait at this point. A smaller spiritual or religious 'service' is more easily dominated by a single group of people,

---

23 cf. Hutton, *The State We're In.* As Hutton notes, this often just compels employees to compete with each other rather than working together (pp. 27ff): the rhetoric divides, then conquers.

24 Oliver, *Ministry Without Madness*, p. 90.

rationales or agenda. It is interesting to note that the notion of the location of 'governing power' seems to have shifted from theologians to bishops, and then finally to the Archbishops' Council over the last two decades. 'Governing power', it seems, lies wherever the main resourcing for the Church of England is coming from. Of course, this radically robbed the *plebs Dei* of their right to power, since power was now concentrated, not shared or dispersed. As we noted earlier, this is neither faithful to Hooker nor to scripture: the whole body is to be a body of *real* power – not just the main agent of the head. This is so for good theological reasons: the incarnation of Christ, like the church, is primarily a risk of embodiment and a negation of power – it only acquires its authority through that action. Any attempt to concentrate or conflate power in the agency (e.g., head) inevitably marginalises Christ and society, leading to a form of introspective congregationalism. In other words, development comes in mutual and open relationships that empower by gift, sacrifice, trust, service and otherness. The *Turnbull Report* lost the Anglican vision for directional plurality which almost defines the Church of England, and replaced it with a form of managerial sharpness – backed by the usual theological discourses – that exorcised power, authority and leadership from the *plebs Dei* and placed them into the hands of a few.

Seventh, and in response to the points above, it therefore follows that there needs to be some evaluation about how the church might turn these agenda around: how does religion *make* society, instead of simply copying it? Scholars such as Charles Davis attempted to sustain the contextual and organic approaches of 'political theology' in the 1960s, which have now largely fallen into disfavour.[25] Davis was suspicious of the exaltation of the defined and different: he sees this as anti-universalist, and therefore a retreat from Truth. In place of this he proposes a universalism of love (socialism or sociality as a moral and religious ideal) as the rationale for the church in relation to society – loving reasoning in praxis.

So perhaps the best way to illustrate the implications of this for *Working As One Body* is to highlight the basic differences between a sharehold-ing and a stake-holding society.[26] The shareholding society, as many will now be aware, has proved to be profoundly disappointing: it has failed to deliver on its promise to give people a say in their public utilities and a share for all in the utilities' success. People know that after the launch (sell-off), new uniforms, 'corporate' logos[27] and first dividends, comes 'streamlining': redundancies, inability to supply all the public (only those who can pay) and massively concentrated power (with salaries to match) in the hands of a very few quickly follow. The rationalising process turns

25 Davis, *Religion and the Making of Society: Essays in Social Theology*. The point is that an established sociality promotes differing opinion, whereas individualism ultimately becomes conformity.
26 For a fuller discussion, see Hutton, *The State We're In*, Chap. 12.
27 At the time of writing, Lambeth Palace has just announced that it has acquired such a logo – a 'gift' to the church from a marketing company that was given at 'cost price'.

what was once a service (possibly weak, but at least *definitively* comprehensive) into a business.[28]

In contrast, a stake-holding society follows the lead of Davis and others, by giving everyone a stake in the economy, not just those with capital, expertise or advantage. Significantly, employees have a say in what their organisation stands for; there is order and mutuality, with power deliberately dispersed.

Moreover, perhaps the difference between the two can be seen in terms of employment. Share-holders believe in contracts and short-termism, which is governed by results. Stake-holders are orientated by the more biblical concept of covenant, in which results only play a part in configuring the bonds of commitment.[29] Here, as has been noted before, *Working As One Body* fails to be inclusive and progressive: the wider sense of participation and belonging which the church should bring is dominated by the managerial class. A stake-holding society does not place effectiveness before people, treating them as resources, products or units. It recognises that institutions often exist for the wider good of all society, not just themselves. In short, the church works for one body (society), but it is not necessarily the case that it works as one identifiable homogenous unit. An incarnate, ambiguous and susceptible body that risks failure may be able to serve society far better than a sharply defined community that is rationalised, strong and sharp.[30]

So, *Working As One Body* attempted to address a number of possible futures for the Church of England in a time of pluralism and financial constraint. It chose one very particular path: a route map for a new future. But there were always other possibilities. The Church of England was beginning, in the 1990s, to try and understand itself as the institution that represents the God whom many believe in yet choose not to belong to. Under such conditions, Christianity retains its dominant social profile, whilst at the same time losing its depth and breadth of articulation.[31] One response to this was to retreat and consolidate into an *associational* or *organisational* pattern, where questions of effectiveness constantly arise. As I have already said, the problem with this vision is that it assumes a gap between the church and England that is not necessarily there.

Another possible response was to rehabilitate the *communal* vision that is both parochial and universal rather than congregational, and is as deeply concerned about the context of religion as about its content. This would be

---

28 I am not suggesting that the report is an anti-service document *per se*. As Hopewell notes, 'mechanists are not opposed to the intentions of service . . . but they argue that unless basic structures are sound and dynamic, any sort of parish *goal* is in jeopardy . . . the primary need of churches today is the rationalisation of the congregational process and the animation of social will to achieve *results*' (p. 26 – italics mine).
29 See Whelan, *The Corrosion of Charity: From Moral Renewal to Contract Culture*; Hutton, *The State We're In*, p. 282.
30 See my 'How to Win Congregations and Influence Them'.
31 See Davie, *Religion in Britain Since 1945: Believing Without Belonging*.

expensive and time-consuming, but may have the advantage of being more expansive in the long-run. For example, at a time when there is considerable tension and competition between European government, Parliament and local government, any established church is quite well placed to facilitate the (re-)building of communities by acting as mediator, agent or initiator. If the church took seriously its obligation to address all needs, it might find that its body was not so small, and that its boundaries were not so obvious.

What was ultimately so unsatisfactory about *Working As One Body* is that the approach it took to itself, the body of Christ, and to individuals, amounted to little more than 'consecrated pragmatism'. I say 'consecrated', because the *Turnbull Report* is an episcopally-driven agenda: more and more power slowly but surely being concentrated in the office of Bishop. A shapely pyramid of power is developing, and it is clear what sits atop. Paradoxically, perhaps, this impetus seems to be coming from the evangelical prelates, who allegedly have a high doctrine of the *plebs Dei* and the priesthood of all believers. But that same group are always in the thrall of business-think and secular reasoning, and the pragmatic fruits of organisational-activism.

Consequently, the Church of England that is the 'Broad Church' – a rich theological tapestry of 'directional plurality' – is quickly being lost to the forces of imposed unity under the cloak or organisational praxis. The age of the informal Anglican *imprimatur* has arrived. As for 'pragmatism', the term has a sliding scale of definitions. At its most basic, it simply means being 'skilled in affairs'; but at its more developed, it can mean 'interfering, meddling, opinionated, dictatorial and dogmatic'.[32]

The creation of a *Kyriarchy*, backed by a theologically-resourced ideology, was a highly problematic development for the Church of England, and it represented a defining moment in its identity. Over two decades later, we can now see that the *Turnbull Report* signalled a retreat from being the church for all, to becoming an episcopal denomination that serves loyal and faithful members. (Those who are not members and avail themselves of services such as occasional offices presumably become 'customers' by default.) In an era of organisational and fiscal reform, this may be inevitable, but the church ought to at least have pondered the costs and future implications of this. It didn't. The church should have been arguing for a more profound view of society, individuals and the church, that began with a theology and an appropriate sociality, and not some borrowed, transient ideology.[33] It didn't.

Ultimately, it is simply not possible to derive a satisfactory ecclesiology from a secular ideology, any more than one can conjure up a satisfactory doctrine of the mission from an emphasis on accountancy. First and foremost,

---

32 *The Shorter Oxford English Dictionary (on Historical Principles)*, p. 1646.

33 We note that Nicholls (*Deity and Domination*, 1989), shortly before his untimely death, was alive to many of these issues. His unpublished critique of *Working as One Body* was to have been humorously entitled *Turnbullshit* (*The Independent*, Obituary, 18th June, 1996, p. 14).

one has to begin with God; not a managerial pragmatism thinly painted over with a theological gloss.

What *Working As One Body* demonstrated was its own desire to routinise, control and stabilise divine and human power in an age of uncertainty. Priests who might be tempted to dissent from prescribed codes or behaviours are more easily dealt with in a rationalised, efficiency-driven body. Targets, goals and aims suddenly replace the ambiguity of sacraments and the dangers of prophetic contemplation. The hazards ahead however, were all too obvious. Turnbull's church which was born in the 1990s is a profoundly safe body – it doesn't rock the boat or question authority. It is comfortable, compliant, centralised, secure, down-sized and maximised; and it speaks with one voice. Therein lies its problem. For bureaucracy brings with it the suffocation of diversity, the emasculation of prophecy, and the dubious gift of a tightly-controlled denominationalism to what was once a national church. So as one writer puts it, and describing the current culture:

> we must also realize that we are living with a major culture shift in the Church where there seems to be little room left for the old tradition of the 'holy companion' type of pastor, still less for the amiable, bungling, and largely ineffectual 'holy amateur'.
>
> At the same time as we are called to be locally and publicly holy and human we are expected to be professional about what we profess. This, with major changes in church economics, all leads to a much more 'managerial' culture in relationships between clergy and people and between clergy and those who call and lead them. This in turn leads to reinterpretations of the basic dynamics of ministry practice so that many clergy are coming to see their work, and even their personal spirituality, as an unending series of project management exercises (though they rarely express it explicitly in these terms).
>
> This kind of cultural and institutional development is likely to have a strong influence on the way we think and therefore the way we speak about the people we lead and serve. If this 'project management' dynamic of ministry is allowed simply to continue without being subjected to careful theological reflection, it can suck the spiritual guts out of the clergy as well as of the churches they lead. The 'language' of the gospel and the language of those who lead in ministry can become foreign tongues of each other without anybody really noticing that it is happening.[34]

Ultimately, as Andrew Chandler suggests,[35] the culture of the Church of England that produced the Turnbull Report, and the Decade of Evangelism – and for all this bullishness – was actually sounding an orderly retreat in an age of doubt. The ascendant evangelical part, assisted by the executive managers and their

34 Oliver, *Ministry Without Madness*, p. 91.
35 Chandler, *The Church of England in the Twentieth Century*, pp. 409ff.

organisational-activists, who began to dominate the Church of England in the 1990s, are now fully in control. But what this coalition has discovered is that they lack 'ecclesial comprehension' – they do not understand the nature of the body they propose to lead, reform and renew. Moreover, this same coalition has also begun to discern that its own narrow spirituality continues to distance the church from society.

As I reflect on this moment, I can also look back on a quarter of a century of my own theological writing. Much of this writing has concerned itself with ecclesiology, and more specifically with Anglicanism and the Church of England. My instincts and inclinations have consistently been shaped by the belief that 'Broad Church' ecclesial polity – generous, orthodox, incorporative, measured, mild, irenic, *via media* – remains the best form of ecclesial polity for national mission and ministry. Moreover, that this polity continues to express the essential essence of Anglicanism – a temperate, accommodating spirituality and theology – that can, at its best, give space to liberal and conservative viewpoints, and catholic and evangelical voices. This is not a church of compromise, however. It is, rather, a vision for dynamic hybridity – the Holy Spirit at work in the whole body of the church.

Moreover, I believe that this 'Broad Church' – that the coalition of evangelicals and organisational-activists so often derides – continues to have a cherished place in the heart and mind of the national psyche. This all suggests that the future of the Church of England may yet turn out to be strangely unresolved. The narrow forms of organisational-activism that currently dominate are likely, in time, to implode. But for the time being, at least, the maps for the present are ones that will only appeal to small minorities of churchgoers. These are the only ones – recipes, if you will – sanctioned by a dominant centre. The maps set out evangelism in clear terms. The maps are clear about who belongs to the church, and who does not. The maps are clear about who will be in leadership, and who will not. It is a puzzling and rather precarious entry into the third millennium for a national church. And it is only to be hoped that the future-maps that emerge will be both more faithful to reality, and at the same time, faithful to the much broader vision that is mapped in Jesus' sketching of the Kingdom of God.

An elegy?

The dedication of this book to Ian taps into some of the book's more elegiac and wistful tones. Ian stands as an exemplar of our highest and finest traditions of devoted parish priests, who have served their communities, and God, with deep commitment and unswerving constancy. Ian is a former doctoral student of mine, and at the time of writing, terminally ill. Ian sent me the poem as an encouragement. He has spent over 35 years in one parish – a once unremarkable pattern of ministry that is almost unheard of in today's Church of England. But his dedication to God – his sense of virtue, and his profound compassion for his people – mark him out as a truly great pastor and priest. Like many doctoral students, supervisors tend to learn much from them, even as they supervise their project and mentor the person. Ian was no exception to this, and his blend of gentle, sharp, incisive, visionary reflective skills, together with his profound humanity – through which the warm radiant grace of God was liberally poured – made both him and his project a joy to work with.

His capacity to reflect on himself, his ministry and community was always remarkable. His eye misses nothing. He is a quintessential participant observer and observing participant. Rather like a family therapist at a large celebratory wedding reception with their own kith and kin, he knows how to join in and enjoy himself; but also when to step back, muse and reflect. He prays for his people; he visits graciously, but does not intrude. He counsels and consoles, yet understanding the difference between empathy and compassion. (Indeed, he heads up the clergy counselling and support network in the diocese.) He is but one sign of God's kingdom in a small English rural village – an unchanging symbol of God's light, love and presence in a world that is distracted and busy.

But lest this sound like the burnishing of the memory of a past long-gone, this same priest has been utterly contemporary and professional in his work, with a methodology and practice of ministry that is responsively dynamic both in and to its environments. He reads assiduously and discerningly, and is up-to-date with the latest and best work on pastoral theology, ministry and more besides. His church has always paid its way as a benefice during his ministry. So one should really view his ministry through the lens of realism, and not romance. Yet the hierarchy of the diocese either sees his work and ministry as 'old-fashioned', and therefore redundant, or, more rarely, romantically idealises his approach.

Neither assessment is really right. The reality is much more nuanced. Ian blends the faithful, unchanging virtues, values, practices and behaviours of a faithful ministry, with all the very best theology, wisdom and work of a thoroughly modern minister. The church hierarchy simply does not seem to comprehend this. So his additional work as a counsellor for the diocese – and this over more than two decades – struggles for recognition despite its dynamic and extensive impact and its thoroughly contemporary, professional approach to ordained ministry.

When I think of Ian and his work, I am reminded of one of my (few) detective heroes, Peter Falk. He plays the TV character known as Columbo, a homicide detective with the Los Angeles Police Department. Sixty-nine episodes, spanning ten series from 1971–2003, introduce us to Lieutenant Columbo – a detective consistently underestimated by his suspects, who are initially reassured and distracted by his circumlocutory speech. Despite his unassuming appearance and apparent absentmindedness, he shrewdly solves his cases by marshalling and sifting all the piecemeal evidence.

Columbo's work is distinguished by a formidable eye for detail and his dogged, dedicated approach. He appears in all episodes as an unassuming man; he is very kind, and befriends everyone to get a better insight into what is really going on; he often pretends not to understand at all – in order to understand more and better; he shuffles around, rarely making eye contact, picking up evidence, stories and impressions here and there, piecing together a broken, bigger picture; he uses all his senses; he analyses; he tends to dress down; he finally makes eye contact at the precise point of epiphany; he is modest; he then shuffles off stage, and into the next episode.

Ian is a reminder of something currently lost to the church; indeed, a church that has somehow become forgetful of itself and so, without a deep sense of constancy, has developed multiple addictions to change and the associated anxieties that come with the consequential cognitive dissonance. Ian has largely stood still in all of this – something that takes courage, virtue and wisdom. He has not adopted his stances out of some sense of superiority; or with slowly-festering bitterness – which some might be prey too. Nor has his distinctive English-Anglican priestly-pastoral wisdom, or his own rich brand of practical theology, been diminished in the new emerging ecclesial culture and climes that this book has been largely concerned with. Finding himself thoroughly counter-cultural and almost eccentrically archaic, simply by standing still and remaining constant and faithful to his calling, Ian is, as the poem says,

> *Someone who loves the mystery of the faith*
> *Whose conversation seems*
> *Credibly to come from heaven . . .*
>
> *. . . a preaching man . . .*
> *who doesn't know how to fake,*
> *A free man, on holiday*
> *In this parish, a still man*
> *Good as an ikon*
> *With a heart full of treasure;*
> *Someone to talk to*
> *When death comes here . . .*
> *Whose eye has missed nothing . . .*
>
> *a man without sanctimony . . .*
> *to handle what is eternal . . .*
> *modest . . . capable of silence*
> *Someone who reminds us now and then*
> *Of your own description*
> *And another kingdom*
> *By the righteousness of his judgement*
> *Or some grace in what's done*
> *In laying down his life even*
> *For his friends.*

Coda
The Churchgoer's Charter

This Coda (or story) is offered as a cautionary satirical tale of what the future might hold for a church that unintentionally embraces the gods of our age – growth and success, with its High Priests from corporations and business – and in so doing, evacuates itself of patience, charity, hope and faithfulness. It is a story of exile, and a Coda that celebrates the return home, the virtues of faithfulness, fortitude, resilience and patience. Written and published some two decades ago in the early 1990s, and at the height of free-market ideology triumphing in Britain, the story asks what might happen if the church were to adopt the same economic, political and ideological pulses that were also shaping the nation?

There are quirky details here that seem quaint now: the invention of the portable fax machine has not come to pass in quite the way one might have envisaged 20 years ago. Technology has developed even faster with mobile phones, tablets and handheld computers. But that is not the point. As church polity is increasingly shaped by market forces, and by targets, strategies and plans – representing a kind of rather inward-looking cluster of concerns that are clothed in apparently missional rhetoric – the story might serve as a timely, even prophetic caution.[1]

The closing parable, although unrelated to the satire, and drawn directly from Bill Countryman's fine *The Truth About Love*, is a brief reminder that though the church may sometimes seem down, it is never out. Just when secularisation or consumerism seems to have triumphed, spring, buds and new life appear. Winter passes, as it must. The one problem the church always faces never changes: namely, coping with the overwhelming abundance of God. Knowing this is how we come to understand that re-charting the church is not only a possibility: it is an inevitability. The re-enchantment of the church will be one where we turn aside from tribalism, and rediscover our breadth; where we learn to value again the deep, mellow, passionate, wise, pastoral corporeal polity we know as Anglicanism. A church rooted in the love of God, the ever-generous providence of the Father, the generative power of the Spirit, and the limitless grace of Jesus Christ; a place where there is no coda or finale – only beginnings and openings.

---

1 Here I refer the reader back to the dedication at the beginning of the book.

Preface to the story: the real present

"We're in the last chance saloon," said Pete Broadbent, bishop of Willesden and one of the architects of Reform and Renewal. "All the demographic evidence shows that, unless we do something in the next five or 10 years, we're shot. There are those who say this [programme] is alien and who want to dig their heels in, but we're facing a demographic time bomb."

The evidence was "indisputable", said John Spence, chair of the church's finance committee and a former Lloyds Bank executive. "Twenty years ago the demographics matched the population as a whole. Now we're 20 years older than the population. Unless we do something, the church will face a real crisis." Among the changes is a redistribution of funding, largely away from struggling rural parishes to churches in deprived urban areas and those seen as innovative and energetic in adapting to social change.

"Some dioceses are being funded to do not very much," said Broadbent. "And some dioceses are underfunded, but are doing an amazing job in trying circumstances. It's about how we divvy up the money to go to places that can use it well and have the greatest need."

Harriet Sherwood, *The Guardian*[2]

The story of *The Churchgoer's Charter*[3]

The time is set some years in the future. The story is in five parts:

Present-future

The bright flash and camera lights of the nation's press reporters filled the Hall at Church House. The Bishop of Southbury, Michael Talent, blinked. Flanked by Bishops, plus other officials from Church House and Sir Marcus Lloyd from the Church Commissioners, Bishop Michael began his speech

> Ladies and Gentlemen. As you will know, today sees the launch of one of the most important documents the Church of England has produced this Century . . . even though we are less than a few decades into a new Millennium. The House of Bishops has felt for some time that the church is too unwieldy in its structure to meet the needs of the people. There has been too much bureaucracy and red tape, and not enough action.

2 http://www.theguardian.com/world/2015/nov/21/justin-welby-church-england-new-synod, accessed 9 August 2016.

3 This was originally published in *Signs of the Times*, Lent 1992, and in a revised form in *Modern Believing*, July 2011, with the addition of the Postscript. It also appeared in Percy, *The Ecclesial Canopy*, pp. 198–204.

Congregations have declined in number: confidence in the Church has dwindled. Today we hope to put the Church of England back on the road to recovery, with the launch of *The Churchgoer's Charter*. This will give power back to the people, and will make clergy and churches more accountable to the parishes they are supposed to be serving . . .

Bishop Michael held up the glossy volume; camera motors whirred, and journalists began punching in copy into their portable faxes. 'This will look great in the papers,' thought the Bishop to himself.' He was right. The headlines and leader columns were fulsome in their praise. *The Times* wrote a lead article under the caption 'Bishop Sees Red (Tape)'; 'Bishop Prunes Vine' reported *The Telegraph*; 'Weeding the Weedy Church' trumpeted *The Sun*, lauding the Bishop in an article on page seven.

   The Churchgoer's Charter had all begun after the government had been re-elected in 2015. It was the Prime Minister's idea. Britain's drift towards becoming a Republic had been sealed with the suspension of the House of Lords, now replaced by a new Upper House of Senators. Key posts, such as 'Archbishop of Canterbury', had become Cabinet positions, the Archbishop now being the 'Minister for Church Affairs'. It was inevitable, really, that the government and church now worked together more closely. Cathedrals had been identified as major tourist attractions and potential income earners as many as 30 years ago.

   When the government had stepped in to help rebuild and refurbish some, and then the Church Commissioners had applied for Euro-loan, it had opened the way for church and state to co-operate at levels unknown since the days of the Reformation. One day, over coffee, the Prime Minister had chatted informally to the Archbishop about 'opening up the church to the ordinary people . . . making ministers more accountable to their parishes . . . streamlining services, and capitalising on investments and ministries'. The fruit of their dialogue was a Republican commission, chaired by the Bishop of Southbury. And now, today, here was *The Churchgoer's Charter*.

Two years later

For the Revd. Maurice Green, *The Churchgoer's Charter* had been a Godsend. His flourishing eclectic church in a prosperous university town had been one of the first to opt out of the diocese of Southbury. As a self-governing body, they were now free from many of the diocesan central structures that they felt had held them back from competing effectively with other churches. They had stopped paying their quota. They had always found it uncomfortable supporting a broad church; all those causes, churches and theological outlooks they had never liked could now fend for themselves. Besides this, they had 'rationalised' their giving to charities and outside bodies, in favour of concentrating their resources on the local situation.

The results had been spectacular. Three fizzy new curates had been hired: the duff old one the diocese provided had been made redundant. The new administrator, together with a new full-time accountant had identified the areas of ministry that were most profitable. Fees for baptisms, weddings and funerals were set at market rates. A new building programme provided further opportunities for income-bearing outreach. The Church Flower Shop provided all tributes, displays and bouquets for weddings and funerals. The new Church Brasserie (The Cana Wine Bar) did the catering for all special events; it was already featured in the *Les Routiers Guide*. A local photographer was awarded the exclusive contract for all weddings at the church, after it had been put out to competitive tender. Certain hymns and prayers had attracted sponsorship from local companies. A local building firm was always mentioned when 'The Church is One Foundation' was sung; the local privatised electricity board sponsored the Collect for Evening Prayer, 'Lighten Our Darkness'.

Alas, other parishes had not been nearly so innovative. Some had obviously just not used their talents as wisely. Of the 14 churches in the town, six had already shut in two years, or been forced to merge. Of course, where possible, the stronger churches had attempted to cover areas that were now no longer served by a parish priest. But in some of the poorer estates on the fringe of town this had proved problematic. Providing a spiritual service at a realistic cost was difficult, especially when some of the people living in impoverished urban areas seemed 'to want something for nothing'. The Revd. Maurice Green did feel some sadness about this. Yet he comforted himself with the proverb that 'Sheep always go where the grass is'. People would come to church if it offered a good service: it wasn't his fault if some clergy buried their talents.

Three years later

Bishop Michael of Southbury sat in his study. The rain poured down outside. 'Ah, where on earth has it all gone wrong?' he sighed. He had some answers, of course; but they were painful to face. For example, there was the share issue in the Church of England, launched in 2020. Called *20–20 Vision: Your Share In the Future,* congregations had been encouraged to buy shares in the national church, which entitled them to discounts for weddings, funerals and baptisms, and a small dividend each year if the Church Commissioners' property speculation had gone well. It had been difficult to get off the ground initially, but the message had soon got home. The Share Issue would allow the public a greater say in how the church was run, and in its future direction.

To Bishop Michael, it had seemed the natural follow-up to *The Churchgoer's Charter,* which had already brought sweeping changes. Administrative posts had been cut by a half in his diocese. Education, Welfare and Social Responsibility officers had been pushed into 'private practice', so churches that needed them could purchase their services when they required them. The poorer parishes that had relied on them far too much in the past were now being encouraged to discover their own resources. Parishes had merged, inefficient clergy had been laid-off, and non-cost-effective areas of ministry identified and re-prioritised. As far as the Bishop was concerned, this was all excellent. However, it had got out of control. The agenda of *The Churchgoer's Charter* seemed like an unstoppable train. Now it looked as though he, the Bishop (of all people), was in danger of losing his job.

The problem had begun six months ago when the more cost-effective parishes in his Diocese had got together with other like-minded churches from neighbouring Dioceses. They had taken a comprehensive look at synodical and ecclesiastical structures. A clergyman from his own Diocese, the Revd. Maurice Green, had argued that Bishops were too many and too expensive: 'they confirm some people in your church once a year, ordain you a new Curate every four years and for that they get a hundred grand, a jolly nice house and a chauffeur-driven car! They're simply not worth it.'

Changes soon followed. Quotas were again withheld by wealthy parishes until all Bishops signed up for the 'ERM' – the Episcopal Exchange Rate Mechanism. The idea was to let Bishops 'float', and open up competition. They would no longer get the exclusive contract for a diocese. Those that did good confirmation addresses or retreats would be paid for their services; those that didn't would be gradually laid off. Some Bishops had already gone into 'private practice', specialising in confirmations, ordinations, dedications, after dinner speeches or radio broadcasts. However, for the Bishop of Southbury, the writing was on the wall: he knew he couldn't compete with some of the younger, more dynamic Bishops. His letter of resignation was prepared, and sat on the table. He was going to go on a very long retreat.

Four years later

Sitting in the Hall at Church House, Michael Talent, now the former Bishop of Southbury, must have thought he'd seen it all before. Masses of cameramen, journalists, photographers and soundmen lined up six or seven deep waiting for him to speak. He was not flanked by other Bishops this time. The only endorsement he had was a letter from his friend, the former Archbishop of Canterbury, who'd retired early due to ill health.

He began to speak, this time holding aloft a copy of a new book written by him, called *Faith in Society*. Its message, he said, was simple. You cannot place a value on spiritual service. Everyone is entitled to ministry, whether they can afford it or not. The National Church Service must be there for all its people, not just a few. The richer churches must support the poorer ones, even if it cost them so much that it hurt them. An apparently weak and 'broad' church is probably better-placed to serve society than a handful of strong eclectic ones. True, the Church is accountable to people, but also to God, the maker and judge of us all.

One journalist asked him where all this fresh vision had come from. In reply, Michael Talent said it was actually quite an old vision. But it hadn't been given a fair hearing. He referred to the Parable of the Talents, pointing out that most people thought that this was about wise financial investment. 'But,' he added, 'It is really about people and truth as well: they need to be invested in too, not buried out of fear. And sometimes apparently attractive gains need to be sacrificed; after all, we are called to lose our lives, not win them.' As he was speaking and replying to questions, journalists shuffled, looked irritated, and then began to leave.

'I bet this won't look very good in the newspapers tomorrow,' he thought. And he was right. They didn't print a word of it.

Postscript – ten years later

Retirement rather agreed with Bishop Michael. It had given him the chance to reflect on the changes that had come about in recent years, especially as a number of them had been something of surprise. For example, he could not have predicted the fate of the Revd. Maurice Green. His church had witnessed enormous growth in the early years of new development. But the constant demands to make the buildings and projects financially viable had led to compromises, and also to divisive and fractious church meetings. The Victorian gallery in the church – a huge space – had been converted into a fitness centre, complete with a glass wall that allowed those attending the gym to watch services as they lifted weights, ran on the machines, and exercised on the benches.

It had seemed like a good idea at the time. Come to church and get fit; pay a subscription too, and witness some worship. And why not stay for a Fairtrade drink in the café after? ('Sweat, Sacrament, Divine', ran the advertisement). But some of the worshippers – even dyed-in-the-wool modernisers – had objected. They did not think that their church was a place for a gym. Some objected that worship was now confused: could people really give their all to God if at the same time they were also thinking about their weight, their fitness, and how they looked? The out-sourcing of the Cana Wine Bar and café to a new catering company who paid good money for the franchise, but sat light to the ethos of the church, had also caused complications.

The church was still making money, and still had many members. But something was missing. Some worshippers felt the soul had gone from the place. Then the economic recession, which hit everyone and everything in its path, bit swiftly and deeply. Suddenly, church meetings were consumed by talks of mergers, redundancies, out-sourcing and rationalisations. Added to which, some worshippers just started to drift off to a local church with far fewer members, and no apparent entrepreneurial outlook at all. But which apparently had something that Maurice's church didn't: a soul. And a sense of awe and wonder, with a priest you could see in the week without going through a plethora of PAs and administrators. The church members were restless for change.

When Maurice's post came up for renewal, everything was basically fine; the recession was weathered; the income streams back on track; the number of worshippers steadied, having stemmed the earlier haemorrhaging. But the Church Council did not renew Maurice's contract. They thanked him for all he had done, but said that they felt God wanted to do something new with the church. To return it to being a place of sacredness and peace; a house of prayer, and an oasis of stillness. People wanted a change of direction; not what Maurice offered.

He left with a handsome pay-off, but somewhat bitter. And also curious. He remembered – from years ago at seminary – another pastor's words. Was it Niemoller, from Germany? He wasn't sure. But the gist of it was this. First the market forces came for the weaker parishes; but I didn't say anything. Then they came for the clergy who were deemed not to be successful or useful; but I didn't say anything. Then they came for the officers and administrators supporting the weaker parishes and clergy; and I didn't say anything. Then they came for the people who had introduced the change-management – for they too were expendable; and I didn't say anything. Then finally they came for me. But there was no-one left to speak for me.

Maurice Green's church had hired a new pastor – a former monk, called Benedict – who had not much in the way of business acumen, and little in the way of charismatic or dynamic leadership. There was not much money about anymore, and little in the way of numerical or financial growth. But Benedict prayed for his people, visited faithfully, and was seen about the parish. The Cana Wine Bar was taken back in to ownership by the church, and the space used to feed to poor. The gym and fitness centre went out of business, and now housed bunk-beds for the homeless.

Had the entrepreneurial church failed? It was hard to say. But the congregation seemed happy enough. There was energy for mission, but no longer the ersatz of chimera-consumerist Christianity. Something earthy and authentic was now coming into existence. Benedict talked about the church in a different way. His church, he said, was a safe space to trespass; a place for finding divine peace; a symbol of diversity in unity; and a Pentecostal laboratory. He said it was a theatre of basic drama and a centre for creativity. It was a temple of dialogue and an academy of committed information; and a place international exchange. He called the church to be a clinic for public exorcism; a broadcasting station for the voice of the poor, and a tower of reconciliation. He suggested that the ministry of the church was to be a motel for pilgrims – and a house of vicarious feasts. It was to be a hut for the shepherd; a dwelling place for God. Just as Christ pitched his tent in the midst of humanity, so should the church live amongst all God's people. The church was to be a sign of pro-existence; an expression of God's utter, total love for all humanity.[4]

4 I owe these insights to M.S. Stancliffe, in his reflections on the place and purpose of a cathedral.

So, gone were the aims, objectives, targets and measuring of outcomes. 'Just how do you measure God's activity?' asked Benedict of his congregation, in a sermon one Sunday. 'The church is not competing in a popularity contest, with Christianity hoping to win more customers and consumers in contemporary culture than other activities. Our faith is about sacrifice and service. Who knows, we might find we're at our best when we're faithful, not successful', he argued. It made people think.

And Bishop Michael had watched this all unfold. It gave him just the smallest pang of pleasure to see the pendulum swing back, to a time long before the *Churchgoer's Charter* was launched. But he knew it might swing again. Meanwhile, some lessons had been learnt.

A parable

There was a woman who lived on her own. She had no neighbours or close friends, but there was an old man who lived half a mile away. The woman had a house and a garden, and at the foot of a garden, she had two apple trees that were her pride and joy. Once she was called away to see a sick relative. She gave the keys of the house to the old man, and asked him to check the house, but he was too infirm to tend the garden. She thought she would be away for a few days, but she was in fact gone for a few years.

From far away she heard of drought and storms, and she feared the worst. But when she did get home, things were pretty well as she had left them. She went into the garden, which was very overgrown. But the apple trees were still there, and in full bloom. She drank it all in, and her heart filled with delight and thanks.

Then she went to the tool shed, got out her pruners, went to the apple trees, and started to cut away at the dead wood. And she thought of the time when there would be apples for herself and for her neighbour.[5]

5 Countryman, *The Truth About Love*, p. 86.

Afterword
Futurescape?

> no one puts new wine into old wineskins. Otherwise, the wine will burst the skins, and the wine is lost as well as the skins. But new wine is for fresh wineskins.
>
> Mark 2: 22

That the Church of England has a future is not in any real doubt. The question is, what kind of future? Moreover, how does this future relate to the wider polity of the global Anglican Communion? As we have begun to see in this study, the trajectory – the direction of travel for the church – is increasingly towards centralised management, organisational apparatus, and the kind of creeping concerns that might consume an emerging suburban sectarianism, instead of a national church, or indeed an international Communion. This, it should be said, is primarily manifested in the current leadership of Anglicanism, and it may not be reflected and reified quite so strongly on the ground, in ordinary parish churches. That said, the signs of the times are there for all to read.

Recent history testifies to this. The official publisher for the Church of England will now rarely, if ever, publish documents on social, national or international issues of common concern. The heyday of *Faith in the City: The Archbishop of Canterbury's Commission on Urban Priority Areas* (1985), and reports like it, seems like another world. Indeed, *Faith in the City* (1985) – which was once the best-selling report ever published by the Church of England – has now ceded that top position to *Mission-Shaped Church* (2004). So, in just a generation, the Church of England has moved from an advocacy of the poor and the marginalised, to promoting its own niche (mainly bourgeois) congregations under the nomenclature of 'fresh expressions'. Today's Church of England mainly publishes texts that specialise in liturgy, missional goals, organisational ephemera or evangelistic activism.

It is a development which contains a salutary lesson. Jesus did not organise 'fresh expressions' of synagogue life and worship; and nor did he advocate 'synagogue-planting'. Jesus's agenda was deeper and broader than the replication of cosy worshipping communities. His mission was to usher in the Kingdom of God. His ministry fashioned the love of neighbours, aliens and strangers. In all its recent evangelistic and organisational fervour, the Church of England has not found a new identity in the twenty-first century; it has, rather, lost itself. It has forgotten that the church is not an end in itself, but rather only a *means* – to help enable that prayer that says 'thy kingdom come, thy will be done'.

The current Archbishop is, apparently, immensely fond of *The West Wing* TV series (according to his closest staff), and he closely identifies with the drama played out in the series and the twists and turns that affect the leadership of President Bartlet. In contrast I rather think the Church of England is far more like the fictional communities featured in *The News from Lake Wobegon* from Garrison Keillor's long-running radio show, *A Prairie Home Companion*. I say this because the current vogueish promotion of 'church planting' has been rather fetishised by the current leadership of the Church of England.

Yet the 'church' is not a 'pre-formed' or nursery-grown shrub that can simply be taken off the shelf, or some mechanistic production line, and 'planted' in a community. A church is a natural, organic community of worshippers, rooted in a wider community. The maturity, stability and longevity of a church is formed out of the community 'soil' that sustains and nurtures it, and helps to form its usefulness, relevance and resilience in a context that has to cope with the challenges and opportunities it also addresses.

Thus, whereas *Faith in City* was rooted in a rich theology of the Kingdom of God, and so asked 'what kinds of communities are these?' and 'how and why might such communities be re-formed to correspond with God's purposes for humanity and society?', *Mission-Shaped Church*, in contrast, asks few such questions of society and naturally assumes God could not be truly present in our communities until bespoke congregations are planted within them. *Mission-Shaped Church* represents a weak and bleak theology of mission: one in which God could not be present in creation and society unless there was an intentional planting. Moreover, *Mission-Shaped Church* assumes the parable of the sower (Mt. 13: 1–9, etc.) is all about the seed and its fecundity. *Faith in the City*, in contrast, read the parable quite differently. God's mission is also about what the church does with the poor and rocky soil.

Ultimately, it will take a lot more to save the Church of England than a blend of management theory, various forms of top-down heroic leadership promising endless transformation,[1] specious secular sorcery with statistics,

---

1 On this, see Tourish, *The Dark Side of Transformational Leadership: A Critical Perspective*, London: Routledge, 2013. Tourish argues that leaders offering heroic, charismatic, visionary, messianic-transformative discourse might actually do irreparable harm to the institutions and organisations that are being led, and only serve to encourage narcissism, megalomania and poor decision-making, and at great expense to the followers.

and evangelical up-speak. Such potions will only have a limited impact on the wider body of the church. A mild tonic, perhaps; but surely not a cure? Better remedies will require a much deeper ecclesial comprehension than the present leadership currently offer. The prevailing culture of missional diagnosis, prognosis and ecclesial pharmacology – coupled to endless new ecclesial 'fitness regimes' (it is not uncommon to encounter seminars and conferences on 'healthy churches' which, by implication, indict those churches that do not sign up for the programme) – tends to demoralise more than it inspires. There seems to be no sagacity, serious science or spiritual substance to the curatives currently being offered.

Indeed, it is already apparent in some Church of England dioceses that the current recipes, far from producing success, are having quite the opposite effect, and only resulting in further stagnation and decline.[2] Yet in his speech at Harrogate for a conference of church leaders run by the New Wine movement (March 2016), the Archbishop of Canterbury praised its leadership for leading a turn-around in the fortunes of the church:

> I believe from the bottom of my heart that the long years of winter in the Church – especially in the Church of England – are changing ... . The ice is thawing; the spring is coming. There is a new spring in the Church . . . New Wine (leaders) have been heroes, and will continue to be. You've borne the burden; you've turned the tide. There is renewal and life springing up.[3]

There is some irony here. For the 'new wine' that is being poured into the Church of England is mainly organisational and activist in character. True, it is missional – but in a narrow, prescribed evangelical dialect – such that it is also warily sectarian. The 'suburban captivity of the church' – which Gibson Winter prophesied would actually *inhibit* the renewal of the churches – has now fully set in.[4] The Church of England is being slowly kettled into becoming a suburban sect; corralling its congregations; controlling its clergy; and centralising its communication. Instead of being a local, dispersed, national institution, it is becoming a bureaucratic organisation, centrally controlling and managing its ministry and mission – and all in a manner that is hierarchically scripted.

Correspondingly, Church of England bishops are becoming less and less the 'chief pastors of their clergy' as they used to be. Bishops increasingly operate like Area Managers – with targets set by London headquarters, replete with vision, 'on-message' tropes and strategies – to load on to the smaller local branch managers (i.e. parish clergy). Bishops still tend to think

---

2 Tim Wyatt, 'Rochester is Skint, says Bishop', *Church Times*, 25 July 2016, p. 5.
3 Tim Wyatt, 'Welby: Church is Entering New Spring – At Last', *Church Times*, 11 March 2016, p. 7.
4 See Winter, *The Suburban Captivity of the Churches: And the Prospects of their Renewal to Serve the Whole Life of the Emerging Metropolis*, New York: Doubleday, 1961.

of themselves as pastors on the ground. But unconsciously and imperceptibly, they are now driving a subordinate workforce – the clergy – with a range of increasing target-led demands. To be sure, bishops still provide pastoral-spiritual accident and emergency and first aid. And bishops still imagine that they have significant advantageous local knowledge. But undetectably, their role has moved from being *receivers* of local information, to becoming *disseminators* of central information to local places. They market and sell a centrally-originated vision to a local context. But they seldom receive the local contextual information in return, or take it to inform and shape the centre of power.

The irony of Archbishop Welby's advocacy of new wine is that it is, in all probability, precisely this issue that the Church of England now wrestles with. The new wine pleads to be understood as an elixir of renewal that is restorative to the body. This new wine contains all the ingredients (i.e. the fruits) of secular organisational theory and practice, blended with evangelical up-speak, which is now being poured into a much older institution. And yet in tasting this new wine, there is plenty to say about its first impressions on the palate. There are hints of pragmatism; it is impactful and arresting; there are hints of secularism combined with biblicism. It is sweet in places, but also has an acidic tang. There are undertones of shrill evangelicalism that are detectable. This is a wine that insists on itself, and tries to takes control of the taste buds. The wine is not easy to drink with anything else, and it displaces subtler flavours that those trying to savour an older wine might remember. It is a strong wine. But it also lacks depth, intricacy and lighter, pleasing notes. It lacks the ageing, quality and character of a long-established vineyard; it lacks the craft that would come through generations of Master vignerons. This new wine may not burst the older wineskins. But it will test their strength and reflexivity to the very core.

The administering of the proverbial new wine – the restorative tonic that is supposed to help the church recuperate – emerges out of a combination of poor ecclesial comprehension, coupled to a conceit that assumes that the present church is an 'unfit' and 'unhealthy' body that can be diagnosed, cured and retrained by those who have perceived how to cure its soul. There is some arrogance here too, which must partly account for why any resistance to the reforming initiatives and agendas of renewal led by the Archbishop is either dismissed or denigrated. As we observed earlier, the Archbishop has set about reforming and renewing the Church of England with a zeal and zest more usually associated with secular management consultants. Yet as the American contextual theologian James Hopewell noted, rather than begin by trying to reform the church, leaders should first make an effort to comprehend it.[5]

Moreover, this same error (i.e. lack of ecclesial comprehension, coupled to an overestimation of and overinvestment in the ability and capacity to

5 Hopewell, *Congregation*, 1987.

deliver reform) is now beginning to have a significant impact on the wider Anglican Communion. For example, the Archbishop of Canterbury's revisionist interpretation and communication from the Anglican Consultative Council (ACC) in April 2016 suggested that the ACC 'endorsed' and 'affirmed' an earlier Communique issued by the Primates in January 2016. This, in effect, amounted to the Archbishop claiming that the ACC and Primates were of one mind on how to handle the Episcopal Church in America (TEC), and address the issue of same-sex-relations and marriage. In fact, the ACC was very clear that it had only agreed to 'receive' the January 2016 report from the Primates – and that such reception did not imply any endorsement or acceptance; or indeed, a rejection. Rather, 'reception' expresses a continuing, open process of receptivity and discernment.

Yet the Archbishop's own 'spin' on the 'reception' of the Communique stated that the ACC meeting of April 2016 '*supports and accepts* all the Primates' Meetings conclusions', including the 'consequences' meted out to the American Episcopal church. A significant number of the ACC dissented, stating that 'there was no plenary discussion or decision with respect to the Primates' Communique . . . there did not seem to be a common mind on the issue other than a clear commitment to avoid further confrontation and division'.[6]

Thus, we see the same mind-set at work: an attempt to centralise, control and manage the Communion – one that is not above a re-narration of recent events, even when this is at odds with the actual history. This is classic, text-book politicking: 'spin' exerted on stories and facts that is attempting to create entirely new memories and impressions of recent events. It is Machiavellian, to be sure – but also risks exposure to malevolence and malpractice. So it seems that the ends might actually justify the means in this new, emergent ecclesial polity of Justin's archiepiscopacy. This is a church where technique, instead of being the servant of organisation, is now its master. It is a church where physique eclipses mystique: Goliath's muscle preferred to David's wisdom. It is a polity where the aesthetic is now sacrificed to the effective. It is a church where values and principles are set aside in favour of pragmatism and vigour.

The problem the Church of England now faces, and that is also being slowly detected across the wider Anglican Communion, might be neatly encapsulated in Ernst Friedrich Schumacher's *Guide for the Perplexed* (1977).[7] In his landmark book, Schumacher distinguishes between two types of problem – convergent or divergent. Convergent ones are those that get a convergent solution – we can all agree on the right answer or principles. But a divergent problem arises out of divergent contexts or institutions. We can't

---

6 *Church Times*, News, 13 May 2016, p. 10. See also Wondra, 'The Importance of Moral Authority: Reflections on Current Events in the Anglican Communion', in *Anglican Theological Review*, Vol. 98, no. 3, Summer 2016, pp. 533–544.
7 Schumacher, *Guide for the Perplexed*, New York: Harper, 1977.

agree on the answer(s), because the values at the heart of the institution are contested. Divergent problems tend to arise from diverse bodies. The Church of England is clearly a highly divergent body struggling with the imposition of convergent structures and solutions. This is not a new problem. One could argue that the post-war era for the Church of England has been a series of epochs, in which convergence has been sought as the socio-public identity of the church has gradually retracted into something more sectarian.

Thus, the divergent nature of the Church of England – a gift to its ecclesial polity, I would argue, and of the Holy Spirit – is being undermined and overrun with convergent processes that seek to deprive the church of its divergent, broad, plural nature. The convergent solutions are often driven by mission-minded middle managers who really do mean well – but also do not understand that the inchoate secular values they have adopted do violence to the body they seek to reform. Schumacher argues that convergent problems are those that belong with the non-living universe, whilst divergent problems are with the universe of the living.

This is perhaps why the focus on mission and management in the Church of England is often experienced as robotic and unfeeling. Bureaucratic processes and criteria are being applied to something that is supposed to be spiritually *felt* and discerned. Moreover, the leadership that is currently operating in the Church of England can sometimes sound like the proverbial Englishmen abroad: unable to make themselves understood by the natives, they simply repeat themselves, only louder each time. At some fundamental level, it has not crossed their minds that they were understood the first time, and that the ensuing silence and increasing disengagement *is* the response to oft-repeated and amplified messages.

The Church of England will need leadership that exhibits much greater theological depth than it is offered at present. Moreover, this will need to be a theological leadership not just for the church, but for the wider public too. Responding to the multiple atrocities that took place in Paris on 13 November 2015, which included the murder of many young people in the Bataclan Nightclub, and over 130 deaths, the Archbishop of Canterbury gave an interview to *BBC Songs of Praise* and stated that the atrocity had caused him to doubt his faith.[8] Matthew Parris, writing in *The Spectator* a few days later, openly questioned whether this personal and rather confessional insight into the quality of the Archbishop's belief was appropriate and adequate for the wider public:

> as we are in confessional mood, here's an anxiety of my own. The Paris atrocity has not occasioned me any new doubts, but Justin Welby's remarks have caused me to doubt Archbishop Welby. Speaking on behalf of God, I have to ask the Archbishop: 'Justin, where are you in

8 Jess Staufenberg, 'Paris Attacks: Archbishop Justin Welby Admits 'Doubt' over God's Presence after Tragedy', *The Independent*, 22 November 2015, p. 8.

all this?' . . . I'm not a believer, but I try to understand what believers believe. Christian theology has a long and distinguished intellectual history; faith's most difficult conundrums have all been raised and answers (acceptable or otherwise) have been offered to all the obvious questions.[9]

There is no way of evading the public's demand for some strong ecclesial leadership that grapples openly with hard questions, and engages richly with the 'long and distinguished intellectual history' of Christianity. To be sure, the Archbishop speaks commendably about his personal life, and exhibits a rare humanity for someone in the constant glare of the media, and in public life. He can speak movingly of his own personal situations, tragedies and losses – past and present. And on the whole, the media appreciate this very much. +Justin Welby also speaks about the religious interlocutors that have apparently shaped his life, and these include the spirituality of the Chemin Neuf community, for example, or that of St. Benedict. Yet there is little sense of how *The Rule of Benedict* shapes the Archbishop's thinking and practice; in fact, his modus operandi seems rather at odds with that of Benedict. And despite his moving personal testimonies and anecdotes of how God might have worked in *his* life, there is a marked absence of salient and culturally resonant 'God-talk', or for that matter of any persuasive public theology.

As Evelyn Underhill once reminded a former Archbishop of Canterbury (Cosmo Gordon Lang) in a personal letter penned in 1930, 'the most interesting thing about religion is God – and the people are hungry for God'.[10] Underhill was concerned about the inner life of the clergy. Her concern was that the multiplicity of the clergy's duties had diminished some priests' grounding in a life of prayer. She was making a plea for the church to talk less about mission, and to say more about God. It was once said of the late Cardinal Basil Hume that he 'had the gift of being able to talk to the English about God without making them wish they were somewhere else'.[11] In the same vein, the Church of England needs less 'personal testimony' from its leaders, and more public theology.

We live in interesting times. The national picture of church-going and religious belief in the United Kingdom has recently arrived at a crossroads. Half the population in the UK now declare themselves to be non-religious – 'nones', as they are dubbed by sociologists and media commentators. It is safe to assume that they will not be won over to return to the church by increasingly organisational, theologically narrow and vogueish sectarian expressions of faith. Yet the fact that the church lives in difficult times is not the problem; that we constantly forget the church has always lived in

---

9 Matthew Parris, 'Has the Archbishop of Canterbury forsaken God?', *The Spectator*, 28 November 2015, p. 12.

10 cf., Beeley and Britton 'Introduction: Toward a Theology of Leadership' in *Anglican Theological Review*, Volume 91, no. 1, Winter 2009, p. 6.

11 Paul Vallely, writing of Cardinal Basil Hume, *The Independent*, 31 December 1999, p. 3.

difficult times – that is the problem. Every generation of Christians that has ever lived has lived in modern times. So, modern times are not the problem. The question is simply, 'what is distinctive about *our* modernity'? Thus, the Church of England now faces a very real struggle – how to continue to be public, pastoral and prophetic in a world that is increasingly privatised, polarised and poverty-stricken.

At present, the church seems to be aping the world, and not offering an alternative. Yet Anglicanism has never sought to be a mere denomination, in some kind of inter-ecclesial 'survival of the fittest' and 'best adaptive polity' contest, set within the context of global churches. Anglicanism is more than this. As a church, it is ultimately a mode for making deep sense of the experience of God. It offers a hopeful theo-social vision for the construction of reality, and for the building of a world. It is meant to be, inherently, a broad church – capacious and generous.

So where and what is the hope in all this? As to where, Anglicanism will have to look deeper into itself for some of the answers here. The polity does have the resources to prevail in the midst of trials and tribulations, and it always has prevailed. It has an in-built reflexivity, resilience and tenacity, grounded in its local congregations and profound incarnational theology, expressed locally and faithfully the world over. It has deep theological and spiritual resources too – including art, architecture, music, literature, poetry and the beauty of its sublime, transcendent liturgy. That will surely withstand some of the forces, fads and fashions that we have discussed throughout this book. And as to what the hope is, Anglicanism will continue to look to God for this. This is a polity that is profoundly rooted in a truly epic spiritual and theological vision of God; one that is, above all, broad, generous and orthodox. And *broad* is the key word here; because narrow Anglicanism is almost a contradiction in terms. It is the breadth that defines Anglican polity. And it is the breadth that will save it, and will surely see that it continues to flourish in a future that is yet to unfold.

Bibliography

Allberry, S. *Is God Anti-Gay? And Other Questions About Homosexuality, the Bible and Same-Sex Attraction.* Epsom, Surrey: Good Book Company, 2013.

Alvesson, M. and Spicer, A. '(Un)Conditional Surrender? Why Do Professionals Willingly Comply with Managerialism?' *Journal of Organisational Change Management,* Vol. 29, no. 1, 2016, pp. 29–45.

Ammerman, N., Dudley, C. and Roozen, D. *Organizing Religious Work.* Hartford Institute for Religious Research, July 2002.

Anderson, B. *Imagined Communities.* London: Verso, 2006 (new edition: original publication 1983).

Applebaum, A. *The Iron Curtain.* London: Allen Lane, 2013.

Arbuckle, G. *Refounding the Church: Dissent for Leadership.* London: Geoffrey Chapman, 1993.

Aron, R. *Main Currents in Sociological Thought.* Vol. 2. Harmondsworth, Middlesex: Penguin, 1970.

Atherstone, A. *Archbishop Justin Welby: Risk-Taker and Reconciler.* London: DLT, 2014.

Augustine. *On The Trinity.* trans. S. McKenna C.Ss.R. Washington, DC: Catholic University of America Press, 1963.

Avis, P. *Authority, Leadership and Conflict in the Church.* London: Mowbray, 1992.

Avis, P. *Church Drawing Near: Spirituality and Mission in a Post-Christian Culture.* London: T&T Clark, 2003.

Avis, P. 'Anglican Ecclesiology'. In *The Routledge Companion to the Christian Church,* eds G. Mannion with L. Mudge, p. 202. London and New York: Routledge, 2007.

Avis, P. *The Identity of Anglicanism: Essentials of Anglican Ecclesiology.* London: T&T Clark, 2007.

Avis, P. *Becoming a Bishop: A Theological Handbook of Episcopal Ministry.* London: Bloomsbury, 2015.

Badaracco, J.L. 'We Don't Need Another Hero', *Harvard Business Review,* Vol. 79, no. 8, 2001, pp. 120–126.

Bailey, M. and Redden, G. *Mediating Faiths: Religion and Socio-Cultural Change in the Twenty-First Century.* Farnham, Surrey: Ashgate, 2015.

Barth, K. *Church Dogmatics.* Edinburgh: T&T Clark, 1958. Vol. IV, Part 2, chapter 15, p. 648.

Bates, S. *A Church at War: Anglicans and Homosexuality.* London: I.B. Tauris, 2004.

Bates, S. 'Living Apart Together', *The Tablet*, 26 September 2015, pp. 8–9.

Bates, S. 'Back from the Brink', *The Tablet*, 23 January 2016, pp. 9–10.

Bayne, S. *An Anglican Turning Point: Documents and Interpretations*. Austin, TX: Church Historical Society, 1964.

Bebbington, D. and Larcen, T. (eds). *Modern Christianity and Cultural Aspirations*. London: Continuum, 2003.

Beeley, C.A. and Britton, J.H. 'Introduction: Toward a Theology of Leadership', *Anglican Theological Review*, Vol. 91, no. 1, Winter 2009, p. 6.

Bellah, R. (ed.). *Habits of the Heart: Individualism and Commitment in American Life*. Berkeley, CA: University of California Press, 1985 (2nd edition: 1996).

Berger, P. 'A Market Model for the Analysis of Ecumenicity', *Social Research*, Vol. 30, no. 1, 1963, p. 87.

Berger, P. *The Sacred Canopy*. Garden City, NY: Doubleday, 1967.

Bermejo, L. *The Spirit of Life: The Holy Spirit in the Life of the Christian*. Chicago, IL: Loyola Press, 1989.

Bernstein, W. *The Four Pillars of Investing: Lessons for Building a Winning Portfolio*. Chicago, IL: McGraw-Hill Professional, 2002.

Bingham, J. 'Welby's Way', *The Tablet*, 2 January 2016, p. 11.

Bird, J., Curtis, B., Putnam, T., Robertson G. and Tickner, L. *Mapping the Futures: Local Cultures, Global Change*. London: Routledge, 1993.

Bonzo, J.M. and Stevens, M.R. *Wendell Berry and the Cultivation of Life: A Reader's Guide*. Grand Rapids, MI: Brazos Press, 2008.

Bowden, J. and Richardson, A. *A New Dictionary of Theology*. London: SCM, 1983.

Bradbury, N. *Practical Theology and Pierre Andre-Liege*. Farnham, Surrey: Ashgate, 2014.

Brotton, J. *A History of the World in Twelve Maps*. London: Penguin, 2012.

Brown, A. *The Myth of the Strong Leader*. London: Bodley Head, 2014.

Browning, D. *A Fundamental Practical Theology: Descriptive and Strategic Proposals*. Minneapolis, MN: Fortress Press, 1991.

Bruce, S. (ed.). *Religion and Modernization*. Oxford: Oxford University Press, 1992.

Bryson, W. *Notes from a Small Island*. London: Black Swan, 1996.

Bühlmann, W. *The Coming of the Third Church*. Slough, Berkshire: St Paul Publications, 1974.

Burleigh, M. *Sacred Causes: Religion and Politics from European Dictators to Al Qaeda*. London: Harper, 2006.

Carr, W. *The Priest-like Task*. London: SPCK, 1985.

Carr, W. *Say One For Me*. London: SPCK, 1992.

Chandler, A. *The Church of England in the Twentieth Century*. Woodbridge, Suffolk: Boydell Press, 2006.

Clements, R. *Exchanging the Truth of God for a Lie: One Man's Spiritual Journey to Find the Truth About Homosexuality*. London: Courage Books, 2008.

Coontz, S. and Thatcher, A. *God, Sex and Gender*. Oxford: Wiley-Blackwell, 2011.

Cornwall, S. *Theology and Sexuality*. London: SCM, 2013.

Cosgrove, D. 'Mapping the World'. In *Maps: Finding our place in the world*, eds J.R. Akerman and R.W. Karrow, pp. 65–115. Chicago, IL: University of Chicago Press, 2007.

'Counting the Doomsday Option: Church of England – Another Public Service is In Crisis', *The Economist*, [USA edition], 1 September 2001.

Countryman, W. *The Truth About Love: Reintroducing the Good News*. London: SPCK, 1993.

Cray, G. (ed.). *Mission-Shaped Church*. London: Church House Publishing, 2004.

Croft, S. (ed.). *The Future of the Parish System: Shaping the Church of England for the 21st Century*. London: Church House Publishing, 2006.

Davie, G. *Religion in Britain Since 1945: Believing without Belonging*. Oxford: Clarendon, 1995.

Davis, C. *Religion and the Making of Society: Essays in Social Theology*. Cambridge: Cambridge University Press, 1994.

Day, A. *Contemporary Issues in the Worldwide Anglican Communion: Powers and Pieties*. Farnham, Surrey: Ashgate, 2015.

DeRogatis, A. *Moral Geography: Maps, Missionaries and the American Frontier*. New York: Columbia University Press, 2003.

DeRogatis, A. *Saving Sex: Sexuality and Salvation in American Evangelicalism*. Oxford: Oxford University Press, 2015.

Douglas, M. *How Institutions Think*. London: Routledge & Kegan Paul, 1986.

Duggan, M. 'The Salt and the Sweetness', *Church Times*, 14 August 2015, pp. 15–17.

Ecclestone, G. (ed.). *The Parish Church?* London: Mowbray, 1988.

Elford, K. *Creating the Future of the Church: A Practical Guide to Addressing Whole-system Change*. London: SPCK, 2013.

Eliot, T.S. *The Idea of a Christian Society*. London: Harcourt, 1960.

Evagrius. 'Chapters on Prayer'. In *The Praktikos and Chapters on Prayer*. trans. J. Bamberger. Kalamazoo, MI: Cistercian Publications, 1981.

Evans, G. and Wright, J. (eds). *The Anglican Tradition*. London: SPCK, 1991.

Faber, F.W. *1854*; 'There is a Wideness in God's Mercy'. In *The New Century Hymnal*, Cleveland, OH: Pilgrim Press, 1995, no. 23.

Faith in the City: A Call for Action by Church and Nation: The Report of the Archbishops Commission on Urban Priority Areas. London: [Christian Action], 1985.

Fayol, H. *General and Industrial Management*. London: Pitman, 1916.

Field, C. and Clements, B. 'Public Opinion Toward Homosexuality and Gay Rights in Great Britain', *Public Opinion Quarterly*, July 2014.

Filby, E. *God and Mrs Thatcher: The Battle for Britain's Soul*. London: Biteback, 2015.

Forster, E.M. *A Passage to India*. London: Allen Lane, 1924.

Foundation, L., Tufano, P. and Walker, P. 'Collaborating with Congregations: Opportunities for Financial Services in the Inner City', *Harvard Business Review*, July–August 1999, pp. 57–68.

Freire, P. *Pedagogy of the Oppressed*. Harmondsworth, Middlesex: Penguin, 1972.

Freire, P. *Education for Critical Consciousness*. New York: Seabury Press, 1973.

From Anecdote to Evidence: Report of the Archbishops' Council. London: Church House Publishing, 2014.

Garrett, G. *My Church Is Not Dying: Episcopalians in the 21st Century*. New York: Morehouse, 2015.

Gittoes, J., Green B. and Heard, J. *Generous Ecclesiology*. London: SCM, 2013.

Goodall, J. 'How to Relish the Parish Church', *The Big Issue*, 28 September–4 October 2015, p. 7.

Graham, E. *Transforming Practice*. London: Mowbray, 1996.

Greaves, M. 'God's Management Consultants: The Church of England Turns to Bankers for Salvation', *The Spectator*, 18 July 2015, p. 20. See: www.spectator.co.uk/

features/9583672/gods-management-consultants-the-church-of-england-turns-to-bankers-for-salvation/, accessed 9 August 2016.

Grierson, D. *Transforming a People of God.* Melbourne: Joint Board of Christian Education of Australia and New Zealand, 1985.

Groves, P. (ed.). *The Anglican Communion and Homosexuality: A Resource to Enable Listening and Dialogue.* London: SPCK, 2008.

Groves, P. and Parry Jones, A. *Living Reconciliation.* London: SPCK, 2014.

Guder, D.W. *Called to Witness: Doing Missional Theology.* Grand Rapids, MI: Eerdmans, 2015.

Guest, M., Aune, K., Sharma, S. and Warner, R. *Christianity and the University Experience: Understanding Student Faith.* London: Bloomsbury, 2014.

Habgood, J. *Varieties of Unbelief.* London: DLT, 2000.

Hardy, D.W. *God's Ways with the World: Thinking and Practising Christian Faith.* Edinburgh: T&T Clark, 1996.

Hardy, D.W. *Finding the Church.* London: SCM Press, 2001.

Hardy, D.W. 'Anglicanism in the Twenty-First Century; Scriptural, Local, Global'. Unpublished paper from Society for the Study of Anglicanism at the American Academy of Religion, 2004, p. 5, quoted in Green, S. *Beating the Bounds: A Symphonic Approach to Orthodoxy in the Anglican Communion.* Eugene, OR: Wipf and Stock, 2014, p. 176.

Hare, D. *Racing Demon.* London: Faber, 1990.

Hauerwas, S. and Willimon, W.H. *The Holy Spirit.* Nashville, TN: Abingdon Press, 2015.

Hefferman, M. *Wilful Blindness: Why We Ignore the Obvious at Our Peril.* London: Simon & Schuster, 2012.

Henwood, G. 'Is Equal Marriage an Anglican Ideal?' *Journal of Anglican Studies*, Vol. 13, no. 1, May (2015): pp. 92–113.

Higgins, C. quoting Bennett in 'The Armchair Revolutionary'. *The Guardian Magazine*, 31 October 2015, pp. 21–29 at p. 25.

Hill, M. *Ecclesiastical Law* [2nd edition]. Oxford: Oxford University Press, 2001.

Holmes III, U.T. *The Future Shape of Ministry: A Theological Projection.* New York: Seabury Press, 1975.

Holmes III, U.T. *What is Anglicanism?* Wilton, CT: Morehouse-Barlow Co, 1982.

Hooker, R. *Of the Laws of Ecclesiastical Polity,* ed. A. McGrade, Cambridge: Cambridge University Press, 1989, pp. 158–176, 161–175.

Hopewell, J. *Congregation: Stories and Structures.* London: SCM, 1987.

Hutton, W. *The State We're In.* London: Random House, 1996.

Issues in Human Sexuality: a statement by the House of Bishops of the General Synod of the Church of England, December 1991. London: Church House Publishing, 1991.

Jaques, E. *A General Theory of Bureaucracy.* London: Heinemann, 1976.

Jenkins, T. *Religion in Everyday English Life: An Ethnographic Approach.* Oxford: Berghahn, 1999.

Jinkins, M. *The Church Faces Death: Ecclesiology in a Post-modern Context.* Oxford: Oxford University Press, 1999.

Kane, R. 'Tragedies of Communion: Seeking Reconciliation Amid Colonial Legacies'. *Anglican Theological Review*, Vol. 97, no. 3, Summer 2015: pp. 391ff.

Kaoma, K. 'An African or Un-African Sexual Identity? Religion, Globalisation and Sexual Politics in sub-Saharan Africa', in *Public Religion and Politics of Homosexuality in Africa*, eds. A. Van Klinken and E. Chitando. London: Ashgate, 2016.

Kaye, B. *Conflict and the Practice of Christian Faith: An Anglican Experiment*. Eugene, OR: Cascade Books, 2009.

Kotter, J.P. *A Force for Change: How Leadership Differs from Management*. New York: Free Press, 1990.

Kotter, J.P. *Leading Change*. Cambridge, MA: Harvard Business School Press, 1996.

Laughlin, R. In *Managing the Church? Order and Organisation in a Secular Age*, eds M. Percy and G. Evans. Sheffield, Yorkshire: Sheffield Academic Press, 2000, pp. 49–77.

LeRoy, E. *Patterns of Polity: Varieties of Church Governance*. Cleveland, OH: Pilgrims Press, 2001.

Lewis-Anthony, J. '"Promising Much, Delivering Little": Ministry Development Review and Its Secular Critics', *Modern Believing*, Vol. 53, no. 2, April 2012.

Linzey, A. and Kirker, R. (eds). *The Gays and the Future of Anglicanism: Responses to the Windsor Report*. Winchester, Hampshire: O Books, 2005.

McAdoo, H.R. *Anglican Heritage: Theology and Spirituality*. Norwich, Norfolk: Canterbury Press, 1991.

MacIntyre, A. *After Virtue: A Study in Moral Theory*. Notre Dame, IN: University of Notre Dame Press, 1981.

Maitland, S. *A Big Enough God? Artful Theology*. London: Mowbray, 1995.

Malloch, T. *Practical Wisdom in Management: Business across Spiritual Traditions*. Sheffield, Yorkshire: Greenleaf Publishing, 2015.

Mannion, G. *Ecclesiology and Postmodernity: Questions for the Church in our Times*. Collegeville, PA: Michael Glazier, 2007.

Marshall, T. *Prisoners of Geography: Ten Maps That Tell You Everything Your Need to Know About Global Politics*. London: Elliott & Thompson, 2015.

Martin, D. *On Secularization: Towards a Revised General Theory*. London: Ashgate, 2015.

Massey, D. *Space, Place and Gender*. Cambridge: Polity, 1994.

May, R. *The Meaning of Anxiety*. New York: WW Norton, 1950 (revised edn 1996).

May, R. *Love and Will*. New York: WW Norton, 1969 (revised edn 1989).

Mead, L. *The Once and Future Church*. Washington, DC: Rowman & Littlefield, 1991.

Milbank, J. *Theology and Social Theory: Beyond Secular Reason*. Oxford: Blackwell, 1993.

Miller, D. and Poling, J. *Foundations for a Practical Theology of Ministry*. Nashville, TN: Abingdon, 1985.

Minkin, L. *The Blair Supremacy: A Study in Labour's Party Management*. Manchester, Lancastershire: Manchester University Press, 2014.

Mintzberg, H. 'Rebuilding Companies as Communities', *Harvard Business Review* Vol. 87, no. 7–8, 2009, pp. 140–43.

Morley, W. (ed.). *Partners in Ministry*. London: CIO Publishing, 1967.

Mudge, L. *Rethinking the Beloved Community: Ecclesiology, Hermeneutics, Social Theory*. Lanham, MY: University Press of America, 2001.

Munoz, D. 'North to South: A Reappraisal of Anglican Communion Membership Figures', *Journal of Anglican Studies*, Vol. 14, no. 1, pp. 71–95, May 2016.

Myers, C. *Binding the Strong Man: A Political Reading of Mark's Story of Jesus*. Maryknoll, NY: Orbis Books, 1970.

Myers, D. and Scanzoni, L. *What God Has Joined Together?* San Francisco, CA: Harper, 2005.

Nicholls, D. *Deity and Domination: Images of God in the Nineteenth and Twentieth Centuries.* London: Routledge, 1989.

Odom, W. *Fifty Years of Sheffield Church Life: 1866-1916.* Sheffield, Yorkshire: J. Northend, 1917.

O'Donovan, O. *Church in Crisis: The Gay Controversy and the Anglican Communion.* Eugene, OR: Cascade Books, 2008.

Oliver, G. *Ministry Without Madness.* London: SPCK, 2012.

O'Neill, O. *A Question of Trust.* Cambridge: Cambridge University Press, 2002.

Orr, D. 'Comment', *The Independent*, 19 September 2015, p. 23.

Parkin, F. *The Marxist Theory of Class: A Bourgeois Critique.* London: Tavistock, 1979.

Parsons, T. 'A Revised Analytical Approach to the Theory of Social Stratification'. *The American Journal of Sociology*, Vol. 45, no. 6 (May 1940): p. 122.

Pattison, S. *The Faith of the Managers: When Management Becomes Religion.* London: Cassell, 1997.

Pattison, S. and Woodward, J. *The Blackwell Reader in Pastoral and Practical Theology.* Oxford: Blackwell, 2000.

Paul, L. *The Deployment and Payment of Clergy.* London: CIO Publishing, 1964.

Percy, M. 'How to Win Congregations and Influence Them'. In *Contours of Christian Education*, (ed.) J. Astley and D. Day. London: Mayhew-McCrimmon, 1992, pp. 177–193.

Percy, M. 'The Priest-like Task: Funding the Ministry of the Church of England' in *The Character of Wisdom: Essays in Honour of Wesley Carr*, M. Percy and S. Lowe. Farnham, Surrey: Ashgate, 2004, pp. 3–22.

Percy, M. 'The Churchgoers Charter', *Signs of the Times*. London: Modern Church Publications, January 1993.

Percy, M. *Power in the Church: Ecclesiology in an Age of Transition.* London: Cassell, 1996.

Percy, M. and Evans, G. (eds). *Managing the Church? Order and Organisation in a Secular Age.* Sheffield, Yorkshire: Sheffield Academic Press, 2000.

Percy, M. *Salt of the Earth: Religious Resilience in a Secular Age.* Sheffield, Yorkshire: Sheffield Academic Press, 2002.

Percy, M. 'Finding Our Place, Losing Our Space: Reflections on Parish Identity'. In *Religious Identity*, ed. S. Coleman. Farnham, Surrey: Ashgate, 2003.

Percy, M. *Engaging with Contemporary Culture: Christianity and the Concrete Church.* Farnham, Surrey: Ashgate, 2006.

Percy, M. *Anglicanism: Confidence, Commitment and Communion.* Farnham: Ashgate, 2013.

Percy, M. *The Ecclesial Canopy: Faith, Hopem Charity.* Farnham, Surrey: Ashgate, 2013.

Percy, M. 'Growth and Management in the Church of England: Some Comments', *Modern Believing*, Vol. 55, no. 3, 2014, pp. 257–270.

Peterson, E. *Under the Unpredictable Plant: An Exploration in Vocational Holiness.* Grand Rapids, MI: Wm. B. Eerdmans, 1992.

Petit, P. *Just Freedom: A Moral Compass for a Complex World.* New York: Norton, 2014.

Pickard, S. *Seeking the Church: An Introduction to Ecclesiology.* London: SCM Press, 2012.

Platten, S. 'Stop the Bean Counters who are Meddling with our Mission', *The Times*, 30 May 2015, p. 27.

Podmore, C. *Aspects of Anglican Identity*. London: Church House Publishing, 2005.

Porter, M. *Sydney Anglicans and the Threat to World Anglicanism*. Farnham, Surrey: Ashgate, 2011.

Porter, M. *A New Exile? The Future of Anglicanism*. Melbourne: Morning Star Publications, 2015.

Pounds, N. *A History of the English Parish Church*. Oxford: Oxford University Press, 2000.

Quattrone, P. 'Governing Social orders, Unfolding Rationality, and Jesuit Accounting Practices: A Procedural Approach to Institutional Logics'. *Administrative Science Quarterly*, June 2015, pp. 1–35.

Radner, E. and Turner, P. *The Fate of Communion: The Agony of Anglicanism and the Future of a Global Church*. Grand Rapids, MI: Eerdmans, 2006.

Reed, B. *The Dynamics of Religion: Process and Movement in Christian Churches*. London: Darton, Longman and Todd, 1978.

Report of the Evangelism Task Force, GS 2015. See: https://www.churchofengland. org/media/2442380/gs_2015_-_evangelism_tg_report.pdf, accessed 9 August 2016.

Ritzer, G. *The McDonaldization of Society*. (Revised edition). London: Sage Publishing, 1996.

Roberts, R. 'Lord, Bondsman and Churchman: Identity, Integrity and Power in Anglicanism'. In *On Being the Church* eds C. Gunton and D. Hardy, pp. 156–224. Edinburgh: T&T Clark, 1989.

Roberts, R. *Religion, Theology and the Human Sciences*. Cambridge: Cambridge University Press, 2001.

Roberts, R. 'Contemplation and the "Performative Absolute": Submission and Identity in Managerial Modernity', *Journal of Belief and Values*, Vol. 34, no. 3, December 2013, pp. 318–337.

Roberts, V. *True Friendship*. London: 10 Publishing, 2013.

'Rome, Constantinople, and Canterbury: Mother Churches?' Fellowship of St Alban and St Sergius at St Vladimir's Seminar, New York, 5 June 2008. See: http:// rowanwilliams.archbishopofcanterbury.org/articles.php/1357/rome-constantin-ople-and-canterbury-mother-churches, accessed 9 August 2016.

Roszak, T. *The Making of a Counter Culture; Reflections on the Technocratic Society and Its Youthful Opposition*. Berkeley, CA: University of California Press, 1995.

Russell, A. *The Clerical Profession*. London: SPCK, 1980.

Ryan, D. *The Catholic Parish: Institutional Discipline, Tribal Identity and Religious Development in the English Church*. London: Sheed and Ward, 1996.

Sachs, W.L. *The Transformation of Anglicanism: From State Church to Global Communion*. Cambridge: Cambridge University Press, 1993.

Sachs, W.L. *Homosexuality and the Crisis of Anglicanism*. Cambridge: Cambridge University Press, 2009.

Saunders, B. *Oh Blest Communion! The Home Life of the Church of England*. London: DLT, 2006.

Scharen, C. (ed.). *Explorations in Ecclesiology and Ethnography*. Grand Rapids, MI: Eerdmans, 2012.

Schumacher, E.F. *Guide for the Perplexed*. New York: Harper, 1977.

Scott, D. *From Office to Profession: The New England Ministry 1750–1850*. Philadelphia, PA: University of Pennsylvania Press, 1978.

Scruton, R. *The Uses of Pessimism and the Danger of False Hope*. London: Atlantic Books, 2010.

Selby, P. *Be Longing: A Challenge to the Tribal Church*. London: SPCK, 1991.

Selznick, P. *Leadership in Administration: A Sociological Interpretation*. New York: Harper, 1957.

Sheppard, D. *Bias to the Poor*. London: Hodder and Stoughton, 1984.

The Shorter Oxford English Dictionary (on Historical Principles), Vol. 2, Oxford: Oxford University Press, 1984.

Shortt, R. *Rowan's Rule: The Biography of the Archbishop*. London: Hodder & Stoughton, 2014.

Sibley, D. *Geographies of Exclusion: Society and Difference in the West*. London: Routledge, 1995.

Sorokin, P. 'What Is a Social Class?' In *Class, Status and Power*, eds R. Bendix and S.M. Lipset, New York: Free Press, 1966, p. 90.

Spencer, S. 'Goals for Growth Expose a Vision's Limitations', *Church Times*, 14 August 2015.

Statistics for the Church of England. London: Church House Publishing, 2012.

Stiglitz, J. *The Great Divide*. London: Allen Lane, 2015.

Talent Management for Future Leaders and Leadership Development for Bishops and Deans: a New Approach. Report of the Lord Green Steering Group. London: General Synod Document no. 1982, 2015.

Talking Jesus: Perceptions of Jesus, Christians and Evangelism in England – a report penned by the Barna Group on behalf of the Church of England and Evangelical Alliance. London: Barna Group, 2015.

Taylor, D.J. *The Tablet*, 31 October 2015, p. 28.

Thompson, K. *Bureaucracy and Church Reform: The Organizational Response of the Church of England to Social Change 1880–1965*. Oxford: Oxford University Press, 1970.

Thung, M. *The Precarious Organisation: Sociological Explorations of the Church's Mission and Structure*. The Hague: Mouton & Co., 1976.

Tomorrow is Another Country: Education in a Postmodern World. London: Church House Publishing, 1996.

Torry, M. *Managing Religion: The Management of Christian Religious and Faith-Based Organizations*. Vols 1 and 2. London: Palgrave Macmillan, 2015.

Tourish, D. *The Dark Side of Transformational Leadership: A Critical Perspective*. London: Routledge, 2013.

Turnbull, R. *Generosity and Sacrifice: The Report of the Clergy Stipends Review Group*. London: Church House Publishing, 2001.

Vasey, M. *Strangers and Friends: New Exploration of Homosexuality and the Bible*. London: Hodder & Stoughton, 1995.

Vasey-Saunders, M. *The Scandal of Evangelicals and Homosexuality: English Evangelical Texts 1960–2010*. Farnham, Surrey: Ashgate, 2015.

Vidler, A.R. (ed.) *Soundings: Essays concerning Christian Understanding*. Cambridge: Cambridge University Press, 1962.

Waters, S. *Temple*. London: Nick Hern Books, 2015.

Watson, N.K. *Introducing Feminist Ecclesiology*. Sheffield, Yorkshire: Sheffield Academic Press, 2002.

Weber, M. *Charisma and Institution Building*. Chicago, IL: Chicago University Press, 1968.

Webster, J. 'The Self-Organizing Power of the Gospel of Christ: Episcopacy and Community Formation', *International Journal of Systematic Theology*, Vol. 3, no. 1, 2001, pp. 69–82.

Western, S. *Leadership: A Critical Text*. London: Sage, 2008.

Whelan, R. *The Corrosion of Charity: From Moral Renewal to Contract Culture*. London: Institute of Economic Affairs, 1996.

Wigg-Stevenson, N. *Ethnographic Theology: an inquiry into the production of theological knowledge*. New York: Palgrave Macmillan, 2014.

Williams, R. *Anglican Identities*. London: DLT, 2004.

Wilson, A. *More Perfect Union? Understanding Same-Sex Marriage*. London: DLT, 2014.

Winter, G. *The Suburban Captivity of the Church*. New York: Macmillan, 1962.

Wondra, E. 'The Importance of Moral Authority: Reflections on Current Events in the Anglican Communion', in *Anglican Theological Review*, Vol. 98, no. 3, Summer 2016, pp. 533–544.

Woodhead, L. 'The Vote for Women Bishops'. See: http://blog.oup.com/2014/07/women-bishops-vote-vsi/, accessed 9 August 2016.

Woodhead, L. 'What People Really Believe About Same-Sex Marriage', *Modern Believing*, Vol. 55, no. 1, 2014, pp. 27ff.

Woodhead, L. and Brown, A. *That Was the Church That Was: How the Church of England Lost the English People*. London: Bloomsbury, 2016.

Wooldridge, A. and Micklethwait, J. *The Company: A Short History of a Revolutionary Idea*. London: Weidenfeld & Nicolson, 2003.

Working as One Body. London: Church House Publishing, 1995.

Yardley, J. and Romero, S. 'Liberation Theology's Revival', *New York Times Weekly*, 31 May 2015, p. 1.

Zaleznik, A. 'Managers and Leaders: Are They Different?' *Harvard Business Review*, Vol. 55, 1977, pp. 67–78.

Index